THE
COMMANDANT
OF AUSCHWITZ

THE
COMMANDANT
OF AUSCHWITZ

THE
COMMANDANT
OF AUSCHWITZ

RUDOLF HÖSS

Volker Koop

FRONTLINE
BOOKS

Published in 2021 by Frontline Books,
an imprint of Pen & Sword Books Ltd,
47 Church Street, Barnsley, S. Yorkshire, S70 2AS

www.frontline-books.com

ISBN: 978 1 47388 688 9

For more information on our books, please visit
www.frontline-books.com, email info@frontline-books.com
or write to us at the above address.

Printed and bound by TJ Books Limited, Padstow, Cornwall
Typeset by Donald Sommerville
Pen & Sword Books Ltd incorporates the imprints of Pen & Sword
Archaeology, Atlas, Aviation, Battleground, Discovery,
Family History, History, Maritime, Military, Naval, Politics,
Social History, Transport, True Crime, Claymore Press,
Frontline Books, Praetorian Press,
Seaforth Publishing and White Owl

For a complete list of Pen and Sword titles please contact

Contents

Introduction vii

Chapter 1. The Life Lies of Rudolf Höß 1

Chapter 2. The Personality 22

Chapter 3. Höß and the SS 42

Chapter 4. The Cynic 75

Chapter 5. Höß and his Fellow Perpetrators 87

Chapter 6. Höß as Head of Department D I 171

Chapter 7. The I.G. Farben Works at Auschwitz 174

Chapter 8. After the Collapse 189

Acknowledgements 206

Appendices 208

Abbreviations 208

Chronology 212

SS Ranks, their Translation and their Equivalents in the
British Armed Forces 218

Facts about Auschwitz Concentration Camp 220

Prisoner Categories 222

Affidavit by Höß during the Nuremberg Main Trial of War Crimes 223

Archives 227

Selected Bibliography 229

Picture Credits 232

Notes 233

Index 247

Introduction

Rudolf Höß is generally considered one of the greatest mass murderers of the Third Reich. Much has been written about the commander of the death camp of Auschwitz. His willingness to speak openly and extensively about his deeds and to co-operate with the prosecuting authorities of the victorious Allied forces and also of Poland is often emphasized. This recognition is unfounded, however, for Höß in his mind had only done his 'duty' as best as he could, just like many perpetrators of the National Socialist system claimed too. If his superiors – foremost Reich Leader SS Heinrich Himmler – had given him another task, he would have made every effort to perform this as well. As he was tasked to expand the Auschwitz concentration camp into the greatest destruction facility of human life of all time, he dedicated himself wholly to this task and showed the Nazi leadership that they could not have found anyone more suitable.

On the occasion of the trial against Adolf Eichmann in Jerusalem, the Jewish philosopher Hannah Arendt spoke of the 'banality of evil' and called the SS Senior Storm Command Leader who organised the transports to the death camps a 'normal human being'. In this sense Höß, who in his spare time tended to his family, read fairy tales to his children or went for rides, led a 'normal' life, too. It is characteristic of him that he did not suffer from the fact of having made a crucial contribution to the death of millions of people and to have been one of the principal actors in the extermination program of the Jews ordered by Hitler and Himmler. He even dared to say with respect to the atrocities at Auschwitz that he had never condoned them and furthermore that he never personally mistreated or killed a prisoner.[1] Perhaps this statement is partially true for his term as commander at Auschwitz – there he let his SS men kill career criminals and other prisoners and do the 'dirty work'. Yet it is also attested that he was personally involved in the trial gassing of Soviet prisoners of war in Auschwitz. Equally, in Sachsenhausen he shot the prisoner August Dieckmann by his own hand – as Harry Naujoks describes.

In the isolation of his cell in Cracow in October 1946, Rudolf Höß wrote down from memory the regulations that applied to all concentration camps of the Third Reich and which also bound him. As 'purpose of the concentration camps' he formulated the following:

> Enemies of the State are to be prevented from their subversive activities among the population and State by secure custody in a concentration camp.
>
> Antisocial elements which until now cause harm to the people as a whole without hindrance are to be turned back into useful people by strict education to order, cleanliness and regular work.
>
> Incorrigible criminals who relapse again and again shall be eliminated from the German people by secure detainment.

At no point did he develop doubts that the prisoners in the concentration camps could be classified into one of the named categories – enemies of the state, antisocial and incorrigible persons. The heads of the National Socialist Party, and hence in view of the equation of the state with the party also the leadership of the state, had categorised these people as such – accordingly they had to be rendered innocuous, in his conviction. He did not need to ponder the legality of it. He was a recipient of orders and executioner and saw his task in protecting the German 'ethnic totality' from such elements.

To the former prisoner Vladimir Matejka from the former Czechoslovakian Socialist Republic, who was committed to the concentration camp Sachsenhausen in November 1935, Höß said: 'You are in a concentration camp. The concentration camp is not a prison, but an educational institution with special methods.'[2] That these 'methods' often resulted in the death of the prisoners Matejka had to painfully experience himself.

In his *Autobiographic Notes*, Höß claimed that he did not know anything of the atrocities in the concentration camps and rejected them:

> I myself have never mistreated a prisoner or even killed him. I have further never tolerated mistreatments at the hands of my subordinates. If I now have to hear in the course of the investigations what awful tortures occurred in Auschwitz and also in the other camps, this sends shivers down my spine.[3]

Of all people, these sentences were uttered by one of the greatest mass murderers of the Third Reich; of all people the commander of Auschwitz arrogated them for himself. Here Höß proves himself to be a liar, since in the character sketches of his subordinates he speaks very clearly of their misdeeds, even though he allegedly was unable to take steps against this as commander and camp senior:

> Unconsciously I had become a cog in the great extermination machine of the Third Reich. The machine has been smashed, the motor has foundered and I have to go with it. The world demands it.
>
> (…) The public may continue to see in me the bloodthirsty beast, the cruel sadist, the millionfold murderer – for the masses cannot imagine the commander of Auschwitz to be otherwise. They would never understand that he had a heart, too, that he was not evil.[4]

Höß implemented Himmler's instructions in a quite businesslike manner. The structure and the administration of a concentration camp, the organisation and execution of the mass murder of the Jews was for him always just the 'job' to be done. The murder of hundreds of thousands of prisoners did not cause any moral problems for Höß, especially since he saw most of them not as 'humans' anyway. Towards Jews he had this attitude without exception. Höß had thus internalised Himmler's demand to silence any form of sympathy while executing the mass murder of the Jews and made it his own.

It is probably little known that the hundred thousands of prisoners who had to experience the terrors of Auschwitz owed the tattooing of the prisoner's number exclusively to Höß. In order to make bookkeeping easier, he asked his superior department for permission to undertake this additional humiliation of the prisoners.[5] Customarily the prisoners' numbers were fixed to the clothing; only in Auschwitz was it tattooed onto the left forearm. The tattoos would eliminate any confusions of undressed corpses as well as enable the identification of escaped and retrieved prisoners.

Characteristic of Höß – as well as for other perpetrators of the Nazi regime – are the terms in which he described his murders. He called it an 'improvement' on the death camp of Treblinka that in Auschwitz a gas chamber with a capacity of 2,000 victims was built, while elsewhere they had to 'make do' with smaller ones in which just 200 victims could be gassed simultaneously. Höß further boasted that the victims in Auschwitz were 'fooled' on their way to the gas chambers by being told that they would be taking part in a delousing operation.

Höß was downright pedantic, and he was a perfectionist. During the trial before the Supreme National Court in Warsaw, the former Austrian concentration camp prisoner Heinrich Dürmayer appeared as a witness. He stated that SS henchmen had told him that only 10, at the most 15, per cent of the prisoners had gone to the camp and that the others had been killed immediately. Höß piped up and according to Dürmayer corrected him with an 'uncanny calm', declaring: 'The witness is wrong. It was only 70 per cent who went into the gas and not 80 or 90 per cent.'[6]

For Höß everything had to have its order. While hundreds of thousands of prisoners were sent directly from the train to the gas chambers at the Birkenau ramp, he took heed as commander that the gardens within the SS settlement were laid out and maintained as uniformly as possible. After a briefing with the director of central construction management in Auschwitz, SS Storm Command Leader Karl Bischoff, Höß instructed the director of the agrarian enterprises, SS Storm Command Leader Joachim Caesar, to procure 600 foliage trees as well as 1,000 different covering shrubs. Höß wanted to create with them a 'green belt as a natural border to the camp' along the crematoria I and II.[7]

Höß was ambiguous in his behaviour without this burdening him. On the one hand he gave orders according to which he prohibited any form of corruption or enrichment, on the other hand he contravened those himself, employed prisoners at his villa and had them procure scarce and consequently valuable consumer goods for him as well as manufacture objects of art. According to statements by prisoners who were employed by Höß at his official villa, which before the German invasion had belonged to the Polish Soja family, one might conclude that it was his wife Hedwig who exercised a particularly unwholesome influence on her husband and further was driven by ambition. When, for example, Höß travelled to Hungary for the preparation of Operation Reinhardt, the mass murder of the Hungarian Jews, Hedwig proudly called her husband the 'special commissioner for the extermination of the Jews in Europe'. According to her, his enemies had failed to destroy him, quite to the contrary: he was now given a significantly more important task and an even more distinguished mission was entrusted to him.[8] Höß had become 'Special commissioner for the resettlement of the Jews' in October 1943, when he became head of Department D I of the Office Group D in the SS Central Economic-Administrative Office [WVHA = Wirtschafts- und Verwaltungshauptamt der SS] in place of Arthur Liebehenschel and he then returned to Auschwitz in order to personally oversee the extermination of the Jews on the RSHA [= Reichssicherheitshauptamt = Reich Security Main Office] transports. The so-called Hungarian transports, which were the responsibility of SS Storm Command Leader Adolf Eichmann, arrived between May and late summer 1944 virtually without pause. More than 2 million Jews died just in the context of this operation.

Höß was camp senior of Auschwitz during this time, while normally this function was performed by the camp commander of Camp A I.

In January 2015 the seventieth anniversary of the liberation of Auschwitz by the former Red Army was commemorated. Höß once stated in an affidavit that 2.5 million people were 'exterminated' there, another time he even gave the number of 3 million, but both estimates do not hold up to scrutiny. Yet even the attested 1.1 million murdered in Auschwitz represent a dimension exceeding any human imagination. This gargantuan killing machine is essentially the work of Rudolf Höß. Any form of sympathy was alien to him – any order was executed by him dutifully. The machine had to run. Difficulties were not allowed to stop it. Prisoner clerk Hermann Langbein describes that in 1944 children were thrown alive into large fires burning beside the crematoria. He reported this to the camp doctor SS Storm Command Leader Eduard Wirths, but the latter did not want to believe him. The next day Wirths merely said: 'This was an order by camp commander Höß. It was given because there had not been enough gas.'[9]

When it was time to destroy the traces of the mass murder, Höß revealed himself to be a perfectionist. SS Standard Leader Paul Blobel, as head of task force 1005, took part in the attempt to cover up the crimes. Among other ideas, he wanted to destroy the corpses with dynamite. Höß investigated such trials carried out in Chelmo and found that the results were inadequate:

> Blobel had had various makeshift furnaces erected and fired them with wood and gasoline residue. He tried further to destroy the corpses through explosions, but this succeeded only very imperfectly.[10]

Therefore other means were employed:

> The ashes were scattered across the extensive woodland area, after they had been ground to dust in a bone mill. (...) The labour itself was carried out by Jewish detachments who after finishing their section were shot. The concentration camp of Auschwitz had to provide Jews constantly for the Task Force 1005.[11]

In the solitude of his cell in Cracow shortly before his execution, Höß found religion again, which he had quit at thirteen years of age. The Polish Jesuit priest Wladyslaw Lohn from Wadowice near Cracow made the sign of the cross above Höß' head and said, 'I forgive you your sins.' After confession and creed Höß received the 'viaticum', the Catholic Eucharist in the hour of death. Höß had had a religious upbringing like many leading National Socialists and SS functionaries, and had even wanted to become a missionary.

If Höß described his actions within National Socialism like no other, if he called the extermination of the Jews wrong, then it was not because he repented his deeds, but he was being pragmatic because through this Germany had drawn the hatred of the world onto itself by such actions.

Höß was more than just a 'cog' in the Nazi system, as he himself wrote in a downplaying manner to his wife in his farewell letter. Without him – or rather without men like him or Eichmann – the Holocaust could have never happened in this brutality. He was given 'a truly sad lot', as he pitied himself, and how fortunate had been 'the comrades who were allowed to die an honest soldier's death'. As commander of Auschwitz he only learned during the investigation and the trial what terrible things had happened there, and it was indescribable how he had been deceived and how his orders had been twisted. 'How tragic,' said he, 'I who am by nature soft, good-natured and always obliging have become the greatest destroyer of human life who executed each order to exterminate coldly and to the last consequence.'

In his functions within the SS, Höß never showed himself to be 'soft and good-natured'. Even his superior, SS Group Leader Oswald Pohl, supposedly saved some prisoners – of Höß the like is not known, with one exception. Stanislaw Dubiel, whom he employed at his official villa, reported that he had been released from the so-called bunker on Höß' instigation and struck from the death list on more than one occasion. The first time Dubiel was supposed to be led to the courtyard of Block 11 and shot together with another 170 prisoners on 12 June 1942 on the behest of the Political Department, in particular its head, Grabner. Höß won through that Dubiel could return to his post. Dubiel wrote: 'In the afternoon of the same day Grabner, in the company of Höß' adjutant and Hößler, entered Höß' garden, where I was working, and demanded my rendition in order to be shot. Höß and especially his wife refused this categorically and asserted their will.'[12] Later Dubiel was once more on the list of persons to be shot in July [probably on 14 July 1942 when around 200 Poles were murdered at the so-called death wall in the courtyard of Block 11]. Another time he was supposed to be shot on 28 October together with 280 prisoners from the Lublin region. This time Höß saved Dubiel's life too. Yet to conclude from this that Höß and his wife had shown sympathy would be wholly amiss. Both hated everything Polish, but did not want to do without Dubiel's services.

In the context of Auschwitz much has been written about Höß. As the author of a biography of Höß, I cannot avoid repeating some of it.

However, crucial are numerous new emphases and corrections of previous publications. For example, sketches are published in this book with which Höß characterised superiors and subordinates during the last weeks of his life and with whom he ultimately wanted to absolve himself.

In many aspects his résumé has to be corrected, starting with the year of his birth as 1901, and not 1900. Britons and Poles who interrogated Höß after the war showed themselves to be pleased by the apparent 'openness' with which he spoke about his activities as commander of Auschwitz. As they did not know the contents of numerous important documents at that stage, they could not always verify the truthfulness of Höß' statements when he seemed to differ agreeably from the denial or inability to remember of other Nazi defendants. Yet as it has been shown, significant concessions have to be made time and again regarding the truthfulness or the attention to detail of these statements.

It is important to the author of this book to pursue as many primary sources as possible. For my research the following archives were consulted among others: official archive Gransee, the Central State Archive Brandenburg, Federal Archive Berlin-Lichterfelde, Federal Archive Ludwigsburg Branch, the Library of the German Bundestag, Federal Commissioner for the Records of the State Security Service of the former GDR (BStU), the Commissioner of the Federal Government for Culture and Media, Archive of the Cathedral Chapter Brandenburg, Municipal Administration/Registry Office/Trade Office Neukirch/ Lausitz, Municipality of St. Michaelisdonn, Local Heritage Society Buberow, Institute for Contemporary History Munich (IfZ), International Tracing Service Bad Arolsen (ITS), State Archive Berlin, State Archive Schleswig-Holstein, State Court Schwerin, Political Archive Foreign Office, State Library Berlin, Town Archives Baden-Baden and Dachau; Registry Offices Dachau, Flensburg, Ludwigsburg, Mannheim, Schwerin, Stuttgart, Office for Public Order (Department Old Files) as well as Centre for Historical Research Berlin of the Polish Academy of Sciences. With regards to the 1st Frankfurt Auschwitz Trial, the Archive of the Fritz Bauer Institute proved itself to be very productive. Furthermore, online research in the archives of the Archiwum Państwowe Muzeum Auschwitz-Birkenau (APMO) and the Institute for Contemporary History Munich (IfZ) was very helpful.

During my research I was struck by the fact that in the archive of the memorial site of the concentration camp Dachau there are hardly any references to Höß, and also in the archive of Sachsenhausen the body of source material is scarce in this respect. Yet with the aid of the archivists of all the mentioned institutions it became possible to draw a picture of the greatest mass murderer of all times, which in many respects stands in contrast to the traditional portrayals.

I have attached special importance to the fact that this book does not deal with the history of the death camp Auschwitz, even though the name Höß stands for this like no other. Gaps were mainly closed in Höß' biography outside his years as a concentration camp commander. A biography is presented that shall show through sources and statements by his contemporaries that have been unknown so far who this person was, who without any empathy viewed the mass murder of hundreds of thousands of people as mere 'work' that he had to execute according to orders.

Chapter 1

The Life Lies of Rudolf Höß

Childhood and Youth

In an interrogation by British military authorities on 14 March 1946, Rudolf Franz Ferdinand Höß explained: 'I was born on the 25th of November 1900. I am the son of the merchant Franz Xaver Höß in Baden-Baden. I have two married sisters who are currently living in Mannheim and Ludwigshafen.' Höß had been warned at the beginning of the consequences of untruthful statements, but here already he had stated a falsehood, a behaviour that accompanied his whole life.

His parents, Franz Xaver Höß and Lina, née Speck, had married on 10 November 1900. If his statements had been true, his mother would have been nine months pregnant with Rudolf at the time of their wedding and would have given birth two weeks later. Yet this is odd. According to the birth certificate kept in the town archive of Baden-Baden, the date of birth is without doubt 25 November 1901 and not 1900. One has to wonder why Höß made himself one year older and clung to this falsehood his whole life.

In a so-called leader questionnaire Höß later stated that his father, who had registered himself on 22 March 1895 at Weinbergstraße 6, Baden-Baden coming from Moos – today a part of Bühl – was a merchant. In reality, however, he was a simple shop servant. In Mannheim address books he is often simply listed as servant. Until 1904 the family lived at Gunzenbachstraße 20 (today no. 46) and in 1907 were listed under the address Hardtstraße 16. In 1907 the family moved to Mannheim. Rudolf Höß was six years old at the time. The family did not find a fixed abode in Mannheim, either, and changed addresses several times, but always lived in rented accommodation, including in the Lindenhof quarter.

1

Höß, baptised in the Catholic faith, received his First Communion in St Joseph's Church of Mannheim. From 11 September 1912 onwards he visited the humanist Karl-Friedrich Grammar School, according to his account 'until the 10th grade'. This statement is wrong. Höß withheld the fact that he was not transferred after finishing seventh grade due to poor performance and had to leave the school on 27 July 1915. Instead he stated in context with the Parchim vigilante murder [Fememord] – Höß, as a member of the Free Corps Roßbach, had taken part in the murder of Walter Kadow, a member of the radical right German National Freedom Party, on 31 May 1923 – during interrogations on 22 August 1923 in Leipzig:

> I visited the grammar school in Mannheim until the 10th grade and left the same in 1916 because I did not want to follow my father's wish to later study theology, but wanted to become a soldier.[1]

Höß mixes here – like so often – truth and lie.

To their credit, the students of the Karl-Friedrich Grammar School Mannheim, on the occasion of the 200th anniversary of their school in the academic year 2005/06, addressed Höß and his performance at school in depth. On 11 September 1912 his daily school life started at the Karl-Friedrich Grammar School. He was not only the second oldest student of his class, but also always belonged to the poorest performers of his year. 'At the end of the 5th grade he held the 28th place of 29 transferred students, at the end of 6th grade the 27th place of 27 students so that it is not surprising that he did not make the grade at the end of 7th grade.'[2] After the death of his father in 1914 his mother therefore took her only now almost fourteen-year-old son from school in summer 1915 and sent him to do an apprenticeship.

His father, Franz Xaver, had allegedly made a vow according to which Rudolf should become a priest. In any case, the Höß household seems to have been very religious. Clergy from all circles went in and out, as Höß described it. Particularly festive occasions for him were those days 'when one of the old, bearded Africa padres who my father knew from East Africa came to visit us. Then I did not move in order not to lose a single word of the conversation.'[3] His father took him on pilgrimages, both at home and to Lourdes and Einsiedeln. He was deeply religious at that time and his father 'prayed for heavenly blessing for me so that I would become a divinely gifted priest some day'.[4] His break with the church occurred at the age of thirteen, when a confessor who was friends with his father did not keep the confessional secret and he felt betrayed and deceived. Only shortly before his execution did Höß return into the fold of the church.

Höß answered the American court psychologist Gustave M. Gilbert in an informal setting during the International Military Tribunal 1946 to his question whether he had had a religious upbringing as a child:

> Yes, I grew up in a very strict Catholic tradition. My father was a true bigot, very strict and fanatic. I learned that when my youngest sister was born he had made a religious vow and dedicated me to God and priesthood: after that he led a Josephite marriage (celibacy). He directed my entire education as a child towards the goal of turning me into a priest. I had to pray and go to church endlessly, had to make penance for the smallest offences – pray as a punishment for any tiny unkindness against my sister or similar trivialities.
>   What made me so stubborn and later probably caused me to close myself off from other people, was his manner to let me feel that I had done him a personal injustice and that he – since I was intellectually much beneath him – was responsible for my sins before God. And I could only pray in order to repent my sins. My father was a kind of higher being to whom I could never get close. And thus I retreated onto myself – and I could not open myself to others. I believe that this bigoted education was to blame for me becoming so withdrawn. My mother was living under the pressure of this fanatical piety, too.[5]

Höß became more and more estranged from the Catholic church, until he broke completely with it in 1922. After he had made this decision, he quite obviously replaced religion with the National Socialist ideology. For him the anti-Semitic propaganda of the National Socialists had been as irrefutable as a church dogma, he said to Gilbert.[6]

In his *Autobiographical Notes*, Höß often creates the impression that his family employed domestics. In this context also belong his later references to the fact that he was allegedly taught by a private tutor, first visited the primary school in Mannheim and then the Grand Ducal Karl-Friedrich Grammar School, which he left with his O-levels:

> In particular it was always pointed out to me that I had to carry out or follow wishes or instructions of my parents, teachers, priests etc., indeed of all adults down to the servants immediately and ought not to let myself be deterred from this by anything.[7]

With this statement Höß apparently wanted to justify that he had already been trained for unconditional obedience from his earliest childhood onward and accordingly carried out later kill orders immediately and fastidiously, too. Not by chance, he further alleged that his father, though a 'fanatical Catholic and staunch opponent of the Reich government', had been of the conviction that despite all opposition the laws and orders of the state had to be followed absolutely.[8] Exactly this attitude then defined Rudolf Höß' later life.

But back to his résumé: Höß registered on 31 December 1917 in the at that time still independent village of Friedrichsfeld. In view of the regulations to be settled, he hence could only become a soldier in 1918 at the earliest, but always claimed – also towards the British interrogators:

> On 1st August 1916 I joined as a volunteer the 21st Baden Dragoon Regiment, replacement squadron, at Bruchsal, Baden. After a short training period I came to the Asia Corps in Turkey and stayed until the end of 1917 in Mesopotamia and then was at the Palestine front until the armistice. I was wounded twice, suffered from Malaria and received several decorations.

From 2 October 1916 until 6 March 1917, according to Höß' statement, he had been deployed in the 6th Turkish Army at the Iraq front and taken part in the battles of Kut-el-Amarna and Baghdad. On 17 February 1917 he received the Iron Cross Second Class, on 6 October 1917 the Iron Crescent and on 19 December 1917 the Baden Medal for Merit. As further decorations, Höß mentioned the Iron Cross First Class (16 May 1918), the Baltic Cross (4 January 1920), the Silesian Eagle (9 June 1921), as well as commemorative medals (1 October 1938 and 27 September 1939) and the Badge of the Wounded Second Class (20 April 1941). He had served since 30 January 1919 in the intelligence department of the East Prussian Volunteers Corps and since 13 September 1919 in the Free Corps Roßbach.

These statements are at odds with the truth, too. Rather it is correct that Höß became a soldier in 1918, thus could not have been wounded in Turkey one year earlier and also could not have received the decorations mentioned by him on the dates given.

Unmistakably his origin and his inadequate school education caused the later concentration camp commander considerable problems. Otherwise it is hardly comprehensible that he often stressed that over many generations his paternal ancestors had been officers, his grandfather had fallen in 1870 leading a regiment and that his father had also been a dedicated soldier. His mother had wanted him to first pass his A-levels, then they could speak about his wish to become a soldier.[9] However, there could be absolutely no talk about A-levels, since Höß had not even managed the transfer to the eighth grade.

In the Free Corps Roßbach

After his stint as a soldier, Höß joined the Free Corps Roßbach,[10] one of the many free corps formed after the First World War. Here – or rather in the Roßbach Committee – Höß came into close contact with National Socialist ideology. The members of the free corps considered themselves soldiers who followed a political idea, and not as mere mercenaries. As such they were evidently considered, however, by the later minister for propaganda, Joseph Goebbels, who noted in his diaries under the entry dated 13 May 1926 that he had sat together with Roßbach's 'mercenaries' in Wroclaw.[11]

Among other places, the Free Corps Roßbach fought in the Baltic states and in Upper Silesia. In October 1919 the minister for the Reichswehr Noske had just announced that he would have anyone shot who tried to reach the Baltic states, but still many formations managed to get there.[12] When Roßbach was supposed to be stopped at the Prussian border, he had some machine guns made ready to fire unceremoniously. The border patrol officers saluted and declared that unfortunately they had to yield to violence.

The fight of the free corps against the Soviet Bolshevists, who had advanced into the Baltic states, and after their retreat against Latvians and Estonians was carried out with unprecedented cruelty. Höß said at that time:

> Countless times I saw the harrowing images of burnt out huts and of charred or scorched corpses of women and children. I believed then that an increase of the human craze for destruction would not be possible after that.[13]

Yet Höß himself later was largely responsible for such an 'increase'.

The Parchim Vigilante Murder

Rudolf Höß always presented himself during interrogations after the war and in his memoirs as somebody who as a member of the SS had only carried out orders and into whose mind the thought never penetrated to refuse obeying an order. Regardless of the 2.5 million people – actually it was probably c.1.1 million – for whose death he was directly responsible according to his own statements, he did not see himself as a 'murderer'. If at all, then the SS as whole was guilty of murder – that was at least his opinion stated after the war.

With such a view Höß suppressed the fact that he personally had tortured and killed, without any order 'from above' at that. For this the murder of the teacher Walter Kadow stands as an example. This is the case of the Parchim vigilante murder, in which Höß took part in

5

a leading role. He belonged at that time to the Roßbach Committee, a successor organisation to the illegal Free Corps Roßbach. Nationalist-racist right-wing radicals like Höß – and by the way Martin Bormann, too – had accused Kadow of betraying the member of the NSDAP cover organisation Greater German Workers Party, Albert Leo Schlageter. During the French–Belgian occupation of the Ruhr area, Schlageter was a militant activist and was sentenced to death by a French military court for espionage and several bombing attacks and subsequently executed. Kadow had allegedly been responsible for Schlageter's death – at least this was the reason later given for his murder and for the heroisation of his murderers.

Walter Kadow, born 29 January 1900 in Hagenow as the son of a smith, visited the elementary and secondary school and from autumn 1915 until Easter 1918 the teachers' college in Neukloster. Subsequently he worked for a year as assistant at the school in Roggenstorf near Grevesmühlen. Since he had no money for further training, he joined the 'Roßbach people' in autumn 1922 and worked as agricultural labourer on the Treuenfels estate in Herzberg. Here he met Höß and Martin Bormann. According to witness' statements, Kadow was highly unpopular among his co-workers. Repeatedly he had aired himself as lieutenant or even senior lieutenant, bragged with decorations that were not his own, borrowed money without paying it back as well as committed embezzlements and dodged bills. He was further accused of being a Communist informer intending to travel to the Ruhr area occupied by France. Höß claimed to have once overheard in a conversation that Kadow had previously been Communist party secretary in Klütz. The later defendant Georg Pfeiffer admitted to secretly stealing Kadow's diary in Herzberg.[14] Therein was entered that Kadow had visited the interior ministry in Schwerin on several occasions. This was seen as proof of him being a snitch. Pfeiffer continued that he had handed the diary to the estate manager, Bormann, for safekeeping. Furthermore, he had found envelopes addressed to the Berlin police headquarters and to the Interior Ministry of Mecklenburg-Schwerin. The estate owner instructed Bormann to fire Kadow.

About Bormann who later had a stellar party career as Hitler's loyal assistant, it is written in the files of the Leipzig Reich chief prosecutor:

> After middle school and grammar school Bormann was drafted in summer 1918 to the field artillery, but did not see any combat duty and was released from the military in spring 1919. Then he went as a trainee to an estate in Mecklenburg and still in the same year joined the knight's estate of the owner von Treuenfels in Herzberg.

For some time he was the manager here and also held this post at the time of the crime. On the same estate were also employed the co-defendants [Georg] Pfeiffer and [Emil] Wiemeyer and the murdered Kadow as agricultural labourers. Bormann is section leader of the German Freedom Party [sic] in the Herzberg region.[15]

From the files of the Reich chief prosecutor about Höß it follows that the latter not only earned his living as an agricultural labourer, but also worked as a film extra. About him is written among other things:

> When Roßbach reinstated his free corps after the Kapp Putsch, he joined this and was in the Ruhr area with them. After the renewed dissolution he worked on several estates in Mecklenburg, Silesia and Schleswig-Holstein with short interruptions during which he found work in the making of the film *Fridericus Rex* in Jüteborg together with other Roßbach men. At the end of 1922 he joined the 'Society for agricultural training in Mecklenburg', obtained with its aid further posts in Mecklenburg and stayed since April 1923 at the brick factory of the estate owner Schnütgen in Neuhof near Parchim, where at the time of the crime he was working – still as a foreman – and where also the co-defendants Zabel and Jurisch were employed. Höß became a member of the German Freedom Party [sic] in January 1923.[16]

The murder victim Kadow and the defendants were thus not only linked by their common employer, but also through their membership of the Roßbach Committee as well as in the right-wing radical German National Freedom Party (DVFP).

The Reich chief prosecutor reconstructed the course of events for the 'vigilante murder' as following:

> Kadow had appeared on 31st May 1923 together with an acquaintance in Parchim and had asked the trader von Haartz for a credit of 5,000 Mark.[17] He received the money as a gift and with his companion made his way to the inn Luisenhof. Bormann had heard of this and he suggested to a labourer named Kühl to make use of this opportunity and to give Kadow a good beating. A few comrades were supposed to drive with the hunting carriage to Parchim. After 11pm the gang of killers to whom also Höß belonged arrived at the inn. Kadow had been drunk for a long time and was lying on a sofa.
>
> Höß had a loaded revolver with him, the others brass knuckles and batons. They loaded Kadow onto the hunting carriage and after a short drive along an avenue the vehicle turned into a forested area on Höß' orders. Kadow wanted to flee, but was stopped by a warning shot from Höß. Höß further broke off a young tree and battered Kadow's skull with it.[18]

It was discussed whether they should wash Kadow and drive him to a hospital, and what else they should do. Finally Höß prevailed with his suggestion to bury Kadow in the forest: 'Thereupon the vehicle started to move once more, and Pfeiffer, as before under Höß' direction, drove along the road for circa 1½ kilometres and then turned right onto a forest plantation. After a further stretch of roughly 400m they halted and Kadow, wrapped in his cape, was lifted down from the luggage carrier and laid on the ground.'[19]

There Emil Wiemeyer cut his left jugular. When Kadow still moved, Höß fired a shot to his head. The corpse was covered in a makeshift way and the vehicle cleaned. The next morning Höß and Zabel drove to the crime scene, buried the corpse and covered the grave with heather. Bormann, who was not directly involved in the murder, advised Höß, Zabel, Pfeiffer and Wiemeyer to vanish from the area. Yet they remained because they feared 'to arouse suspicion by their simultaneous, sudden disappearance'.[20]

It should be interposed at this point that there is a risk of relying on secondary sources. This is shown in particular by the Parchim vigilante murder. The French historian Jean-Claude Pressac wrote that five days after Schlageter's execution Bormann gave the 'order' to murder 'the old teacher Kadow'.[21] However, there was no talk of an order and at the time of his death Kadow was no teacher and furthermore only twenty-three years old.

Some months later, seven of the associates in the crime were arrested. After the department of public prosecution Schwerin had initially classified the case as an apolitical brawl among drinking companions with a fatal outcome, the prosecutor at the Reich court in Leipzig, Ludwig Ebermayer, claimed the case for himself on the basis of the Law for the Protection of the Republic, so that the responsibility was transferred to the state constitutional court in Leipzig. Höß at first confessed to the crime in front of the county court Haynau, but later recanted.

In the course of the Parchim vigilante murder trial chaired by Judge Alexander Niedner on 15 March 1925 Höß was sentenced to ten years in prison and Bormann, who had tried to cover the traces of the murder, to one year in prison for aiding and abetting. The other associates – Bernhard Jurisch, Karl Zabel, Georg Pfeiffer, Emil Wiemeyer and Zenz – received prison sentences between five and a half and nine and a half years for grievous bodily harm and manslaughter.
Höß later said:

> We had beaten Schlageter's traitor to death. And one who had participated himself notified the *Vorwärts* – the leading Social

Democratic newspaper – of the case, allegedly because his conscience pricked him, in reality, as it later transpired, in order to make money. How the entire case had unfolded in reality could not be untangled. The notifier [this means Bernhard Jurisch] was not sober enough during the incident to be able to recall the exact details. Those in the know kept silent. I myself took part, but neither as ringleader nor as main perpetrator. When I realised during the investigation that the comrade who was the actual perpetrator could only be incriminated by myself, I took on the blame myself, and he was already released while in custody. I do not need to emphasize that I agreed with the death of the traitor due to the motives described above. Moreover since Schlageter was an old, good comrade of mine with whom I had fought some hard battles in the Baltic states and the Ruhr region, with whom I had collaborated behind the enemy lines in Upper Silesia and with whom I had walked many dark path organising weapons. I was then – and am still today – firmly convinced that this traitor had deserved his death. Since in all likelihood no German court would have convicted him, we did, according to the law which we had given us ourselves born out of the necessity of the times.[22]

It is evident that Kadow's murder was a particularly cruel and brutal manslaughter. Evidence for the fact that Kadow was a traitor does not exist. It is hardly surprising that Höß whitewashed the 'vigilante murder' with this description and – like so often – resorted to lies. In addition he glossed over his own role and even projected an image of himself as a martyr by claiming to taking the blame in order to protect the actual perpetrator. He justified Kadow's murder and later even went so far to deny his part in the crime. On 28 March 1928 he wrote from his imprisonment at Brandenburg to a Mrs Härtel in Nördlingen: for the battering with the tree he had received one and a half years of jail, for the actual killing nine years. Yet he was innocent at that. During the killing of Kadow he had been with the horses and held them fast.[23]

In Brandenburg Prison

After his custody in Leipzig Höß served part of his sentence in the Brandenburg jail. About this time he wrote:

A new world, unknown to me so far, opened up. At that time serving time in a Prussian gaol was certainly no recreational holiday. [24]

(...) Already during the first days of my serving time I became *finally* wholly aware of my situation. I came to my senses. (...) So far I had been living from one day to the next, had accepted life as it presented itself without any serious thought about my future. Now I had leisure enough to think about my life so far, to realise

9

my mistakes and weaknesses and to prepare for my later, more meaningful life.

I had learned – in between deployments with the free corps – a trade which I enjoyed and loved and in which I had the opportunity to progress. I had a passion for agriculture and had already achieved some success, this was confirmed by my references. But the true meaning of life, that which truly fulfils a life, I was lacking and it was not clear to me at that time.[25]

(...) I got used to the rough tone of the junior officers, who indulged all the more in arbitrary power games the more primitive they were. I also got used to follow willingly and without inner rebellion, even with an inner smile, the orders given by such officers limited in every sense, which were often totally nonsensical. I got used to the crude, mean tone with which most prisoners confronted each other there. Yet I could *never* get used it, although this happened daily, if the prisoners frivolously and spitefully pulled everything good and fair in life to pieces and that which was sacred to many people; they became especially unkind if they realised that they could hurt a person with this. Such talk always upset me. A good book has always been a good friend to me.[26]

(...) I continually received from comrades and acquainted families good and valuable books covering all areas of interest. In history, the study of races and genetics, however, I was particularly interested and preferred studying those.[27]

Höß spent nine months in custody in Leipzig and after his sentencing began his term of ten years for grievous bodily harm and manslaughter on 10 April 1924 in the Brandenburg jail, which was, however, shortened to five years due to a Reich amnesty. The personal files for this time are found in the Central State Archive Brandenburg in Potsdam and provide information on his daily life in prison, his visits and his petitions to the jail's directorship, his thoughts and his relationship to National Socialism. Although Höß spent a defining – and for his character revealing – period in Brandenburg prison, this important episode has so far largely been ignored by his biographers.

With a letter by the Reich chief prosecutor to the penitentiary Brandenburg the 'agricultural labourer Rudolf Höß was brought for internment',[28] whereby 'the sentence has to be calculated from 15th March 1924 6pm and to be administered as solitary confinement in accordance with the Reich chief prosecutor'. Höß was given the prisoner number 2934/28 and on 10 April 1924 received among other things the following kit:

- 1 pair of Manchester trousers, brown
- 1 jacket, grey, and 1 pair of riding trousers, grey linen

- 1 linen shirt, short
- 1 pair of socks, grey wool
- 1 pair of boots, high
- 1 tie, self-binder
- 1 handkerchief, white

Furthermore, he was handed a hair brush, a white body belt, a tin of shoe polish, a shoe brush and a toothbrush.

In his personal statement for the directorship of the penitentiary dated 22 April 1924 Höß wrote that at the time of the crime he had received an income of three hundredweights of rye from his last employer, the brick factory Neuhof near Parchim.[29] This was by no means unusual, for in the time of high inflation payment in goods was more welcome and stable in value as a payment of the wage in Reichsmark.

As his last residence he stated the village of Brüel in Mecklenburg and named his sisters Maria and Margarete, who both worked as playschool nurses in Mannheim, as next of kin.

He admitted to the deed laid to his charge with a 'Jawohl', although from then on he would always deny it. To the question about his plans after his release Höß only answered: 'Uncertain, as the sentence is too long.' He explicitly rejected spiritual support during his imprisonment. Several times he petitioned for the subscription of magazines, but the director of the penitentiary rejected on 4 June 1924, for example, the petition to subscribe to the magazine *The Comrade*, as it was too nationalistic and 'directed as a battle organ against the existing government and eventually towards a violent overthrow'.[30]

Höß turned to the prison's administration quite frequently with requests of various kinds. On 3 February 1924 he requested permission to write a letter to a 'former comrade' and asked for the delivery of books and writing material. In addition he wanted to have 'one tooth made at his own cost'. He repeated his request for the dental treatment on 1 May 1924 and explained at the same time that he would ask the 'people of the Roßbach association' to send the money for this. This was allowed as well as the Ullstein dictionary *1,000 Words in English* on 14 August 1924 and permission for physical exercise on 7 October 1924. On 22 January 1925 he requested that the light in his cell be left on until 9pm, and on 25 November 1925 he asked for an extension until 10pm. As he justified these petitions with wanting to further educate himself in the evening, they were usually granted to him. Soap and toothpaste were regular entries on his 'wish list'. As the circumstances required, he

11

received an advance on his wages for these, as for example on 25 April 1925. On the same day he further asked to receive photographs of his parents.

In order to round off Höß' portrait, further wishes are listed here as examples:

- 7 October 1924: request for the permission to exercise, on 25 November 1925 request for the permission to buy plimsolls.

- 22 January 1925: request for four notebooks and a dozen writing nibs, atlas and textbooks on geography.

- 3 July 1926: request for the delivery of picture frames already approved.

- 22 September 1926: request to write a letter to Mrs Härtel, to keep his clothes in his cell and for a second hour of exercise.

- 16 November 1926: request to be allowed to accept a birthday package.

- 9 and 30 December 1926: request to write further letters to Mrs Härtel.

- 5 March 1927: request for warm shoes because of rheumatism – denied.

- January 1928: request to buy a blotter.

- At the beginning of 1926 his heel got caught, he fell down and dropped a pail. The damage of 10.50 Reichsmark he wanted to pay out of his 'assets'.

A Visit by the Free Corps Leader

Höß received visitors relatively frequently, for example from his last employer, the estate owner Rudolf Schnütgen, who wrote in his request for a visit dated 11 June 1924: 'I am bonded to Höß through nationalist-racial ideas.'[31] He was 'a selfless man'. Bruno Fricke from Berlin, lieutenant of the meanwhile dissolved Free Corps Roßbach, visited him several times, including on 8 June 1925, and had spoken in his request of the 'comrade ensign Rudolf Höß'.[32] A certain 'Beckmann from Kalsow' took care of the prisoner and on 25 October 1924 inquired of the penitentiary administration if he could send Höß pictures for his walls and how often he was allowed to visit him.[33] The answer was given on 1 November 1924. There were no objections to the sending of pictures, but it must be left to the 'judgement here whether they were suitable to be hung up'.[34] Among the visitors were the aforementioned

Bruno Fricke, Mrs D. Härtel from Altenau in the Harz on 24 July 1926, as well as the former Senior Lieutenant Roßbach. He gave his address as Berlin-Wannsee, 'at the moment Munich', and wrote on 3 March 1926 that he wished to 'visit the prisoner Rudolf Höß on the occasion of my passing through Brandenburg'.[35] From a letter by Höß he had surmised that the former would be delighted to see him, 'his old leader', once again. Most of all Roßbach considered 'this visit expedient in the interest of the prisoner's state of health'. That he did not pursue any other interests with his visit, he felt he did not need to explain, wrote Roßbach. Likewise it must be known to the board that he himself had nothing to do with the 'Parchim matter', i.e. the vigilante murder. The answer came on 10 March 1926: the jail's administration had no objections to the visit.[36] Nevertheless, the director insisted on accompanying the visitor personally to Höß. Roßbach, who was considered by the Reich Commissioner for Monitoring the Public Order as 'leader's deputy for Northern Germany', said he would arrive at the town of Brandenburg on 1 April 1926 and estimated that he would be at the penitentiary around 10.45am.[37]

Among the 'old comrades' who visited Höß were further known members of different free corps, so from Berlin Dankwart Belling and Hans-Gerd Techow. The latter was involved in the murder of Foreign Minister Walther Rathenau on 24 June 1922, had been sentenced by the state court Leipzig and now belonged to the Berlin SA leadership. Werner Lass, founder of the radical right-wing Schill Youth, arrested in 1928 with his financial advisor Techow because of bombing attacks, but released due to lack of evidence, also visited Höß. To several inquiries the letter writers received the answer that Höß was not allowed to receive food packages – exceptions were only granted for the Christmas holidays.[38] For instance, the Sports School Ekkehard in Stuer[39] had sent a 'care package with sausage, butter, bacon, cheese, and gingerbread biscuits' and a letter, which in view of the approaching Christmas holidays were handed to him. At any rate, the prison conditions were eased for Höß again and again. He was a Grade III prisoner who enjoyed all kinds of privileges.

Höß was allowed to write letters, but this permission was restricted to relatives. In his autobiography he mentions a 'bride', which 'comrades' had already organised him in Leipzig, since he was only allowed to correspond with relatives, among which 'brides' were also counted.[40] This girl wrote to him 'faithfully and obediently' all those years and reported on all events in his circle of acquaintances. These letters have been lost, merely a letter to 'Miss Helene Huber' which was returned to the penitentiary with advice of non-delivery, was taken into the personal files and still provides information today.

There is no final certainty about the identity of this 'fiancée'. According to the thorough research by Karen Strobel of the city archive of Mannheim, the inner city of Mannheim was at the time divided into squares. Höß erroneously gave 'R.2.1.' as her address. Strobel's search yielded that 'R.2.1.' was then the address of the Protestant Concordia Church. She established, however, that in square 'S.2.1.' a family called Huber was registered and had a daughter named Helene.

Helene Huber had until 30 May 1923 lived with her parents in 'S.2.1.' and had then moved to Gelsenkirchen, before she returned to her parents on 5 January 1927. It is thus very likely that Höß had written to her in Mannheim not knowing that his 'bride' was now living in Gelsenkirchen, and therefore the letter returned with advice of non-delivery. A connection to Mannheim also existed for Höß by the fact that during the time in question both his sisters lived in Mannheim. It cannot be excluded that they assisted in the search for a 'bride'.

Letters to the Mannheim 'Bride'

The undelivered letter to 'Helene Huber, Mannheim R.2.1.' which thus remained preserved for posterity sheds light on his version of the murder and his relationship to the 'leader'. In view of its importance for contemporary history it shall be reproduced at full length and verbatim. Höß wrote to 'dear Helene' that he received her parcel and letter on the second day of the trial and then continued:

> Ten years the state court here considers approximately necessary for bettering me. Half a year was struck off for the custody. A quarter of year we did not get struck off, such trivialities are beneath the state court. Now for the earth-shaking deed itself. There was among us in Mecklenburg a certain Kadow, a failed teaching candidate who pretended to support our cause body and soul, but in reality was a Communist snitch, furthermore he was an informant for the French. After he had made himself very obnoxious to us, embezzled money, contracted debts in the name of comrades, stolen their clothes and more, he was dismissed and vanished without a trace. Reappeared in the Ruhr area and was one of Schlageter's traitors. On 31st May last year he suddenly appeared again in Parchim in order to lure many of us to the Ruhr area. Yet we wanted to give him a sound walloping. We found with him, when he was drunk, his diaries in which he had noted all his misdeeds, and in addition his Communist party membership card. Imagine our anger: five days previously Schlageter had been shot. All the beatings which we

14

had received in the raids of the Communists on sparsely protected gathering thanks to the treason of this wretch. We were quite drunk, too, and no longer reflected on anything.

We drove on a cart out of Parchim towards our living quarters in Neuhof near Parchim. On the way he received a sound walloping, but he still denied everything. We stopped on a meadow and confronted him again. He denied everything and assured his innocence. Our anger turned into rage, nobody paid attention how or with what he was beating him. Kadow collapses. What to do now? We drove into a forest in order to leave the avenue. The others dragged him into the underbrush, I remained with the horses. Then the terrible thing of the event happened. One had a fit of rage, rushed Kadow lying on the ground like mad and cut his throat. Another fired two shots through his skull.

The next morning he was buried in the thicket of the forest. One who was present, an indolent fellow, disappeared, travelled to Berlin and wanted to make money by reporting the entire matter to the 'Vorwärts'. Now arrest upon arrest was made, I made my escape to Silesia, but was arrested in my bed in Kaiserswaldau [Okmiany] at 3:30am through the denunciation by a Communist who knew me from before. Then I was transported like a Sternickel [infamous serial killer/arsonist before the First World War] or Großmann [contemporary serial killer] to Leipzig – make your own judgement! – I could at most be charged with grievous bodily harm. My defender (Judicial Council Dr Hahn, Berlin) reckoned with 3 years maximum. But no, the charge was even premeditated murder, but was turned by the high court into complicity in manslaughter under recognition of all mitigating circumstances after four days of trial. Ten years gaol because of the 'enormous agitation' which this deed has caused among all circles of the population.

Since 9 April I have been here in the jail. Solitary confinement. Occupation. Braiding raffia (60 metres per day). Of my comrades everyone was distributed to a different home. By incarcerating us together the republic would be in danger! Well, it isn't over until the fat lady sings. Here you will find total riff-raff. Communists, separatists, high traitors, war traitors and national traitors, spies and so on.

Every now and then the International can be heard. All are hoping for an amnesty. Not me, since for the Roßbach people and folkish-nationalists there is no mercy. We are after all, according to everyone's opinion except that of our comrades and those who know us, the scum of humanity. I don't care. I have never given anything on the opinion of the many. I trust in the victory of our cause and in my leader and my comrade. Come what may – we remain the same – even in the gaol. I am not dishonoured by this.

How are you? With all of you in Mannheim!

In the newspapers there our heinous deed was probably hashed over. In the Leipzig papers they even showed our pictures. All this honour! Hopefully my sisters did not learn anything of this.

Kind regards Rudi[41]

Braiding Raffia in Solitary Confinement

In his *Autobiographic Notes*, Höß states that during the first two years of his imprisonment he was allowed to receive and write a letter every three months.[42] However, it can be gathered from the jail's files that he was allowed to write and also to receive a letter every two months. After two years he obtained some easing of detention conditions, could from now on write monthly, receive as many letters as arrived, was allowed to order books, and the light only went out in his cell at 10pm. From the fourth year of imprisonment the obligation to work was rescinded, his wage rose to 8 Pfennig per day, and he was even allowed to write every fortnight.

As the jail's 'attestation of employment, non-employment, detention, sickness etc.' implies, for most of the time Höß was in solitary confinement[43] and had to perform raffia braiding in April 1924. On several occasions he had to carry out tailoring for other prisoners, for example in April 1925 and April 1926. In 1927 he was employed in the property room, which he termed the 'collecting point for news in the penitentiary'.[44] In November 1927 Höß was accused of having assisted in the smuggling of letters from the jail. One was allegedly addressed to a newspaper, another to the Prussian State Parliament. This he refuted in a report dated 28 November 1927. In these letters it had been alleged that he – Höß – and another prisoner 'had women in our cells at night and performed intercourse with these women'. Further, the letters stated that four prisoners mentioned by name, among them also Höß, 'performed homosexual acts with each other'. A fellow prisoner would try to find out more about their contents. He only reported these matters 'so that the penitentiary is informed'.[45] The penitentiary administration decreed in writing that the incident should be resubmitted after a week and 'discrete investigations', but apparently the matter came to nothing.

In previous biographies it was not mentioned that Höß, as the principal party in the Parchim vigilante murder, was sentenced by the State Court Schwerin on 1 June 1926 to pay the mother of the murdered Walter Kadow, who was living in the Hanseatic town of Wismar, a lifelong pension of 30 gold Mark a month from 1 August 1926 onwards.

On 1 October 1926 she informed the Brandenburg jail's administration of this sentence. At the same time she announced that she would now 'proceed against the convict with the means of foreclosure'.[46] The penitentiary board, however, could not give her any hope of being able to enforce the claim: 'Rudolf Höß being imprisoned here does not have any cash funds. The wages to be paid cannot be confiscated by means of foreclosure, as they only become his property by being handed over upon his release.'[47] When Höß regained his freedom, the payment of a pension was no longer an issue.

It is noteworthy that no further documents on Höß' sentence exist apart from the files kept in the Central State Archive Brandenburg. The Central State Archive Schwerin stated regarding this matter that numerous documents had been lost during the war and even more through later inadequate storage.

Rejected Petitions for Pardon

'I no longer counted on being released before the end of the ten years. With confidence I hoped to survive the "remainder" of my sentence in physical and mental good health. I had already thought about how to keep myself occupied further: languages, further professional training. I thought of all kind of things, anything but release,' so it is written by Höß:

> And it came over night! In the Reichstag a majority had been found suddenly and unexpectedly on the extreme right and the extreme left which both had a great interest in liberating *their* political prisoners. Almost without preparation a political amnesty came about, and together with many others I got free, too.[48]

Höß had addressed several petitions for pardon to the Reich president, but these had been rejected. Herein he found supporters on the extreme right. In a petition to the Reich minister for justice, Oskar Hergt, for example, it was said on 5 September 1927:

> The former ensign Rudolf Höß was sentenced on 15th March 1924 for grievous bodily harm and manslaughter to ten years of jail. Six months of custody have to be counted towards the sentence so that in October of this year four years will have been served, thus almost half of the sentence. We therefore ask Your Excellency to recommend to the Reich president a pardon for Rudolf Höß.[49]

Julius Friedrich Lehmann, head of the Munich publishing house Lehmann, wrote to Minister of Justice Hergt on 18 April 1928 and made the prisoner's case: 'Mr Höß is said to be a very splendid fellow.'[50]

A little later, in the meeting of 15 June 1928, the Reichstag debated the issue of an amnesty for political prisoners. The Mecklenburg MP Friedrich Everling of the German National People's Party was one of the spokesmen.[51] He called the members of the numerous free corps 'soldiers' who in carrying out their duties might at most have killed negligently, but never committed 'political assassinations'. He found support with Wilhelm Frick, member of the Reichstag for the NSDAP and since 1933 Reich Minister of the Interior. Frick was indignant that Reich president Paul von Hindenburg could easily pardon roughly a dozen of 'so-called vigilantes languishing in jails', but did not do so on the advice of Minister of Justice Hergt:

> Here ought be mentioned first and foremost the cases of Höß and Pfeiffer. This is about a so-called vigilante murder in Mecklenburg which already dates back to the time of inflation and the passive Ruhr resistance. According to the information of one of the participants the traitor Kadow then disposed admitted himself that he delivered Schlageter into the hands of the French.
>
> Because of such a traitor German men, the aforementioned Höß and Pfeiffer, are still sitting in the jail today, and the German National minister has so far found no occasion to pardon these two German men for which he would have the ability at any time.[52]

The National Socialists demanded a general amnesty 'because the so-called vigilante murders represent a great legal scandal'.

It is symptomatic that Frick claimed: 'This agitation against the vigilantes is solely instigated by the Jewish press and the League for Human Rights.' This fitted Höß' world view, which was by now heavily influenced by anti-Semitism. The amnesty was preceded by many intense, partly tumultuous meetings in the Reichstag. The Communists demanded it for their arrested members, the National Socialists for theirs and for their sympathisers. Characteristic of this are the speeches during the Reichstag meeting on 15 June 1928.

Early Release

Höß was released from jail earlier than he expected. On 16 July a telegram of the Reich chief prosecutor reached the penitentiary, 'Rudolf Höß 1112j 236/23 on leave from penal sentence to be released immediately, if no superimposed custody.' On 18 July 1928 the Reich chief prosecutor confirmed to the penitentiary board that 'the convict Rudolf Höß has served his sentence which has been reduced by the Reich amnesty law of 14 July 1928 from 10 to 5 years imprisonment.'

In the Reichstag minutes of the third meeting of 15 June 1928 it can also be read that the later Nazi minister of the interior, Wilhelm Frick, campaigned for Kadow's murderers. 'I would like to state further that Kadow's case is a political deed by the right. These people are still imprisoned today and they have not been presented with any other alleviation than that which is granted to every common criminal automatically, that they would be released after having served three-quarters of their sentence.'

Frick claimed that there were a dozen cases of vigilante murders for which the perpetrators had been punished.[53] This was wrong, replied Minister of Justice Hergt. Rather there was only one more case and five additional prisoners:

> The killed in this case is called Cadow [sic]; the names of those who are serving a penal sentence as convicts I will not mention here, they are of no interest to the parliament, either. Solely this case might be called a vigilante murder at a pinch. Indeed it is called a vigilante murder by those persons who have addressed a petition for pardon to the Reich president, but differs quite significantly from that which we usually understand as a vigilante murder. We do not deal here to wit with any military organisation at all. It is not a case in which the convicted perpetrators perhaps stated that they had carried out the killing on military principles. This case is not about the fact that the killed had anything to do with the Schlageter matter according to the results of the entire process, the preliminary investigation and the main trial, in particular that he had betrayed Schlageter.[54]

On 17 July 1928 the gates of the jail opened for Höß. He received in wages 122.21 Reichsmark as well as 5.17 Reichsmark that he had had to hand in at commitment. He registered in Berlin, Friedrichstraße 200, and allegedly he was taken in there by a friendly family.[55] Despite thorough investigations, also by the Central State Archive Berlin, I was unable to trace the owner or tenant of this apartment at the time.

Once again, on 21 July 1928, Höß wrote to the penitentiary board. He needed a copy of the Leipzig amnesty telegram, since Tiergarten police station was making difficulties for him over the issuing of an in-country passport. Initially he was supported by the Patriotic Prisoners Aid, which the teacher for business correspondence and national history, Friedrich Carl Holtz, had founded in 1927 in order to look after the 'vigilante murderers' during their sentence and in order to obtain an amnesty for them. The committed anti-Semitic Holtz had also founded the magazine *Fridericus*, to which Höß subscribed in jail.

It is noteworthy that the minister for propaganda Goebbels did not even mention the name Höß in his diaries, but that of Gerhard Pfeiffer, the 'vigilante murderer from Mecklenburg who had just been released from the jail'.[56] He had taken him to Wannsee. After four years of ordeal, Pfeiffer had looked very embittered, Goebbels noted.

On 18 October 1930 the Reichstag accepted an amnesty law that granted immunity from prosecution for political crimes committed before 1 September 1924 and not directed against members of the Reich government. Among those profiting from several amnesties by Reich president Hindenburg was incidentally also Hermann Göring who – wanted for arrest since the failed Hitler Putsch of 1923 – was living in exile in Italy and Sweden and whom only an amnesty allowed the return to Germany.

Höß and the Artaman League
Soon after his release Höß joined the Artaman League founded in 1924. Among them may have been many idealists who were willing to pay their wages as labourers on the estates of big landowners into a common coffer except for negligible pocket money. From these means large estates were bought and made productive for the long term in order to be then divided into individual farms of an average 15 hectares. This group settlement favoured by the Artamans was, however, no collective enterprise. Only during the development and setting up of the settlement did they proceed collectively.

Höß later said that he had wanted to help 'during a set-up for the long term with an ambitious goal – I wanted to settle! In the long years of isolation in my cell *this* dawned on me: *there was only one goal for me for which it was worth to work and fight – the farm established by my own hands with a large, healthy family. This should become my purpose and goal in life.*'[57]

Immediately after his release he therefore made contact with the Artaman League, who campaigned among other things for replacing the 130,000 Polish seasonal summer labourers (on average). A healthy rural lifestyle was their focus, combined with a strict moral code. In many aspects the Artaman League anticipated National Socialist ideology: the settlement of the east and the reincorporation of the territories lost to Poland after 1918 into the German Reich were fixed components of the Artaman programme. To this was added the strict moral code that demanded of its members a virtually ascetic lifestyle. Its elementary demands included voluntary severity and absolute abstinence of alcohol and nicotine, 'a pure relationship to the other sex (…), voluntary poverty and simplicity in the midst of an over-refined world having become materialistic'. If we observe, however, who was Artaman, then this image is put into perspective. To this movement belonged, for instance, Richard Walter Darré, who during the Third Reich was Peasant Leader and Reich Minister for Food and Agriculture, who espoused the ideology of blood and soil.

Höß resigned from his position as agricultural civil servant and broke off with his present circle of friends and acquaintances. Shortly after he met Hedwig Hensel and spoke of an 'accordance in trust and understanding'.[58] In 1929 the two got married.

In 1934 Himmler allegedly prompted him to join the SS. Yet here again we find a correction of his biography typical for Höß: he had joined the SS on 1 April 1934 as a candidate and had been promoted to SS storm trooper on 20 April 1934. Yet to British interrogators he stated that already in 1933, on the Sallentin estate in Pomerania, he had established a group of mounted SS. From his personal files kept in the Federal Archive Berlin-Lichterfelde it follows that Höß had belonged to the Storm troop 2/R/5 in Stargard in Pomerania from 20 September 1933 until 10 June 1934. During a visit to the estate, Himmler, whom he already knew from the Artaman League, took notice of him and prompted him to take on the administration of a concentration camp. So he had gone to Dachau in November 1934.

In the official register of the town of Dachau, the date of the move of the Höß couple is given as 1 January 1935.[59] Höß' position is stated as company leader [Scharführer]. On the registration card was found the handwritten note:

> Criminal record: sentenced for grievous bodily harm on 15th March 1924 by the Reich Court for the Protection of the Republic Leipzig and for manslaughter to ten years' jail. Terminated on 18th July 1928 due to Reich amnesty law from 14th July 1928.

It was further noted that the police headquarters Mannheim communicated on 31 January 1935 that his sister, Maria Luise Höß, born 13 August 1927, had received her certificate of citizenship. According to the Dachau register, on 5 May 1939 the Höß family moved to Sachsenhausen-Oranienburg.

Into the Dachau period fell the birth of son Hans-Jürgen, which was certified on 1 May 1937 under registration number 7/1937 at the registry office Etzenhausen.[60]

Chapter 2

The Personality

Nazi Ideology as Surrogate Religion

Höß received the SS membership card with the number 193 616. On 20 April 1934 he became a SS storm man [Sturmmann or lance corporal], on 20 November 1934 SS Under Company Leader [Unterscharführer or sergeant], on 1 April 1935 SS Company Leader [Scharführer or platoon sergeant major], on 1 July 1935 SS Senior Company Leader [Oberscharführer or company sergeant major] and on 1 March 1936 SS Head Company Leader [Hauptscharführer or battalion sergeant major]. From December 1934 to January 1935 he completed special training in infantry with the guards of the Dachau concentration camp. There he was transferred to Department II on 1 March 1935 and finally became report leader on 1 April 1936. In this position he was directly subordinate to the Protective Custody Camp Leader, had to review the prisoner population, to manage the prisoners' office and to allocate the guards. In addition, he had to perform camp punishments or to monitor their execution and was primarily the supervisor of the guards, who in turn had to monitor the block leaders and room chiefs, scribes, etc.

In the eyes of his SS superiors he always performed outstandingly in the evaluations, and also his 'racial' appearance corresponded with SS ideas:

> Nordic with a Mediterranean element
> Character: honest, faithful and open
> Will: very diligent, asserts himself
> Common sense: yes
> Knowledge and education: above average
> National Socialist world view: very good and firm

Appearance and conduct at and outside duty: modest, but vigorous, hardly drinks, smokes moderately

Training courses including special training: completed equestrian training

Degree and firmness of training: (among others) 2. in service to the SS: special training in Dachau

Qualification for which position: report leader at the camp for protective custody

Dachau, 24 June 1936

SS Senior Leader [Oberführer; no equivalent in British or US military; between colonel and brigadier general] H. Loritz, camp commander

Statement of the superior offices:

Entirely suitable as company commander. Faithful, calm, dependable.

On 22 July 1936 the 'leadership corps' of Dachau concentration camp gathered to sponsor the SS Head Company Leader Rudolf Höß considered for promotion to SS Under Storm Leader [Untersturmführer or 2nd lieutenant].[1] The meeting during which the promotion was agreed upon was headed by the camp commander SS Senior Leader Hans Loritz.

In further personnel reports and evaluations it is stated:

Prior convictions: none

Injuries, persecutions and punishments in the battle for our movement: 10 years jail, stab wound in the left upper arm

Racial overall appearance: medium height, Dinaric with Nordic elements

Character: open and sincere

Will: firm, carries through decisions made

Common sense: yes

Knowledge and education: good general knowledge, organiser

Perceptivity: quick and assured

Appearance and conduct on and outside duty: respected by his subordinates, strict but fair. Outside duty modest and restraint. Very moderate drinker and smoker.

Suitability for promotion: yes

For which position: Adjutant at the concentration camp Sachsenhausen

Oranienburg, 15th July 1936

On 12 July 1938 Höß was transferred to Sachsenhausen concentration camp. This was due to the following directive: 'The leader of the SS Death Head Units and concentration camps, SS Main Office, is requested to relieve SS Under Storm Leader Rudolf Höß for functional reasons from his position as leader at the commandant's headquarters of the concentration camp Dachau effective 1st August 1938 and to transfer him as adjutant to commandant's staff of the concentration camp Sachsenhausen.'

Two years later, on 18 July 1940, followed the 'promotion' of Höß to camp commander of Auschwitz. The inspector of the concentration camps, Richard Glücks, called upon the SS Main Office for Personnel to transfer 'SS Under Storm Leader Rudolf Höß, SS no. 193 615, from the commandant's staff at the concentration camp Sachsenhausen to the staff of the concentration camp inspector for special deployment while retaining his official position as camp commander of the concentration camp Auschwitz/Upper Silesia' effective 1st August 1940.'

Höß became SS Head Storm Leader [Hauptsturmführer or captain] and on the suggestion of the inspector of the concentration camps was put forward on 20 January 1941 as 'SS Storm Command Leader [Sturmbannführer or major]. Höß is camp commander of the large-scale camp Auschwitz where primarily agriculture is conducted and in which the Reich Leader SS takes a great interest. The Reich Leader SS has agreed to the promotion of Höß to SS Storm Command Leader'.

The Reich Leader SS and Head of the German Police, SS Central Economic-Administrative Office (WVHA) wrote on 27 July 1942 to SS Main Office for Personnel in Berlin:

> As per communication by the head of Office Group D the Reich Leader SS on the occasion of his visit at the concentration camp Auschwitz on 18th July has promoted the camp commander SS Storm Command Leader Rudolf Höß to SS Senior Storm Command Leader [Obersturmbannführer or lieutenant colonel] effective 18th July 1942. The issuing and remittance of a certificate of promotion is requested.

SS Group Leader [Gruppenführer of Major General] Maximilian von Herff, head of the SS Main Office for Personnel, wrote on the occasion of a trip of inspection through the General Government in May 1943:

> Concentration camp Auschwitz, camp commander SS Senior Storm Command Leader Höß.
>
> Good soldierly appearance, athletic, equestrian, knows how to behave in every situation, quiet and simple, but still assertive and rational. Does not push himself to the fore, but lets his actions speak for him.
>
> H. is not only a good camp commander, but has also performed pioneering work in the area of the concentration camps with new thoughts and new educational methods. He is a good organiser and good agriculturalist and the ideal German pioneer for the Eastern

24

space. H. is definitely capable to be employed in a leadership position within the concentration camp sector. His particular strength is practice.[2]

Nevertheless, the SS Central Economic-Administrative Office Berlin transferred Höß from Auschwitz concentration camp to the staff of Office Group D – SS Central Economic-Administrative Office – effective from 10 November 1943. On 2 May 1944 the SS Central Economic-Administrative Office called upon the SS Main Office for Personnel 'to confirm the SS Senior Storm Command Leader Rudolf Höß with effect from 1st May 1944 as head of Office D I in the SS Central Economic-Administrative Office'. Until then Höß had merely been temporarily in charge of D I.

For Höß the National Socialist ideology was quasi a surrogate religion. He had joined the NSDAP early and he always gave the low number 3240 as his membership number. Yet this was only partly true, as he had started his 'SS career' outside the party, before he was readmitted and received the very high membership number 5 357 166. The latter he himself never mentioned at any time.

It is correct that Höß had joined the NSDAP in 1922, without standing out by undertaking any particular activities. After the failed Hitler putsch of 9 November 1923, the Commander-in-Chief, Hans von Seeckt, to whom Reich President Friedrich Ebert had transferred executive authority on the basis of Article 48 of the Weimar Constitution, imposed a ban on the NSDAP throughout the Reich. As a result, Höß' membership became void. When the NSDAP was founded again in February 1925, Höß was doing time in Brandenburg jail due to his participation in the Parchim vigilante murder and in this situation was not able to apply anew for NSDAP membership. Even after the general amnesty for political crimes and after his release in 1928, it took another nine years until he received another NSDAP membership card.

Although Höß had become a member of the SS in 1934 and was already proving successful as Himmler's henchman at Dachau, party membership remained a long way away for him for the time being. The administration of Dachau wrote on 14 May 1936 to Nazi regional leadership [Gauleitung] in Munich:

> When Höß was released in June 1929 [from the jail] he took over a camp of the Artaman League (today rural aid [Landhilfe] of the Hitler Youth) in Brandenburg. According to his information, he was not allowed to belong to the party as camp leader. From there he was transferred to the concentration camp Dachau on the order of the Reich Leader SS.

Furthermore, party comrade Höß informs us that he reminded Reich Leader Martin Bormann, whom he personally knows well from the time of our struggle, of the whole affair during his most recent visit on the 8th of this month here at the camp, and the Reich Leader promised him to submit this matter once more to the Reich treasurer. SS Standard Leader Mackensen [SS-Standartenführer or Colonel] from Hess' staff has joined the party together with Party Comrade Höß 1922 in Munich.[3]

The answer that the 'Regional Group Death Head Unit Upper Bavaria of the NSDAP' received on 24 November 1936 from the Munich party headquarters regarding the 'alleged membership of the national comrade Rudolf Höß, membership no. 3240', was very unsatisfactory for the latter:

Rudolf Höß reported by you with the membership number 3240 is not on record with the Reich leadership. Under this number is listed a party comrade Walter Beddig. After the Reich leadership has not given another number for Rudolf Höß, and you have informed us that Höß does not have a membership card yet, said comrade has to be inferred from the archive of the regional group and is no longer listed in the regional files, either. A re-registration by you may only be undertaken if Höß can produce also his membership card aside from the yellow de-registration certificate of his former regional group.[4]

This demand was typical German bureaucracy. For it was obvious that Höß could not produce a 'de-registration certificate'. After all, he had not left the party, but the latter had been prohibited. To this was added that the re-established NSDAP had imposed a freeze on admissions on 19 April 1933, which was only completely lifted in 1939. Höß thus had to hope for an exception, which was long in coming, though.

In this context earlier speculations on Höß possibly leaving the party are interesting. Andrea Riedle, who took over the academic management of the Concentration Camp Dachau Memorial Site in 2011, writes that no date for leaving the party has been recorded for Höß, unlike for other members of the SS.[5] Yet as elaborated, such a date could not exist.

Höß had meanwhile been promoted to SS Head Storm Leader [SS-Hauptsturmführer or captain] and transferred to Sachsenhausen, yet even in 1939 he had not received a new membership card yet. At least Bormann, who was calling the shots among the staff of the Führer's deputy Rudolf Heß, had intervened in the meantime, though rather reluctantly. From him the NSDAP Reich treasurer Franz Xaver Schwarz received under the subject 'SS Head Storm Leader Rudolf Höß, membership number 5 357 166, Sachsenhausen (northern railway), Friedlandstr. 11' the following request:

> Reich Leader Bormann has recently noticed while advising his old comrade-in-arms Rudolf Höß regarding his application for receiving the Blood Order that Höß has still not received news regarding his party membership. (…) Chief of Staff Bormann would be therefore grateful to you if you would from now on investigate the whereabouts of the membership card at your own initiative. Perhaps it is possible for you to give Höß a preliminary notification of his successfully joining the party for now so that he has some kind of record of this in his hands.[6]

Indeed Höß, 'residing at concentration camp Sachsenhausen', then received his membership card issued on 3April 1939 and containing the note that he had joined the party on 1May 1937 – and not in 1922.

Höß thus belonged retroactively from 1937 to the NSDAP with a very high membership number and could not expect much from the party. In vain he hoped to receive the Blood Order for his participation in the Parchim vigilante murder and in view of his subsequent jail sentence. Quite unusually, Höß himself had applied for the Blood Order – and did not receive it. His 'comrade-in-arms' and 'accomplice' Bormann, in contrast, had merely received a sentence of one year, had styled himself a martyr in various essays in the party organ *Völkischer Beobachter* [National Observer] and had been decorated for this with the Blood Order that Höß desired so much, yet in vain.

There is hardly anything written on his relationship to Bormann in Höß' *Autobiographic Notes*. In Cracow prison, however, waiting for his execution, he wrote that he had been Bormann's guest in spring 1935 together with some comrades from his time in the free corps in Mecklenburg. At that time Bormann was living in Pullach near Munich. His property was bordered by a newly built Jesuit school. Höß explained regarding this:

> According to Bormann's knowledge and account this is apparently furnished completely in line with modern requirements and managed in an exemplary manner. During our visit a class of these Jesuit students were running towards the playing field, all of them tall, slim yet strong figures of a uniform type. They could have been immediately absorbed into the 1st company of the Leibstandarte [Bodyguard Standard]. Bormann now turned the subject to the Jesuits and their principles of education. Their basic principle, to

unconditionally subordinate one's own will to the idea, has to be essential for the SS, too, if it ought to become the sword arm of the National Socialist movement. Soon after an essay appeared in the 'Black Corps' ['Schwarzer Korps'], the journal of the SS, which addressed this thought in more detail under a pseudonym.[7]

Not for nothing had Hitler, Goebbels and Himmler attended Jesuit schools, Höß wrote as an aside.

Not only was the Blood Order withheld from Höß, but also the 'Golden Party Badge'. How much this affected him becomes evident from the fact that years later – after the end of the war – he even complained about this in interrogations by the victorious British. Also his last rank – SS Senior Storm Command Leader corresponding in rank to a lieutenant colonel in the Wehrmacht – was not exactly an expression of high regard by the party leadership.

When Höß commenced his duty as adjutant and then as protective custody camp leader in Sachsenhausen, he remarked:

> Through a comrade in the liaison staff Heß I heard much from the Führer's circle. Another old comrade held a leading position in the Reich Youth leadership, another in Rosenberg's staff as press secretary, another in the Reich Medical Association. I now often met these old comrades from the free corps times in Berlin and became more than previously acquainted and familiar with the ideas of the party and its intentions.[8]

The truth is that Höß met with the 'old comrades', but he did not belong to them. He must have looked enviously upon his former comrades-in-arms of the Roßbach Committee or of the Artaman League:

- Heinrich Himmler, Reich Leader SS and then – besides many other offices – Reich Minister or the Interior and commander of the reserve army
- Martin Bormann, head of the NSDAP party chancellery and 'secretary of the Leader'
- Richard Walter Darré, Reich Peasant Leader
- Alfred Rosenberg, head of the NSDAP Office of Foreign Affairs, the Leader's Commissioner for the Supervision of Intellectual and Ideological Education of the NSDAP, head of operations at Staff Rosenberg, Reich Minister for the Occupied Eastern Territories
- Baldur von Schirach, Reich Youth Leader

- Walter Granzow, Minister President/Governor of Mecklenburg
- Kurt Daluege, SS Supreme Group Leader (SS-Oberstgruppenführer or General), head of the regular police force
- Karl von Eberstein, SS Senior Group Leader (SS-Obergruppenführer or Lieutenant General), General of the Waffen-SS [military arm of the SS] and police
- Karl Ernst, SA Group Leader and member of the Reichstag
- Hans Hayn, SA Leader
- Edmund Heines, SA Group Leader and member of the Reichstag
- Oskar Heines, SA Senior Storm Command Leader
- Wolf-Heinrich Count von Helldorf, SA Senior Group Leader
- Otto Hellwig, SS Group Leader
- Hans Kammler, SS Senior Group Leader and General of the Waffen-SS, head of the SS and army building sector
- Willi Klemm, SA Brigade Leader [brigadier]
- Paul Röhrbein, SA Brigade Leader
- Fritz Schlessmann, SS Group Leader

In contrast with these careers, Höß had to content himself with the SS Death Head's Ring awarded on 7 January 1943 and with the War Merit Cross First Class with Swords bestowed on 20 April 1943, which probably caused some inferiority complexes that he possibly wanted to compensate for by an especially perfected system of mass murder. To this was added that at the same time the head of the Central Building Department (ZBL) at Auschwitz concentration camp, SS Storm Commando Leader Karl Bischoff, had received the same decoration, too. Bischoff held equal rank to Höß at that time, which probably significantly lessened the value of this order for the latter.

Höß would possibly have also received the Knight's Cross in addition to the War Merit Cross. In the context of Operation Reinhardt,[9] the mass murder of the Hungarian Jews in German-occupied Poland and the Ukraine, Höß – who by now was head of department in Oranienburg – was sent to Auschwitz in order to increase the death rate. People were ceaselessly driven into the gas chambers and burnt in the crematoria. Höß urged the mostly drunk SS men who were on duty at the extermination sites to the greatest hurry, as SS Under Company Leader Pery Broad wrote, especially as Lublin was already in Russian hands and hence its gas chambers beyond reach for the 'Hungarian operation'.[10] The imminent end of the war prevented Höß receiving the decoration that he firmly believed he deserved.

In contrast to Operation Reinhardt, Operation Schmelt is not widely known. Albrecht Schmelt was Special Commissioner of the Reich Leader SS for Foreign Labour and head of the operation named after him. Schmelt organised the work details of Jews in road construction and in armament factories: and was responsible for approximately 180 labour camps. He had forced labourers who were no longer capable to work as well as the old and the sick selected and sent to Auschwitz for extermination. The greatest murder programme so far began on 12 May 1942; until August 1942 roughly 35,000 Jews from Upper Silesia were gassed. The selections were carried out by functionaries of Operation Schmelt, in particular by Friedrich Karl Kuczynski. Schmelt's office had its own barracks at Auschwitz. Camp commander Höß had even authorised on 9 July 1943 – after the end of Operation Schmelt – the construction of six barracks to house his people.

Mass Murderer Without a Sense of Guilt
Beside statements by perpetrators and witnesses during the trials at Nuremberg, Warsaw, Cracow, Jerusalem and Frankfurt and written orders or correspondence, Rudolf Höß' *Autobiographical Notes* count among the most important sources for descriptions of the origin of Auschwitz and the monstrous atrocities committed there.

It is obvious that Höß' statements and his notes take up a lot of space in the description of the mass murder of the Jews – and not only of them – with authors dealing at length with this complex account. The author of this book does not get around doing so, either. Yet how trustworthy was Höß? In a multitude of detailed questions, lies can be proven against him, which in part pervade his entire life, for example his date of birth. How far can we therefore believe his *Autobiographical Notes*? The answer is that we cannot, as will be shown in the following.

Despite the mass murder he organised and despite the numerous kill orders given by himself, Höß felt no personal guilt whatsoever. In this he was no different from the others who – after Hitler and Himmler – were responsible for the Holocaust. Adolf Eichmann, for instance, claimed to have only executed orders, the same as Oswald Pohl, SS Senior Group Leader and head of the SS Central Economic-Administrative Office. Both were masterminds of the organisation of mass murder. Even one of the worst among the perpetrators, the sadist Amon Leopold Göth, asked his Polish judges for clemency in order to become a 'useful member of society'.

It is telling for most of the perpetrators that they claimed to have known nothing and could not recall anything. Most denied any personal guilt, however, and washed their hands in innocence. Despite his undisputed willingness to talk, Höß was no exception:

> My life was colourful and varied. Through all the highs and lows of life fate has led me. Life was often tough for me, but I always struggled through. Never gave up. I had two guide stars giving my life direction, since I returned from the war as a man, into which I had gone as a schoolboy: my fatherland and later my family. My boundless love for the fatherland, my national consciousness, brought me to the NSDAP and to the SS. I considered the National Socialist world view to be the only appropriate one for the German people. In my view the SS was the most active champion of this outlook on life and only it was capable of gradually leading the entire German people back to an appropriate life.[11]

And further below it is written:

> Unwittingly I had become a cog in the great extermination machine of the Third Reich. The machine has been shattered, the motor has perished and I have to go along. The world demands it.[12]

His self-perception is contradicted, however, by the statement of the concentration camp prisoner Isaak Egon Ochshorn, who in September 1946 put the following remark by the commander of Auschwitz on record: 'Our system is so terrible that nobody in the world will believe that it is possible at all. Even if a Jew manages to flee and to tell the world what he saw: the world would brand him as a fantasist and liar, and nobody would believe him.'[13]

Similarly full of self-pity as Höß were other perpetrators, including Oswald Pohl. He had brought Höß as head of Office D I into the headquarters of his office. From May 1944 to July 1944 he sent him back to Auschwitz as camp senior, after Operation Reinhardt had stalled there. Höß had evidently gained a reputation among the SS leadership as the organiser of the virtually industrial killing of people.

Pohl wrote in his treatise *Credo* in the light of his impending execution:

> On 1st December 1947 the prison gates shut behind me: the last station of my earthly existence had swallowed me who had been sentenced to death.
>
> Outside the gates remained my life, which had led me without patronage and without 'connections' from a simple worker's son to the highest ranks of the military craft: through industry, sobriety

31

and sacrifice for a cause to which I dedicated myself from the beginning with enthusiast idealism. My life's work was shattered.

I do not feel called upon to examine National Socialism as a political ideology in its devastating effect on the individual and on society. (...) In this context only the share of my personal 'guilt' tormented me. (...) I had neither killed anybody nor invited or encouraged others to do so, I had demonstrably and energetically opposed inhumanities as far as I gained knowledge of them – but did this clear me of 'guilt'?[14]

Pohl had been 'converted' and had returned to the fold of the church, but he had learned nothing. He recalled the people who had once acted in concert with him. What had become of them, he asked and immediately gave the answer:

Since I was incarcerated and thus prevented from observing their behaviour in the outside world, I watched the more closely the selection of those who appeared as witnesses and defendants at the Nuremberg trials. Aside from a few exceptions I did not recognise them. Was this the proud courage of conviction which in glorious times had thundered through the German regions and with which the high and highest leaders of all organisations especially manifested their sanctity and infallibility? Where was now the sermonised ideal 'Loyalty is the marrow of honour' (Hindenburg) and 'Your honour is loyalty' (Himmler)? I saw scarecrows who had apparently dreamed away the years of the Third Reich as lifeless dummies and acted as such, who knew nothing or little.[15]

Just like Höß or Eichmann, Pohl did not wish to recognise, either, that his actions had been shaped by inhumanity. The same holds true for the aforementioned SS Head Storm Leader Amon Göth, who from March 1943 until September 1944 was commander of the Plaszow concentration camp near Cracow. He wreaked his obsessive sadism on the prisoners and murdered many of them with his own hands out of sheer pleasure. Together with Höß he was surrendered to the Polish after the war. Both arrived in Cracow by train on 30 June 1946. In a petition for mercy addressed to the Polish state president dated 5 September 1946, Göth claimed to have only followed orders as a soldier. Amon Göth was sentenced to death for mass murder and hanged on 13 September 1946.

SS Senior Company Leader Wilhelm Boger of the Political Department at Auschwitz tortured prisoners with the so-called Boger swing 'invented' by him. It consisted of two vertical posts at which the prisoners were hung head down from a pole by the hollows of their knees where the wrists were tied to the ankles or the pole. In this helpless position they were interrogated by Boger and his henchmen and beaten with sticks and whips, some of them to the death; this gained him the name 'beast of Auschwitz'. Boger cynically called this torture instrument the 'talking machine'. He did not want to know of any fatal mistreatments, either: 'The 'intensified questioning' had fulfilled its purpose when either the confession was made or a state was reached in which absolutely nothing more could be gained from the witness. Yet nobody was killed.'[16] If prisoners later died, they were perhaps shot, but nobody found their death through 'intensified questioning'.

None of the Nazi perpetrators felt guilty, and Höß least of all. And yet he was involved in everything terrible happening at Auschwitz down to the last detail. As proper as it was that Höß had to pay for his deeds at the gallows in front of his commandant's villa, so it is regretful that he could not comment upon the accusations made by other SS perpetrators against him during later trials. This would have been instrumental in one case or another during the 1st Frankfurt Auschwitz Trial. As it was, Höß could be blatantly portrayed as the actual prime mover of the mass murder in order to qualify their own part in the Holocaust.

SS Storm Man Horst Huley, for example, had joined the guard battalion at Auschwitz in 1941 and had to perform cordoning off duties when new prisoners arrived at the infamous ramp. He confirmed that 'Mr Höß' was frequently present and carried out the selections – also with SS Head Storm Leader Heinrich Schwarz, commander of Auschwitz III – which decided upon immediate death or the extension of a torturous life.[17]

Leopold Heger was also SS Storm Man when he was ordered to Auschwitz and became Höß' driver. Yet Höß only made use of him for longer journeys, for example to the Majdanek extermination camp where Höß wanted to find inspiration for the improvement of the Auschwitz machinery of murder. He confirmed, however, that Höß drove his own car to the outer ramp when the Birkenau ramp had not been completed yet. Höß fetched the car from the motor pool or had Heger bring it to his villa. Heger was deputy head of the motor pool and left – according to his statement – his post only when Höß requested him. Incidentally, even in 1964 he did not say a bad word against Höß: 'I do remember Baer, but I had no contact to him. I had contact with Höß. I even got along very well with Höß, but not with Liebehenschel and not with Baer, either.'[18] Approached on the subject of the driving orders for the vehicles that brought the people to the gas chambers, Heger said that there had been only oral instructions issued by Höß or his deputy.

The Questioning of Rudolf Höß and Otto Moll

The absurd attitude taken by numerous Nazi perpetrators by claiming downright that they had merely followed orders became especially apparent during the joint interrogation of Höß and one of his closest assistants, SS Head Company Leader Otto Moll. In 1935 Moll was drafted as an SS cadet to the SS Death Head Standard 'Brandenburg' in Oranienburg and permanently accepted into the SS on 16 November 1936. His 'career' as concentration camp torturer began in 1938 as detail leader in the plant nursery of the Sachsenhausen camp. On 2 May 1941 he was transferred to Auschwitz, where he was at first involved in agricultural operations and subsequently spread fear in the punishment battalion. After that, until the initial operation of the crematoria of the extermination camp in Birkenau, he managed in various functions the special unit for the burning of corpses in pits near Bunkers I and II. Moll distinguished himself by particularly sadistic behaviour and was therefore also called the 'Auschwitz angel of death'. In Auschwitz-Birkenau he personally committed numerous murders such as the shooting of women and children. Höß appointed him 'commissioner for the extermination of the Hungarian Jews'. He drafted the so-called Moll Plan, which intended the bombardment of the camp complex after its evacuation and thus the killing of the remaining prisoners, which could no longer be put into action, however.

During the main Dachau trial, Moll had requested to be questioned with Höß – a wish that was granted on 16 April 1946. The interrogation was conducted by Lieutenant Colonel Smith W. Brookhart.[19]

The arrogance of the perpetrators revealed itself when, at the beginning of the interrogation, Moll declared that it was an insult to him to see that the commander 'walks freely while I am cuffed to a guard'. Yet Brookhart told Moll curtly that his feelings were of no consequence whatsoever.[20]

On Moll's tasks, Höß made the following statement:

> Firstly he had to ensure that the people undressed in an orderly fashion, and that after their killing the corpses were disposed in an orderly manner, and later, when the extensive extermination complex had been completed, he had responsibility for the whole complex.[21]

Moll showed himself self-confident and even boasted to have carried out his 'work correctly in all weathers':

> I was never drunk while on duty or with prisoners, and I have never mistreated a prisoner. I have achieved great success with regards to the prisoners' labour because I pitched in myself during their work. The prisoners respected me because I behaved towards them like a model soldier, and therefore I was put onto all difficult tasks coming up.[22]

On 30 April 1943 Moll received the War Merit Cross 1st Class with Swords and said three years later to Brookhart 'for work like this I did not want to have an order'. He explained this so far unfamiliar opinion of his with the fact that his work had not been 'honourable'. He claimed to have asked Höß several times why these 'things' had to be done, why they could not stop them. Höß allegedly explained that he did not like it, either, that he must execute such strict orders and that they could not change anything in this regard. Moll: 'He suffered like us all under this work, and none of us was still really sane.' Upon the question of when he lost his mind, Höß corrected Brookhart conducting the interrogation: 'I believe you mean when our nerves no longer put up with the strain.' Once more he claimed 'superior orders': 'I had to do these things because nobody else was there who would have done them in our stead. There were strict orders and they had to be followed. Many others felt like me, and subordinate leaders came to me, such as Moll has done, and spoke about it and had the same sentiments.'[23]

Moll also made more precise distinctions: 'I did not mean to say that I was crazy for a shorter or longer period, but that I was a nervous wreck again and again.' He was signed off work due to the state of his nerves, but he was never declared unfit for duty because of it or because of Paragraph 51 of the Penal Code.

As not to be expected otherwise, Moll bridled at the accusation of having been responsible for the death of people himself:

> If you say 'responsible', then I would like to emphasize once more that I do not agree with using this word in any manner to the actual killing of people, as I was not responsible for the actual physical termination, and I will not admit to this, as it does not correspond with the facts.[24]

Moll described that it took about half a minute until death occurred in the gas chambers and based his statement on the following facts and circumstances:

> The gas was inserted through an opening. Roughly half a minute after the gas had been inserted – of course I can only estimate this, as we had no stop watches to measure this and we were not interested in it anyway, at any rate after half a minute there were no longer any loud noises, and also otherwise no sounds could be heard from the gas chamber any longer.[25]

He had to listen to the crying and screams of the people 'because I was close by with my work detail. I could do nothing against it, as I had no possibility to change anything'. Again he strictly denied any responsibility:

> I was not responsible for the preparations because there were no special preparations. The victims were led into the gas chamber by the leader on duty, there was a work detail of the administrator who told them to get undressed. There was another detail of the actual administration responsible for collecting all valuables from the people. The whole affair took place in a very correct manner, and in no case there was reason to intervene. I had no right to intervene, the entire procedure was supervised by a medical doctor.[26]

During the evacuation of the concentration camp Moll distinguished himself by particular cruelty.[27] If prisoners lagged behind on the death march due to malnourishment and exhaustion, they were shot on the spot by a detail under his command.

When the Majdanek concentration camp was dissolved in June 1944, SS Senior Company Leader Erich Mußfeldt was transferred to Auschwitz-Birkenau. Here he worked under Moll as leader of the special unit at the Birkenau II and III crematoria; from September 1944 until the evacuation of the camp in January 1945 as head of all crematoria.

For the record: Höß emphasized that the victims undressed 'in an orderly fashion' and that 'the corpses were disposed of in an orderly manner'. Moll insisted that he was not responsible for the 'actual physical termination' of the victims' life and that 'the whole affair' proceeded 'correctly'. And just like Höß and even his daughter Ingebrigitt declared, if not they, then others would have been ready to murder, Moll uttered this pseudo-argument, too. To call the procedure of murdering people 'correct' reveals one of the starkest perversions imaginable.

Moll was sentenced to death by an American military court and this was carried out on 28 May 1946 in the Landshut prison for war criminals. Mußfeldt was executed at the end of January 1948 in Cracow.

Höß also claimed during this interrogation to have only executed orders, this time those of Eichmann. The latter did not only order the extermination of the Hungarian Jews, but also the killing of the work details at the crematoria in three-month intervals. He did not follow the latter order, however, because he did not deem it right. Höß states another falsehood with this.

Blind Obedience

In Nuremberg the American psychologist Gustave M. Gilbert conducted long conversations with Höß, and in the Polish prison in which the commander of Auschwitz was held from 25 May 1946 until his execution on 16 April 1947, the psychologist Stanislaw Batawia and the legal expert Jan Sehn tried to comprehend his psyche.

Gilbert had been brought in as court psychologist to the Nuremberg trials of the International Military Tribunal and had talked to every defendant person to person. Before, during the war, Gilbert, who was born in New York in 1911, had conducted interrogations of prisoners. In preparation for the trial against Ernst Kaltenbrunner, who from 1943 until the end of the war was head of the Security Police and the Security Service as well as head of the Reich Security Main Office [Reichssicherheitshauptamt], he questioned Höß while in custody on 9 April 1946. Reich Marshal Hermann Göring had doubted whether it was technically possible to murder 2.5 million people, and Gilbert now expected an answer to this from Höß.[28]

They spoke about Höß' work during his time as commander at Auschwitz. Willingly Höß conceded that this, which he always called the 'extermination operation', had begun in summer 1941 and that under his administration almost 2.5 million Jews had been killed.[29] He declared this not difficult at all, and that it would even have been possible to exterminate even more people. To the question by Gilbert about how many people could be killed in one hour, the former concentration camp commander answered that for such a calculation one had to assume a twenty-four-hour-day: in Auschwitz there were six extermination chambers – 2,000 people could be gassed in each of the two large chambers and in the four smaller chambers up to 1,500 people could be so killed, which amounted to a total capacity of 10,000 victims per day.

Gilbert showed himself shocked. He tried to imagine how the murder proceeded, but Höß corrected him: 'No. You do not imagine it correctly. The killing itself took the least time, but the cremation cost so much time. The killing was easy; one did not even need a guard detail to drive them into the chambers; they simply went into them because they assumed they would take a shower there, and instead of water we turned up the poisoned gas. The entire affair went very quickly.'[30] He reported all this in a 'calm, apathetic and sober tone'.

On 12 April 1946 Gilbert questioned the former commander of Auschwitz once more in the latter's cell.[31] He wanted to know whether he had ever wondered if the Jews murdered by him were guilty or deserved such a fate in any way. Höß answered that he had been living in an entirely different world: 'Don't you understand, we SS men were not supposed to ponder such questions; it never crossed our mind. And furthermore it had become a certain matter of course that the Jews were to blame for everything.'

This seems to be contradicted by Höß' answer before the Nuremberg tribunal, when Kaltenbrunner's defence counsel, Kurt Kauffmann, asked him: 'Did you yourself ever feel sympathy for the victims in view of your own family and children?' Höß replied with a very curt, 'Yes, sir', probably because it was expected of him.[32] To the enquiry why he had nevertheless been able to carry out the mass murder, Höß spoke of 'doubts', but for him 'the unconditional order by Reich Leader Himmler and its reason given was always exclusively determinant'.

To Gilbert, Höß confirmed that it had always been clear to him that Germany had to be protected from the Jews. Only after the collapse of National Socialism did he begin to have doubts:

> Yet nobody said something like that beforehand; at least we did not hear of it. Now I would only like to know if Himmler believed all that himself or only provided me with the means to justify all of that which he wanted to have done by me. At any rate this was actually not crucial. We were all drilled to execute orders without thinking. The thought of not executing an order simply occurred to nobody. And somebody else would have done it anyway, if I had not done it ... Himmler was so strict in details and had SS men executed for minor offences – we took it for granted that he stuck by a strict code of honour.[33]

It had not always been 'a pleasure to see the mountains of corpses and to smell the incessant cremation. Yet Hitler [he probably meant Himmler] had ordered it and had even explained its necessity. And I have actually never wasted much thought on whether it was wrong. It simply seemed to be necessary.'[34]

In all conversations Höß presented himself – at least in Gilbert's opinion – very rational and dispassionate, showed some 'delayed interest in the enormity of his crime', but gave the impression as if this would have never occurred to him if nobody had pointed it out. Gilbert's judgement: 'He is too apathetic to believe in any remorse by him, and also the prospect of being hanged does not seem to disturb him unduly. He leaves the overall impression of a man who is intellectually psychologically normal, but shows a schizoid apathy, insensitivity and lack of empathy, as it occurs hardly less extreme in a real schizophrenic.'[35]

Gilbert thus explains only in part why Höß acted during his interrogations markedly rationally, described details of the mass murder without emotion and saw himself as a mere recipient of orders whose task it had been to do his part for the extermination of the Jews.

Höß was not apathetic at any time, however, and he probably did not do his 'work' with enthusiasm, either. He fulfilled that which had been assigned to him as his duty – no more and no less.

The Anti-Semite

Höß confessed himself to be a strict anti-Semite and justified this among other things with the fact that for years he had read every week Goebbel's leading article in the *Reich*, equally his books and speeches, further Rosenberg's *Mythus des 20. Jahrhunderts* [*The Myth of the 20th Century*] and of course Hitler's *My Struggle* as well as most of his speeches.[36] To this were added ideological pamphlets and other training material of the SS. Streicher's *Stürmer* [*Attacker*], on the other hand, had seemed to him too superficial. Those who had regularly read the *Stürmer* were mostly people with a very limited grasp. Goebbels, Rosenberg and Hitler stimulated his thoughts more, and it was written by all of them that Judaism was Germany's enemy:

> I, as an old fanatical National Socialist, accepted this as fact – just like a Catholic believes in his church dogma. It was simply the truth you were not supposed to rock; I had no doubts about it. I was absolutely convinced that the Jews were the antithesis of the German people and that sooner or later there had to be a conflict between National Socialism and World Jewry – I thought this already during the peace. On the basis of these doctrines I assumed that sooner or later other nations would also recognise the Jewish threat and equally take up position against it. In these books and writings and speeches it was stated that the Jewish people were in all countries a minority. Yet because the Jews were so strong financially, they influenced and dominated the people so extensively that they could

maintain their power. It was shown how they ruled the German people through the control exercised by them over the press, film, radio and the educational sector. We assumed that it was the same in other countries and that with time other countries would break their power just like us. And if anti-Semitism did not come through, then the Jews would succeed in causing a war that would destroy Germany. Everybody was convinced of this; you could hear and read it everywhere. This was even before the war. Then, after the outbreak of war, Hitler declared that the world Jewry had begun a conflict with National Socialism. This was in a speech before the Reichstag at the time of the French campaign. The Jews had to be destroyed. Of course at that time nobody thought that this was meant literally. Yet Goebbels expressed himself ever more fiercely against the Jews. He accused England or Holland or France not so much of being our enemy as he did the Jews. And he called Roosevelt and Morgenthau and others the people who intended to bring Germany down to a primitive standard of living. And it was always emphasized that world Jewry had to be exterminated if Germany ought to survive, and all of us considered this to be the truth.

That was the image in my mind. And when Himmler summoned me, I took on the task as something which I had already accepted earlier – and not only I, but everyone. I considered it absolutely right despite this order which would have shaken the strongest and coldest people – and just at this moment this stark order to exterminate thousands of people (I did not know at that time how many) – and although it terrified me temporarily ... After all it fitted perfectly with that which had been preached to me for years. The problem itself, the extermination of the Jews was not new – only that I was supposed to be the one to carry it out frightened me at first. Yet after I had received the unambiguous, direct order and even an explanation for it – then nothing remained but to execute it.[37]

If Höß spoke of being summoned by Himmler and given the order to exterminate the Jews, then this is most likely an expression of great confidence by the Reich Leader SS in Höß. Regardless of that, Himmler had generally ordered the 'eradication of the Jews'. The head of Department D II, SS Senior Storm Command Leader Gerhard Maurer, had forwarded this instruction on 5 October 1942 to the commanders of all concentration camps.[38] According to this, Himmler ordered 'that all concentration camps on Reich territory must be made free of Jews. Therefore Jews in those concentration camps ought to be transferred to Auschwitz or Lublin.' The numbers of the prisoners held should be reported immediately.

Höß was ready for unconditional obedience, but not until self-abandonment. No, the extermination of non-Jewish enemies of the state and Jews was in any case something with which he could identify himself perfectly. When on 19 May 1946 Gilbert wanted to probe the indications of sadistic tendencies in Höß, he asked him if Himmler had possibly chosen him for the post as commander because he had known of his past as a vigilante killer. Höß denied this most vigorously:[39]

> He could have just as well chosen any other SS officer. We were all drilled for unconditional obedience regardless of the nature of our orders. I was at that time commander of Auschwitz by pure chance, and he had decided to make Auschwitz the principal eradication camp. Nothing else remained for me to do but to execute the orders. Every other SS man would have done the same. The same happened to Eichmann, who had been tasked with the entire programme of eradication, and also to the leaders of the deployment groups, as for example Ohlendorf.[40]

From this Gilbert concluded: 'He believed that if he was guilty of murder, so was the entire SS; for they were all trained to do the same without the slightest scruples.' Yet Gilbert's opinion has to be amended insofar that the choice most certainly did not fall on Höß by chance.

Incidentally, only former Reich Marshal Hermann Göring and former Grand Admiral Dönitz[41] were willing to comment upon Höß' statements on the mass murder of the Jews and other ethnic groups in Nuremberg.[42] Gilbert assumed that their remarks had been previously agreed upon in the dock: Höß was no Prussian but evidently a Southern German; a Prussian would never have brought himself to do such things. Solely Hans Michael Frank, the former General Governor of occupied Poland and the 'butcher of the Jews of Cracow',[43] said to Gilbert: 'That was the nadir of the entire trial – to hear a man say with his own words that he murdered two and a half million people in cold blood. Of this people will still speak in a thousand years.'

Chapter 3

Höß and the SS

Adjutant and Protective Custody Camp Leader in Sachsenhausen Concentration Camp

From November 1939 until May 1940 Höß was leader of the protective custody camp at Sachsenhausen concentration camp with the rank of SS Head Storm Leader and thus responsible for the entire area of the prisoner camp. It is telling that of all people he had chosen the Sachsenhausen camp commander SS Senior Leader Hermann Baranowski as a role model. The prisoners had got to know Baranowski as a hard and brutal SS leader who stopped at nothing. He could watch the whippings for hours and cheer on the SS men to strike even harder: 'Then his laughter roared through the night, he bellowed and slapped his thighs. To the prisoners he called: "If I laugh, the devil laughs",'[1] the camp senior Harry Naujoks shudders even after decades.

Höß, in contrast, described Baranowski as:

> very strict and hard, but of a scrupulous sense of fair play and fanatical sense of duty. As a very old SS leader and National Socialist he became my role model. I constantly saw in him a grander reflection of myself. He also had moments where his good nature, his soft heart revealed themselves, and yet he was hard and uncompromisingly strict in all matters of duty. So he constantly brought home to me how the hard 'must' demanded by the SS had to silence all soft stirrings.[2]

These lines reveal Höß' conception of himself, as he also expressed it in his farewell letters: he had only done his duty, but had a heart and was basically a good man.

During Höß' time as adjutant and camp leader in Sachsenhausen, the first systematic mass shootings of opponents of the regime and

Soviet prisoners of war took place under his supervision. For this purpose the Gestapo [Secret State Police] had invented an installation that enabled killings in series without causing unrest and suspicion among the prisoners:

> The installation for shots in the back of the neck intended for mass shootings was camouflaged as a medical station. SS men dressed up in white coats received the prisoners and feigned examinations. The look into the mouth of each prisoner, however, only served to identify gold teeth or prostheses which were supposed to be pried out after the killing. Finally the men were led one by one into a room where seemingly their height was to be measured. Actually the bar in front of which they had to stand served only as cover. By a narrow gap it marked the neck of the prisoner for the SS man posted in the soundproof and darkened room next door, who thus could place the fatal shot in the neck right on target.[3]

Regardless of the extent to which Höß had ordered shootings himself: according to his own standards he, as protective custody camp leader, always had to be informed on all incidents in the camp 'by means of an appropriate monitoring system'.[4] Further, it was his task to appoint the 'prisoner supervisors' – the block seniors and kapos [a foreman-like prison functionary].[5] Unsuitable 'prisoner supervisors' had to be relieved immediately, which Höß clearly neglected in the case of Palitsch, to which we will return later. Should prisoners be punished, it was the protective custody camp leader's responsibility to interview them first and then to suggest a level of penalty to the commander. Furthermore, he was supposed to instruct the entire personnel in the conduct with prisoners, especially in the prohibition of mistreatment. If these standards are applied, Höß clearly failed as protective custody camp leader at Sachsenhausen, and this is true to a far greater extent for his service as commander of Auschwitz.

Mass Murder as Purpose in Life

By the end of 1939 the inspector of the security police and the SD [Security Service] had already proposed the establishment of a concentration camp in occupied Poland with the Higher SS and Police Leader in Wroclaw, SS Senior Leader Wiegandt, because he expected mass arrests among the Polish population of Upper Silesia. Wiegandt's conviction was that the Polish resistance to the German occupation had to be broken by all means, and for this purpose they needed sufficient accommodation for the high number of prisoners to be expected. At first Himmler decided to establish a 'quarantine camp' in

Upper Silesia, which soon turned into a concentration camp. Wiegandt began his search on the ground and found a seemingly suitable spot at the Sola River, a tributary of the Vistula: Auschwitz with 12,000 inhabitants, among them 8,000 Jews – other sources speak of 7,000 – as well as roughly 3,000 'free' Polish.[6] This location had been taken by the Wehrmacht on 4 September 1939 and had been incorporated directly into the German Reich, while most parts of occupied Poland were consolidated in the 'General Government'.

The seed for the largest extermination facility for human life ever seen by the world were empty barracks of a Polish artillery regiment as well as some buildings of the Polish Tobacco Monopoly Company. From the planners' viewpoint Auschwitz was conveniently located, but most of all it did not seem vulnerable to aerial attack – before the background of the looming Second World War this was an important aspect. On 27 April 1940 Himmler gave the official order for the establishment of the concentration camp. Already, on 18 and 19 April 1940, Höß had explored the area around Auschwitz and familiarised himself with the local conditions.

Prepared for his new task, Höß was transferred to Auschwitz on 1 May 1940 with the guideline to collaborate closely with the mayor. The initial point was to renovate the existing barracks. For this the Jewish community had to provide approximately 300 Jews.[7] Furthermore, a prisoner detail of thirty-nine men from the Dachau concentration camp was deployed until mid-June 1940 in order to erect a first fence line around the future camp. Guard duty was performed by a commando of the SS equestrian division stationed at Cracow.

Höß arrived with five members of the SS and at first conducted his 'official duties' from a hotel near the train station. His future official villa was initially claimed by SS junior leaders and other SS personnel. To Höß' inner circle belonged as adjutant SS Senior Storm Leader Josef Kramer, as first protective custody camp leader SS Senior Storm Command Leader Karl Fritsch and as his deputy SS Under Storm Leader Franz Xaver Mayr. In addition, they had to find accommodation for the SS members and German civil servants of the administration. In spring 1941 Höß and the representative of the Reich Commissioner for the Strengthening of the German National Character from Katowice and the mayor of Auschwitz, Grünweller, visited the location on the right bank of the Sola.[8] It transpired that a large part of the apartments, as far as they had Polish owners, was in excellent condition. In contrast, the members of the committee recorded that the residences in the Jewish quarter could not be renovated for Reich and ethnic Germans, even with great effort, and thus were unsuitable. It was determined that

Polish and Jews ought to be 'evacuated', namely under the premise of the provision of housing for Germans. A first transport was supposed to contain up to 250 people, a second 800. The necessary plans were to be drafted by Höß and to be co-ordinated with the mayor.

During the visit the committee had further noted that there was still 'metal essential to the war effort' inside the houses. A 'collection' was prompted accordingly. Furthermore, a history of the town of Auschwitz was to be written, namely by a SS Head Company Leader who was a primary school teacher, and belong to the commander's staff of the concentration camp. He was offered a monthly remuneration of 250 RM maximum. Additionally he was to be assisted by a female Polish teacher who was permitted to be paid up to three Reichsmark per day. Furthermore, it was expressly allowed to use the services of 'intellectual Jews' if required for the success of the chronicle.

In a letter to the representative of the Reich Commissioner for the Strengthening of the German National Character in Katowice, Höß complained at the same time that farmers to be resettled were allowed to sell large livestock.[9] He listed some examples for which the East German Land Management Company had allowed this. Butchers had bought the livestock and had already slaughtered it for the largest part – Höß imputed that these were 'black slaughters'. The 'remaining livestock' he had had confiscated and brought to the camp.

In addition to his task as commander, Höß was assigned the leadership of a special commission determining the guidelines for the extension of the concentration camp and the number of persons to be settled in Auschwitz. The entire environs of Auschwitz were supposed to form a so-called Wehrmacht estate district. That meant that the German Reich was viewed as its proprietor and the area, with seven municipalities, was administered by the Waffen-SS. A requirement for this was a functioning mayor's office and this was to be established by Ludwig Damm among others.

The civil servant Damm had been ordered to Auschwitz at the beginning of August 1942 and here he had some experience of Höß. During a visit home Damm had hinted at the monstrous events in the camp and was advised by the court officer of the garrison command to report this immediately to his superior on his return. The consequence for SS Storm Man Ludwig Damm was a stern reprimand by commander Höß dated 5 January 1943:

> I punish you according to the German Professional Code for the mobile state § 8 Section C subparagraph 2 with a stern reprimand, because you acted against existing orders and regulations during

45

your period of leave. Reason: during your period of leave in December 1942 you talked to soldiers and party comrades about the Jewish issue and made statements concerning the solution of the Jewish question at Auschwitz. With this behaviour, which under circumstances might have caused unrest among the population, you acted against the orders known to you. I abstained from a more severe punishment merely on the basis of your impeccable conduct so far and a favourable assessment by a third party and expect that this incident serves as a lesson to you for the future.

Höß, Senior Storm Command Leader and Commander[10]

Less lucky was Jan Pilecki, who was brought to Auschwitz with one of the first transports. He was a specialist in the field of electrical engineering and initially belonged to the electricians detail at Auschwitz. There, however, he listened with fellow sufferers to foreign broadcasts, which caused Höß to send him to the infamous punishment battalion.[11]

Höß himself described the beginnings of the concentration camp Auschwitz as follows:

From my superior department, the former inspection of concentration camps, I received the order to create a quarantine camp for prisoners coming from Poland on the grounds of the former Polish artillery barracks near AUSCHWITZ.[12] After HIMMLER's visit to the camp in 1941 I received the order to develop the camp as a large concentration camp for the east and especially to employ the prisoners in the agricultural enterprise which was to be expanded as much as possible and thus to cultivate the entire swamp and inundation area along the Vistula. Further he now ordered the provision of 8,000 to 10,000 prisoners for the construction of the new Buna works of the I.G. Farben. At the same time he ordered the building of a prisoner of war camp for 100,000 Russian prisoners on the area of BIRKENAU.

The number of prisoners rose from day to day. As the sanitary facilities did not suffice at all, sickness was unavoidable. As a result mortality rose, too. Since the burial of prisoners was not allowed, the first crematoria were constructed.

(...) 1941 the first transports of Jews arrived from SLOVENIA and the Upper Silesian region. Those unfit to work were gassed in the antechamber of the crematorium on an order given to me by Himmler personally.

In June 1941 I was ordered to a meeting in Berlin with HIMMLER, and he explained to me the following: the Führer has demanded the solution of the Jewish question in Europe. A few extermination camps existed in the General Government (BELZEC near RAVA RUSKA, Eastern Poland, TREBLINKA near MALINA at the River Bug, and

WOLZEK near Lublin). These camps were under the control of the task force of the security police led by high officers of the security police and guard details. These camps were not very efficient and could not be extended. I visited the camp TREBLINKA in spring 1942 in order to inform myself on the spot of the conditions.The following methods were applied for executions: small chambers equipped with pipes were used to introduce fatal exhaust fumes from car motors. This method was unreliable, as motors came from old, captured transport vehicles and very often malfunctioned. (...) According to the camp commander of TREBLINKA, 8,000 people had been gassed within half a year – for Himmler too few.[13]

For the murderous plans of the National Socialists Auschwitz, in a sparsely settled region, proved itself as the location suitable for a mass extermination facility. It was situated at a railway junction where four lines crossed and which enabled the sending of prisoner transports from all countries occupied by Germany directly to the camp. During his stay in Berlin Höß received instructions from Himmler to present within four weeks a plan for the construction of this camp. Moreover, he impressed on Höß that this task was so difficult and important that he had actually considered assigning this task to a further high-ranking SS officer. However, in the end he did not deem it advisable to entrust two officers with the same task. Höß received the order to carry out the extermination of the Jews – Höß himself speaks of 'deliveries' by the Reich Security Main Office (RSHA). During this he was supposed to maintain close contact with SS Senior Storm Command Leader Adolf Eichmann of Department 4 (an office headed by SS Group Leader Müller) regarding the arriving transports.

First, however, thousands of Russian prisoners of war, who according to Himmler's written order to the local Gestapo leaders were to be 'annihilated', i.e. killed, were brought to Auschwitz from the Gestapo headquarters at Wroclaw, Opava and Katowice. Since new crematoria were not to be completed until 1942, the prisoners were killed in makeshift gas chambers and then buried in pits.

Very early on, namely on 1 March 1941, Himmler visited the Auschwitz camp in the company of the NSDAP regional leader of Upper Silesia, Fritz Bracht, the district president Springorum, the Higher SS and Police Leader Erich von dem Bach-Zelewski and the inspector of concentration camps Richard Glücks, as well as representatives of I.G. Farben.[14] Höß states that already on that occasion he reported on difficulties during the establishment of the camp; regardless Himmler ordered its expansion to 30,000 prisoners. In addition, up to 10,000 prisoners were to be provided for the construction of an

I.G. Farbenindustrie works. Jews were to be resettled in the area earmarked for agriculture, but the Polish population was allowed to remain for now to be exploited for their workforce. Allegedly, Himmler also ordered the construction of a camp for 100,000 Russian prisoners of war, however, the number given by Höß seems rather unrealistic.

Ahead of this visit the camp had been 'spruced up' as much as possible. Himmler was presented exclusively with well-fed and cleanly dressed prisoners, as Wieslaw Kielar wrote, himself a prisoner at Auschwitz:

> The hospital took on the look of a real hospital. At least on the outside. The sick were lying in individual beds on sheets with clean covers. Under the beds were bedpans, feeding cups and chamber pots. The kitchen provided milk soup for those having stomach trouble, salt-free food for those with kidney problems and white bread for those on a special diet. The corpse carriers had to keep their activities hidden.[15]

Himmler's visit had also its positive aspects, as Kielar states further, for part of the feigned benefits remained in place for some time. Yet the number of dead increased nevertheless, because epidemics broke out again and again.

Incredible Intransigence

Auschwitz was originally conceived as a mere 'quarantine camp' and transit station for Polish prisoners for the 'Old Reich', but it rapidly developed into the largest installation for mass murder experienced by humankind.

Höß was responsible for the frictionless functioning of the murder machinery and he did everything he could so as not to disappoint the expectations placed on him by his commander, Himmler. Much has been written about the coolness with which Höß pursued his task. His account is barely believable in its brutality and lack of empathy:

> Two old farm houses situated on the road to BIRKENAU were made airtight and fitted with wooden doors. The transports were unloaded at the edge of BIRKENAU. Prisoners fit for work were selected and brought to the camps. The luggage remained behind and was brought to the camps later. The others who were to be gassed had to march to the extension a kilometre away. The sick and people incapable of walking were brought there by vehicles. In front of the farm houses all had to undress behind walls made from branches. The door had a sign 'disinfection room'. The junior leaders on duty had to explain to the prisoners that they should take care of

their possessions in order to find them again after delousing. This prevented unrest. When they were undressed, they marched into the room, which was large enough for 200 to 300 people at once. The doors were closed and two or three cans of Zyklon B were dropped into the room through holes in the walls. It consisted of a coarse substance of hydro-cyanic acid. The duration was 3 to 10 minutes, depending on the weather. After half an hour the doors were opened and the bodies were removed and burnt by the prisoners detail permanently deployed there. Before the corpses were burnt, gold teeth and rings were removed. Firewood was placed between the corpses, and when roughly a hundred bodies were inside the pits, the wood was set on fire by rags quenched with paraffin. If the fire burnt well, more corpses were thrown upon it. The body fat collecting at the bottom of the pits was poured with buckets onto the fire in order to accelerate the process during rain. The burning took six to seven hours. The smell of the burnt bodies was noticed inside the camp, even if the wind was blowing from the west. After the pits were emptied, the remaining ashes were broken up. This happened on a cement platform where prisoners pulverised the remaining bones with wooden hammers. The remains were brought to a remote location at the Vistula and then dumped into the river. (...) After the first two large crematoria had been finished in 1942 – the two additional ones followed half a year later – mass transports from Belgium, France, the Netherlands and Greece began. Transport trains halted at a purpose-built ramp with three tracks situated between crematorium, camp and the BIRKENAU camp. The selection of prisoners and the distribution of luggage took place on the ramp. Prisoners fit for work were distributed among the various camps, and prisoners to be executed were brought to one of the new crematoria. There the first ones went into one of the large subterranean rooms to undress. This room was furnished with benches and clothes hooks, and the prisoners were told by the translators that they would be bathed and deloused here and that they should take care of their belongings. They continued into the next room equipped with taps and shower heads in order to give the impression of a bathroom. Two junior leaders remained inside the room until the last moment in order to prevent unrest. Sometimes it happened that the prisoners knew what was coming. Especially the transports from BELSEN knew, when they returned from the east and the trains reached Upper Silesia, that they had been brought to the extermination site. When trains from BELSEN arrived, the security measures were increased and the transport was divided into smaller groups brought to different crematoria in order to prevent riots. SS men formed a narrow cordon and forced resisting prisoners into the gas chambers.

It was very rare that prisoners resisted the measures we had put in place. I remember well the following incident: a transport from BELSEN arrived, circa two-thirds, primarily men, were in the gas chamber, the remaining third was in the divestment room. When three or four SS junior leaders came into the divestment room in order to speed up the undressing, a riot broke out. Electric cables were ripped out and the SS men overpowered. One of them was stabbed and all were disarmed. When it was completely dark inside the room, a wild shootout broke out between the guards near the exit and the prisoners inside. When I arrived, I ordered the doors closed and the termination of the first part of the gassing, and then I went inside the room with guards equipped with flash lights and we drove the prisoners into a corner, from where individual people were driven into another room of the crematorium and shot with small calibre weapons on my order.

It happened repeatedly that women hid their children under their clothes and did not bring them into the gas chamber. The clothing was searched under SS supervision by a permanent prisoner detail, and the children found were sent to the gas chamber. After half an hour an electrical ventilator was switched on and the corpses were brought up to the incinerators by an elevator. The burning of roughly 2,000 prisoners in five ovens took approximately 12 hours.

In AUSCHWITZ there were two extensions, each had five double incinerators. In addition there were two further extensions, each with four larger ovens, and provisional offshoots as described above. The second provisional offshoot was destroyed. All the clothes and all the prisoners' possessions were sorted at the camp by a prisoner detail permanently active and also stationed there.

Valuables were sent monthly to the REICH BANK in Berlin. Clothes were sent to the armament firms and after their cleaning used for forced labourers and deported persons. Dental gold was pried out and sent monthly to the medical department of the Waffen-SS. The medical ordnance master SS Group Leader UEBERREUTER was responsible for this.

I have not personally shot or struck dead anybody. As a result of the mass of arrivals, the number of those fit for work increased immensely. My protests to the RSHA (Reich Security Main Office) to reduce the number of transports was rejected each time. The reason was given that the Reich Leader SS had issued the order to speed up the extermination and that each SS leader had to fulfil this. Corresponding to the immense overpopulation of the existing barracks and the insufficient sanitary installations, epidemics such as spotted fever, typhoid, scarlet fever and diphtheria broke out from time to time, especially at BIRKENAU. Doctors were subordinate to the camp commander in military matters. They had their own routines regarding medical decisions and were under the command of the head of the medical corps of the SS Central Economic-Administrative Office, Standard Leader Dr LOLLING, who himself answered to Reich Physician SS Senior Group Leader Dr GRAWITZ.

In one respect the rules mentioned were broken. Local Gestapo leaders had been ordered by the RSHA to make contact with us. Prisoners who were kept in concentration camps for the Gestapo and were not sentenced for political reasons could be transferred to any other camp. I received the names of persons myself from the head of the Gestapo, and I brought them to the doctor responsible in order to finish them off. This was usually done by a benzine injection. The doctors were instructed to write a proper death note. As cause of death they could name any kind of illness. (…)

In January 1945 there were circa 63,000 prisoners in all camps. I estimate that in AUSCHWITZ roughly three million were put to death, 2.5 million of them in the gas chambers. These numbers were officially mentioned by EICHMANN in a report to HIMMLER. Most of them were Jews. I recall that as commander of AUSCHWITZ I received the order by the Gestapo to gas 70,000 Russian prisoners of war. The largest number of prisoners killed in one day in the gas chambers of AUSCHWITZ was 10,000. I also recall the large transports arriving: 90,000 from Slovakia, 65,000 from Greece, 11,000 from France, 20,000 from Belgium, 90,000 from the Netherlands, 400,000 from Hungary, 250,000 from Poland and Upper Silesia and 100,000 from Germany and Theresienstadt.[16]

Höß did his 'duty' and only assumed an air of sensitivity after the war was lost:

If an incident had stirred me a lot, it was not possible for me to return home to my family. Then I mounted my horse and in such manner chased away the horrific images, or I often wandered at night through the horse stables and found tranquillity with my darlings.[17]

Family Environment

In order to get an idea of Rudolf Höß, we also have to consider his personal environment, especially his family. This is only possible to a limited extent, however, since very little is known of his wife, Hedwig. At best her character can only be sensed from her sparse statements in the Frankfurt State Court in 1964 or from the statements of former Auschwitz prisoners, especially by Eleonore Hodys. Important clues are further provided by Hans Peter Janssen, who went to school with the Höß children in St Michaelisdonn in Schleswig-Holstein.

The most promising source of details about Höß's family life seem to be the statements of his second oldest daughter, Ingebritt.[18] The British journalist Thomas Harding tracked her down in 2013 near Washington D.C. After promising not to reveal her name or her place of residence, she agreed to an interview.[19] Harding's book is an important source, but it should be pointed out that not all her statements withstand verification. This holds also true for the book by Höß' grandson, Rainer, which however contains previously unseen photos of the family's life. In contrast, Hermann Langbein, who suffered as a prisoner in Auschwitz and had an essential part in the realisation of the Frankfurt Auschwitz trials, is unreservedly reliable.

Yet first let us consider his wife. Hedwig was born in 1908 as the daughter of Oswald Richard and Lina Florentine Hensel in Oberneukirch in Upper Lusatia. Höß met her in summer 1929 on the Liebenberg estate near Buberow in Brandenburg. Together with her brother, Fritz, Hedwig had arrived there in 1929 some months before Höß.

Höß describes his encounter with his future wife in a rather emotive manner:

> During my first days [with the Artaman League] I met my future wife who – inspired by the same ideals – had found her way to the Artaman League together with her brother.
> At first sight our belonging together was a forgone conclusion on both sides. We found ourselves in a harmony of trust and understanding, as if we had lived together since youth. Our approach to life in all areas was the same. We complemented each other in every respect. I had found *the* woman for whom I had longed during the long years of solitude.[20]

As will be shown later, this wife of Höß's dreams exercised considerable influence on her husband, enjoyed life as the commander's wife wholeheartedly and soon no longer wanted the simple life at the Artaman League.

On 17 August 1929, only three months after meeting, the two married while living in Neuhäsen[21] near Löwenburg in the north of Brandenburg.[22] One entry in the birth certificate of Hedwig Hensel lists under the registration number 12/1929 the municipality of Buberow – today a district of Gransee – as the location for the civil marriage.[23] Yet the two actually tied the knot in the registry office in Gutengermendorf. The witnesses were the inspector Theodor Gender, as well as twenty-three-year-old Artaman Ilse von Seckendorff.[24] The Artaman League had settled in the Buberow region just as in Mesenberg and in Häsen, or the Badingen region. In the notice of intended marriage Höß is named as 'Artaman leader', Hedwig simply as 'Artaman'.[25]

Höß' grandson Rainer claims that the wedding was celebrated in the baroque castle of Meseberg.[26] This would be piquant in so far that the castle serves today as a guest house of the federal government. As Jörg Grau from Buberow's heritage society told the author of this book, however, this claim has never been proven by corresponding documents. Likewise, inquiries with the Federal Chancellery and the Foreign Office could neither confirm nor refute Rainer Höß' description.

At the time of their marriage Hedwig was already three months pregnant, which led to speculation that Rudolf had married her simply out of a sense of duty. On 6 February 1930 their son Klaus-Bernd was born.[27]

Hedwig's brother, Fritz, played an important role in her life and later in Höß'. Fritz became a renowned painter, predominantly in northern Germany. On 31 October 1939 he signed up for military service and was deployed from 1942 onward as war artist in Russia, Romania and Hungary.

He had an order to produce monthly pictures for the homeland and thus to report from the various war zones. Fritz visited Auschwitz several times, most likely mainly to see his sister. During those visits he made drawings and paintings with motifs from the Auschwitz landscape. He was wounded during front-line duty in February 1945. In April the same year he moved to Flensburg. There he helped his brother-in-law to acquire a new identity. Fritz himself was thought to be the wanted Rudolf Höß and he was arrested by the Allies for a short period of time, but soon released again.

From the descriptions of daughter Ingebritt – frequently also written Inge-Britt – numerous details of the family life of the concentration camp commander can be gathered, although her memories are occasionally inaccurate.

Born on 18 August 1933, Ingebritt grew up in the vicinity of concentration camps: first Dachau, subsequently Sachsenhausen at the age of five to seven and then from the age of seven to eleven in a plush villa on the edge of Auschwitz. Here the Höß family commanded chefs, nannies, gardeners, drivers, seamstresses, hairdressers and cleaners, who for the most part were camp prisoners, as for example Eleonore Hodys.

To Harding, Ingebritt described the villa at Auschwitz as a grey two-storey stucco building, which her mother even called 'paradise'. Immediately next to it, however, was hell for the millions of people who were tortured and murdered in Auschwitz. Regardless of this, Hedwig once said – the numerous perks and advantages as commander's wife in mind – that she wanted to live there until the end of her life.[28]

On 1 March 1941 Reich Leader SS Heinrich Himmler visited Auschwitz and in preparation the villa was renovated from top to bottom. The rooms were painted, the kitchen modernised. Paintings and tapestries stolen from Jews decorated the walls. To these were added some paintings by Hedwig's brother, Fritz. Almost all the furniture was made by prisoners. The wooden floor was covered by large carpets and the windows framed by colourful curtains.

On the ground floor was a kitchen with an oven and pantry. Then there was a room with a sofa, three chairs and two coffee tables and a standard lamp, next to it a dining room with an oval table and chairs for eight people. Höß had an office, which could only be entered from the dining room. The large desk was adorned with family photos. Further furniture comprised two leather armchairs and a narrow shelf for books, documents and vodka bottles.

The first floor included three bedrooms and a playroom. The couple's bedroom contained two beds made of walnut, a leather armchair big enough to sleep in and wardrobes. Above the bed hung a large painting showing wild flowers. The guest room had two dark wooden beds, a wardrobe and bookshelf. The attic had been divided into three rooms in which the servants slept who were at the family's beck and call.

According to Ingebritt in her conversation with Harding, the children were supposed to be brought up 'normally' and attended school in Auschwitz. At weekends the family gathered in the living room, Höß had the children describe their daily routine to him or read them stories or fairy tales, e.g. Max and Moritz or Hänsel and Gretel. Ingebritt recalled communal lunches and dinners and playing in the garden.[29] At Christmas the children were taken to a church service in one of the neighbouring municipalities in a horse-drawn sleigh.

On Sundays Höß took his children to the horse stables. Photos show a pond in the garden and a large picnic table. Prisoners built two toy planes for the boys, which were tall enough to sit in and drive through the garden. The girls flirted with the soldiers guarding the camp entrance. Despite this idyll the children were well aware that their father supervised a prisoner camp. Men in striped clothes worked in their garden. The Höß children dressed up as prisoners with black triangles and yellow stars pinned to their clothes and chased each other, until their father put an end to this. Höß' grandson, Rainer, recounts in the story of his family that on one occasion Rudolf and Hedwig Höß were at the officers' mess, the head supervisor Maria Mandl was looking after the children and the seamstress Mia Weiseborn made armbands and badges:

> Then they called the cook, Sophie Striepel, her sister and further servants, tied them to chairs and – as a 'game' – hit them with towels

into which soap bars were wrapped. Into this scene burst Hedwig and Rudolf: immediate break-up, tongue-lashing, punishment.[30]

Maria Mandl was characterised by sadism, but at the same time enjoyed the confidence of the Höß family. On 27 March 1944 Höß supported a 'bonus for the head supervisor of the women's concentration camp Auschwitz, Miss Mandl' and justified this as follows:

> Miss Mandl is subject to an increased risk of epidemic due to her role as head supervisor, especially since the sanitary and hygienic conditions of the women's camp are still inadequate. Her extensive range of duties further requires much overtime daily, which is increased in particular by the fact that on top of her work she has also to carry out the overall management of the female supervisors in the staff office.[31]

As a result, Mandl received a bonus of 100 Reichsmark in addition to her monthly overtime pay.

In her conversation with Harding, Ingebritt showed herself to be convinced that her father was a sensitive man, and asked herself why so much evil was ascribed to him. She was of the opinion that he had been sad inside. She had read his *Autobiographical Notes* and did not know what to believe. There must have been two sides to him: the one she knew and another. To the remark that he had been responsible for the death of millions of Jews, she replied: 'He had to do it. His family would have been endangered if he had not done it. He was only one of many in the SS. There were many who would have done it, if he had refused.'

In the 1950s Ingebritt left Germany in order to start a new life in Spain, where she worked for three years as model for the fashion label Balenciaga. In 1961 she married an Irish-American engineer working in Madrid. When she told him of her family background, they came to an unspoken agreement not to mention it again in future. In 1972 the family, now with a son and daughter, moved to Washington D.C. She found a part-time job in a fashion boutique, where she worked for thirty-five years. The couple divorced in 1983, the daughter passed away, but her son is living with her.

The Affairs of Hedwig and Rudolf Höß

If Höß once thought that his approach to life harmonised completely with that of his wife, it was shown in Auschwitz that this was not true for all spheres of their life. When Höß admitted to his wife that beyond the fence of the Auschwitz villa thousands of Jews were murdered, her reaction was ambivalent. On the one side she saw the 'necessity' for

Jews to be exterminated, on the other hand she found it disconcerting that this mass murder took place in her immediate neighbourhood. According to Höß' own statements, after finding out about the killings she allegedly refused to have sex with him from then on. This must have taken place at the end of 1942, as Höß explained during his interrogation in Nuremberg on 15 April 1946: 'At the end of 1942 my wife was alerted to the goings on in my camp by remarks of the then regional leader of Upper Silesia. My wife asked me if this was true, and I admitted it to my wife.'[32] Hedwig could not have been consistent because daughter Annegret was born on 20 September 1943.

On 12 April 1946 Höß spoke about his relationship with his wife, his family, and in particular his sexual life, with the American court psychologist Gustave M. Gilbert while in his Nuremberg cell:

> After today's test had been concluded, HÖSS said: I assume you wish to learn by this method if my thoughts and habits are normal.
>
> GILBERT: Of course!
>
> HÖSS: I am completely normal. Even when I carried out the extermination task, I was leading a normal family life and so on.
>
> GILBERT: Did you have a normal life with respect to other people?
>
> HÖSS: Well, perhaps this is a peculiarity of mine, but I always preferred to be alone. If I had worries, I tried to cope with them by myself. That was the issue which aggrieved my wife the most. I was always content with my own company. I never had friends or close relationships to anybody – not even in my youth. I never had a friend. And I sometimes took part in social events, but never with all my heart. I was happy if people were cheerful, but I could never partake in this joy.
>
> GILBERT: Did you ever regret this?
>
> HÖSS: No, never! Even now, when I was hiding on the farm, I felt most at ease, when I was alone on the fields with the horses.
>
> GILBERT: When you had to hide, this is understandable. But how was it before that?
>
> HÖSS: Yes, I was always alone. Of course I loved my wife, but it was not a true mental companionship.
>
> GILBERT: Did you notice this, and did your wife notice it?
>
> HÖSS: Yes, I noticed it, and my wife, too. My wife believed I was not happy with her, but I told her that it was simply my nature and she had to accept this.
>
> GILBERT: I asked him about their sexual relationship.
>
> HÖSS: Well, it was normal – but after my wife had found out what I did we rarely felt the desire for intercourse. To the outside everything looked normal, but looking back now I believe that there was an estrangement ... No, I never had the need for friends. I had

never had a truly trusting relationship with my parents – and to my sisters, either. I only realised this after they had married that they were like strangers to me. As a child I always played alone. Also my grandmother said that I had never had playmates as a child.[33]

Sexuality never played a significant role in Höß' life. He never felt the urge to start or continue a love affair, although he had fleeting sexual affairs. And in his married life passion was rare. He also claimed to have never felt the urge to masturbate.

Just as Höß courted the female prisoner Eleonore Hodys, about whom we will learn more below, Hedwig allegedly had an affair, too. Anieli Bednarskije,[34] a young woman from Auschwitz working at the Höß villa, reported that Hedwig had an affair with the German kapo [prisoner supervisor] Karl Bohnera, who among other things polished the shoes, fried fish and so on, and who could move about relatively freely.[35] One day Höß returned unexpectedly and caught the two in unmistakable circumstances in the garden shed. After a violent scene, Hedwig was able to calm her husband. Bohnera avoided the villa from then on. However, Bednarskije claimed that the two continued to see each other when Höß was not there.

Yet how dubious this and other sources are is shown by the fact that the Catholic priest Manfred Deselaers, who moved to Auschwitz in 1990 to dedicate himself to the German–Polish reconciliation, does not speak of a 'shoe shiner', but of the 'German kapo Karl Böhner, head of the canteen of the shoe factory in Chelm'.[36] Deselaers names Stanislaw Dubiel as another of Hedwig's lovers. He is described as a good-looking man who recounted his affair with Hedwig after the war.[37]

Into that period falls the affair of the concentration camp commander with Eleonore Hodys. That Höß pursued her has to be accepted as fact, although not every detail is necessarily true in view of Hodys' colourful personality. During an interrogation in October 1944 by SS judge Konrad Morgen she painted a picture of her relationship with Höß about which he himself never said a word:

I met Höß upon my arrival at Auschwitz. He or the SS Head Storm Leader Schwarz usually asked the new arrivals for their profession, if they could type. I named pharmacy assistant as my profession. Dr van Brodemann wanted to have me for the hospital. Senior Storm Command Leader Höß arranged through the female supervisor Langenfels [sic] for a room of my own in Block 4. A few days later I was ordered to the commander because he wanted an artisan embroideress. I was received at the commander's residence by Mrs Höß, who showed me a carpet in the hallway and asked if I could mend it. I took on this task and completed it in two days.

During that time I saw the commander come and go. He asked me if I was Hodys and did not ask any further questions of me. He remarked that he was actually not allowed to employ prisoners in his house, but that his wife had various tasks. I further made two tapestries, a silk Gobelin cushion and bedside rugs and covers. I liked working in the commander's house. During the night I stayed in the camp. As long as I worked in the commander's house, I was fed there. I ate alone in a room and received the same food as the commander. The food consisted of soup, starter, meat, vegetables, baked goods or biscuits, fruit salad and coffee. It was extraordinarily good and comparable to that of a grand hotel during peacetime. The two Jewish seamstresses, whose names I have forgotten and who were working there, received the same food. One of them is still alive. I talked to her a few days before going to Munich. These two girls worked from 1942 onward until two or three weeks ago in the commander's house without interruption. Where the commander or his wife got the astonishing amount of cloth I do not know. Mrs Höß was very simply, I would say too simply, dressed.[38]

This description of the rather simple appearance of Hedwig Höß corresponds with the latter's statement of her lack of socialising that she gave during the 1st Frankfurt Auschwitz trial on 19 November 1964.[39] The then fifty-seven-year-old stated that she was widowed, living in Ludwigsburg and was without employment. To the question if she could recall a Senior Storm Command Leader Hartjenstein, she answered: 'Yes, but in principle we had little contact. I was rarely in the officers' mess and it [sic] was only superficial.'

On the other hand, the historian Kathrin Kompisch states:

His wife [Hedwig] organised the social life of the SS leaders there, had dinner parties and hosted high-ranking guests. Mrs Höß must have known what was happening in the camp, since their villa was situated in the immediate vicinity of the camp prison, for which reason her husband complained about the screams of the people tortured there disrupting his after-lunch nap. Furthermore, Mrs Höß had camp inmates working at her house and reported those who were not industrious enough in her opinion to her husband for punishment.[40]

Interesting is the description by Rainer Höß, who recalled that he had worn a fluffy cardigan as a child and later realised that this must have belonged to a Jewish boy murdered at Auschwitz.[41] In this context he mentions the request logs of the tailor room in Auschwitz: 'All of them showed the signature of my grandmother: suits, shirts, tablecloths with matching napkins (…) My grandmother had ordered them herself in the concentration camp's 'Canada' depot.'

On the other hand, Höß forbade the SS men 'to call the prisoners to the wire fence and hand them shoes or clothing for repair'. That was not only prohibited, but extremely dangerous, as the wire fences were under high voltage.[42] Such was Höß' admonition of his subordinates in February 1941. He was not guided by this in his own conduct with the prisoners.[43]

Abuse of Privileges

Hedwig abused her position as commander's wife shamelessly, as Hermann Langbein describes:

Marta Fuchs, a dressmaker from Bratislava who had been deported for racial reasons, had to tailor for many months in the Villa Höß. An attic room was turned into a workshop. The cloth evidently came from 'Canada'.[44]

Another Jewess with the nickname Manza was employed as a hairdresser for Mrs Höß. She made cunning use of the tendency to have prisoners working for her and prompted Mrs Höß to request someone else for her children's knitwear. So another prisoner found good, secure employment and Mrs Höß obtained one more personal slave.

When too much was spoken about the clandestine employment in the villa of the commander, Mrs Höß had a tailor workshop established in the staff building and the work continued there, by which means the wives of other SS leaders were given the opportunity to profit likewise thereof. Yet even during that time, Martha Fuchs and another seamstress were still ordered to work at the Villa Höß on short notice, where two Jehovah's Witnesses were also employed, one as a cook, the other as a chambermaid. The name of one is known: Sophie Stipel from Mannheim.[45]

We owe further insight into Hedwig's behaviour to the prisoner Stanislaw Dubiel, mentioned above. His statements before a Polish court can be read in Hermann Langbein's book *People in Auschwitz*. If the commander's wife needed groceries, Dubiel frequently had to organise those:

Initially I carried the goods in a basket out of the food store for prisoners which was managed by SS Under Company Leader Schebeck, later I used a cart.

For the private household of Höß I fetched from the store sugar, flour, margarine, different baking powders, soup spices, macaroni, oats, cocoa, cinnamon, semolina, peas and other produce.

Mrs Höß was never satisfied and always started conversations with me about what was still missing in her household. With these groceries she not only provided her own household, but sent these to her relatives in Germany, too.

I also had to supply Höß' kitchen with meat from the slaughterhouse and with milk. He never paid for anything that went from the food store and the camp slaughterhouse to the Höß household.[46]

Dubiel fetched 5 litres of milk daily from the camp dairy for the Höß villa, although the allowance for the family would have only been 1.25 litres. Further he provided in the course of a single year three 85-kilo sacks of sugar to the Höß household. There he saw among other things boxes with 10,000 Yugoslavian 'Ibar' cigars each, which had been delivered for the prisoners' canteen, but with which Hedwig paid illicit labour.

Just how corrupt the SS members and prisoners employed in the food and clothes magazines were can best be shown with the example of Schebeck. Friedrich Skrein, a prisoner who was temporarily employed as lumberjack, describes this very vividly:

Detail Leader Reichenbacher had instructed me to go either each Friday or each Saturday to Under Company Leader Schebeck, who headed the prisoner stores, i.e. the food store, and usually to bring him a sack of sugar, margarine, sausages or meat. These were meant for his family.[47]

In return Schebeck received things from the clothing stores for his personal use.

On 7 August 1946 Stanislaw Dubiel described to the investigating judge, Jan Sehn, how each winter he had to organise 70 tons of coke to heat the villa and the hothouses. In addition, thousands of flower pots, seeds and seedlings had to be brought from the nursery in Rajsko, an outpost of the camp, to the villa, as well as vegetables as winter stock during autumn. He knew from Mrs Höß that the commander was very keen on staying in Auschwitz. Furthermore, she was convinced that her husband's transfer to the Oranienburg central despite his promotion within the hierarchy of the Central Economic-Administrative Office did not reflect his importance and abilities. Rather he viewed his transfer as a scheme by the head of the agricultural department in the camp, SS Senior Storm Command Leader Joachim Caesar. In reference to Hedwig, Dubiel made the further statement: 'She hated everything Polish: "The Polish all have to pay for the atrocities in Bydgoszvcz. They are only here to work until they kick the bucket."' On Jews

Hedwig had a preconceived opinion, too: they had to vanish from the earth to the last person, and in due course it would be the turn of the English Jews, too.

Dubiel claims to have heard that Hedwig once exclaimed that here, in the villa, she wanted to live and die.[48] When she learned from a prisoner working in her garden that his equally imprisoned wife had given birth in the women's camp, she sent a pink baby jacket to the woman.[49] The medical doctor Ella Lingens confirmed this incident in front of the Frankfurt State Court. Yet she mainly reported on the horrific conditions in the women's camp, Birkenau. Children born there could not be bathed and were barely rubbed down with crepe paper, but: 'I do recall that the wife of the commander Höß once sent a pink jacket into this hell.'[50]

In spite of this singular case it is attested that Hedwig reported prisoners who in her opinion worked too sloppily to her husband for punishment. Also her son, Klaus-Bernd, made such reports, as Martha Mináriková-Fuchs, who was working as a dressmaker in the commander's villa, reported.[51]

The wife of the commander made use of opportunities that were actually not her due and contradicted her husband's orders. According to Garrison Order 27 / 42 dated 7 October 1942, the following regulations were in place for the allocation of prisoners to a household:

A. Male prisoners
The allocation of prisoners for the restoration and maintenance of gardens belonging to Reich-owned residences will in future be made only by the administration. The offices managing these houses will be charged RM 0.30 per daily labour for these prisoners.

B. Female prisoners
The allocation of a female prisoner is made at a charge of RM 0.30 per daily labour for those SS members living in rented accommodation as well as SS families with many children.[52]

It is typical that Höß on the one hand abused his position as commander without scruples, or rather tolerated such behaviour by his wife, but on the other hand castigated just this in his orders. In a circular letter 'To all SS leaders at the concentration camp Auschwitz' dated 6 February 1943, he stressed that in view of the war situation it could not be acceptable to 'continue the allocation of an SS man for the personal attendance' of the SS leaders.[53] He had therefore permitted 'that the leaders will have female prisoners (IBV)[54] assigned for the cleaning and care of their things'.

In the 'Garrison Order 22/43' regarding the allocation of prisoners to households Höß then stated more precisely:

> With effect from 1st June 1943 and on the order of the SS Central Economic-Administrative Office RM 25.00 are being charged monthly for the female prisoners assigned to the households. The invoice is issued at the end of each month.
>
> The allocation of more than one household assistant for any household has been prohibited. In general household assistants are primarily assigned only to households with many children after prior agreement with the SS Central Economic-Administrative Office, Office Group D. (...) The households affected will be assigned in certain intervals labour details for special household tasks (laundry days, spring clean etc.).[55]

Höß, in whose villa numerous prisoners were working, had them make objects of art, as mentioned elsewhere, but prohibited this for all others:

> I have noticed that SS members have received various objects made by prisoners, be it pictures or other so-called art objects like sheet metal roses. Material that is today very difficult to obtain is wasted here in an irresponsible manner, not to mention that prisoners are supposed to be occupied with useful tasks. I herewith prohibit such illicit labour rigorously and will report any SS member who in future allows such nonsensical and tasteless tasks to be performed or puts in the commission for them to the Reich Leader SS for punishment, irrespective of the person concerned or of their rank.[56]

An important role in the Höß household was played by Erich Grönke, who had been convicted several times for theft and rape and had been committed as a professional criminal first to Sachsenhausen and then to Auschwitz.[57] There he was initially employed as a kapo in the leather factory, before Höß supported his release in 1941 and Grönke became head of the factory. Regarding his relationship with Höß, he stated before the Frankfurt State Court that he had sometimes been at the Höß villa several times a day, because the head of the household always had new requests, for example the maintenance of the horse tack and the family's shoes. Grönke became friendly with Höß, accompanied him when hunting and was on first-name terms with him. One of the Höß' sons even refused to go to sleep if Grönke had not said good night to him. Grönke got on equally well with Hedwig and often went on leisurely drives with her.

SS Senior Company Leader Robert Sierek also supplied the Höß family. In Herman Langbein he is quoted as saying:

> I was only cautioned by the camp commander Höß. Höß undertook nothing against me primarily because he was dependent on my assistance and support, as I always had to organise something for him, mainly cloth. Such procurements were possible because I was frequently out and about as the buying agent for the camp administration.[58]

On 10 November 1943 Höß was entrusted with the tasks of Office Group D at the SS Central Economic-Administrative Office (WVHA) in Berlin and on 1 May 1944 he was appointed head of Office D I at the same institution. From May until July 1944, on the order of the WVHA, he was once more in the Auschwitz-Birkenau camp as garrison commander in order to take care of the smooth operation of the extermination of the Hungarian Jews. When the Höß family moved away from Auschwitz for good, the garrison doctor wrote on 26 November 1944 to his family: 'He [the commander Baer] had told me of Höß' house and garden that it was a shame how everything was furnished there, irresponsible. The move had been carried out with two railway cars and countless boxes.'

Jerzy Rawic, who was a prisoner in Auschwitz and wrote the preface to Jadwiga Bezwińska's book *Auschwitz in den Augen der SS*, had worked in the leather factory detail and was witness to the almost daily illicit tasks that were performed on Grönke's orders for Höß and his wife:

> The things there! Leather-covered armchairs and chandeliers, briefcases and handbags, suitcases, shoes, furniture, all kinds of objects made from leather and metal, toys for the children and carpets. (…) The prisoners working at the commander's house – and there were many in service to Höß – received special 'Canadian'[59] clothing. The point was to make them look presentable, mainly to dress them in clean clothes. For the Höß family were in panicked fear of the infectious diseases prevailing in the camp, especially of spotted fever. Therefore Mrs Höß received these clothes to distribute them among the prisoners. Yet she did not dispense them, but kept them for herself, and to the prisoners she gave old clothes worn by the family. The Höß family wore the clothes of the gassed, their children wore the clothes of other children murdered by their father.[60]

One of the suppliers of food for the Höß family – meat, sausages and cigars – was SS Senior Company Leader Friedrich Engelbrecht, head of the canteens. Regarding this, Jerzy Rawic writes:

> The commander did 'not notice' the excess of all this food, he did not take an interest in where the meat products, exotic fruits,

alcohol etc. came from on his table, during a period of the strictest rationing of bread and skimmed milk in the Third Reich. When he travelled to Hungary, however, in order to assist Eichmann in the operation of transporting the Hungarian Jews to the gas chambers of Auschwitz, he sent entire baskets of wine from there to his wife, who had remained in Auschwitz.[61]

An important contemporary witness is Janina Szcurek, who lived in Auschwitz and on 13 January 1963 gave the following report:

I visited Hedwig Höß at her residence and offered to sew at her house. For good measure I took along my apprentice Bronka Urbanczyk to the Höß villa: at the Höß' residence I met prisoners for the first time, among them Bronek Jaron from Cracow, Wilhelm Kmak from Grybow near Tarnow, and Kwiatkowski.

Jaron and Kwiatkowski were working in Höß' garden, but were also often employed in the house, where they performed the heavier tasks. Jaron always polished the shoes. On his request I made contact with Mrs Stankiewiczowa and her daughter, Helena Kwiatkowska. The father-in-law of Mrs Kwiatkowska was the owner of a drug store in Auschwitz town, and from them I brought injections, vitamins and grey salve to the Höß residence. The medications were most often received by the prisoners themselves or by Mrs Höß' housemaid, Angela Bednarska, a resident of Auschwitz. Angela hid the parcels in the garden, to which she added food 'supplied' from Mrs Höß' kitchen. Angela very often gave me money from her wages, and I bought medication for the prisoners with it. After a few days I stopped going to work because I only received one 'stew' and a 3 Mark payment. If I sewed at home, I could earn much more. Mrs Höß called me back through Angela, increased my wage to 10 Marks and gave me better food, of which I gave part to the hungry prisoners who were secretly looking for potato peel in the rubbish dumps, although they were beaten for this by the kapos. I very frequently came to Mrs Höß to sew, and she even called me in for ironing. When I went home, Angela picked a bunch of flowers for me from the garden on Mrs Höß' orders. She then used this occasion to slip me some food. Meanwhile I stood at the gate and watched for nearby SS men. The best time for laying out the food was in the evening, when the Höß family were going to the theatre or cinema.

The prisoner Kmak[62] mentioned above was often at the Höß residence. He painted walls and doors, on which the Höß' children were constantly drawing. Kmak carried out the tasks slowly and asked me not to disturb the children while drawing, because his work at the Höß residence was his only contact to the outside world.[63]

The Lover of the Concentration Camp Commander

Höß committed a crime in Auschwitz on the prisoner Nora Mattaliano-Hodys (Eleonore Hodys), with whom he evidently had a love affair. When she was pregnant by him, he had her isolated in the so-called command arrest area – this was at least her accusation. He did this of his own accord and not on anyone's orders.

The affair came into the open because SS judge Konrad Morgen investigated SS members in Auschwitz for embezzlement. The trigger had been a field post package confiscated due to its conspicuous weight. It contained three gold lumps, one having the size of two fists and two smaller ones. This was high-carat dental gold sent by a simple medical orderly from Auschwitz to his wife. Morgen estimated that this amount of gold corresponded with roughly 100,000 robbed corpses. He assumed that only a part of the killed had gold teeth. Morgen decided to investigate the matter on site. He travelled to Auschwitz, reported to Höß and announced that an investigation was under way. During this meeting Höß was supposedly very uncommunicative and merely said that many of his SS men were not able to cope with the difficult task. Similar assessments are incidentally found in the character sketches that Höß made during the weeks and months before his execution in Cracow prison.

The description of the conditions then discovered by Morgen during his walkabout is testament to the fact that Höß could organise mass extermination, but otherwise did not have 'his' camp under control:

> An SS officer showed me the entire camp and also explained to me the death machinery in all its detail. The crematoria did not draw any attention. The ground was deepened at a sloping angle, and an outsider could only notice that the vehicles disappeared in a depression in the ground. A tall gate led to the so-called changing rooms. There were numbered places and even cloakroom tickets. Arrows on the wall pointed to the shower rooms. The labels were written in six or seven languages. In the huge crematorium everything was spick and span. Nothing indicated that just the previous night thousands of people had been gassed and burnt there. Nothing remained of them, not even a speck of dust on the incinerator's fittings. I wanted to meet the SS personnel and went to the SS guardroom at Birkenau. There I experienced a real shock for the first time. While guardrooms were usually of Spartan simplicity, here SS men were lying on sofas and dozing off with glassy eyes. Instead of a desk, a hotel hob was standing inside the room and four to five young Jewesses of oriental beauty were baking potato fritters and feeding the SS men, who let themselves be served

like pashas. The SS men and the female prisoners were on first-name terms.

Seeing my appalled, questioning expression, my companion only shrugged and said: 'The men just had a difficult night, they had to process several transports.'

During the subsequent locker check it was revealed that in some a fortune of gold, pearls, rings and hard currency of all kinds had been hoarded. In one or two lockers we found the sexual organs of recently slaughtered bulls that were said to increase sexual potency.[64]

In the context of this investigation Eleonore Hodys' name was mentioned, too. Morgen attended to her, especially since she was extremely frail at that point. She claimed that Höß had ordered that she face aggravated conditions in a standing cell without food in order to kill her and to cover up their affair. Höß denied knowledge of these conditions during an inquiry in 1944. As this investigation was dropped on Himmler's behest – probably in light of the beginning dissolution of the Third Reich and its concentration camps – this matter remained unresolved. Morgen, however, repeated the accusation during the 1st Frankfurt Auschwitz trial in 1964 that Höß had intended to let the woman starve to death.

Hodys was a decidedly colourful personality whose last civilian address had been Löwengasse 4 in Vienna.[65] For inexplicable reasons she claimed to have been an 'illegal member' of the NSDAP in the years before the annexation of Austria, to have paid membership fees and to have fought for the party in the underground. Before her arrest this issue triggered a lively exchange of letters between various Nazi offices. For example, on 17 August 1939 the NSDAP membership office contacted the Vienna regional treasurer Johann Anderl about 'queries we have received by the national comrade Hodys regarding her alleged membership of the NSDAP for your attention to be returned after processing. In the course of clarifying this matter we ask you to determine how far the statements of national comrade Hodys are fact.'[66] In particular they wanted to find out which membership card had been handed in by Hodys at the National Socialist Public Welfare office Vienna III in May 1938. It was noted that there were no documents regarding potential membership of the 'national comrade' at the Reich Chancellery or in the files of the former national management in Austria. Hodys was arrested, and the chief prosecutor commenced an investigation of her 'for fraud, the attempt of fraud, assuming a false title, perhaps also treachery.' On 15 October 1938 the chief prosecutor noted: 'The defendant has, among other things, worn or carried the NSDAP badge. She claims to have been an "illegal" member of the NSDAP in Vienna since 1928 and to have paid fees until April 1938.'[67]

On 30 April 1940 the Munich NSDAP membership office reported to Hanover that there was no evidence of Hodys' party membership. Meanwhile, her father had renounced his daughter, and the district economic advisor of District Vienna III even called her an international con artist.[68] At that time she was already in Lübeck-Lauerhof prison, and it would not be long until she was transferred – via Ravensbrück – to Auschwitz and would meet Höß there.

The case of Hodys was mentioned among others before the International Military Tribunal at Nuremberg. A witness was the former SS judge Konrad Morgen. He had been able to prove – aside from perjury – at least one attempted murder by Höß together with the SS Head Storm Leaders Schwarz and Aumeier.[69] Regarding the investigations into the 'Hodys case', during the trial erroneously called the 'Czech Nora Hody', he made the following statement on 7 August 1946:

> The married standard leader Höß had begun a love affair with a Czech female prisoner called Hodys, and the female prisoner had become pregnant. So that the matter would not come to light, he had his lover brought to the bunker in Block 11. In the basement there were standing bunkers. I later had them removed. These were small rooms, roughly one to one and a half square metres in size. At the bottom was a small hole through which one could only crawl, and there the prisoner concerned had to stand as long as the camp command wanted. And in the case of Hodys he had even given the instruction to no longer provide food to this pregnant woman. She was supposed to starve there. (...) And from this torture I liberated the woman. I brought her to a Munich clinic run by a Catholic order and gradually won her trust. (...) And then this woman made a complete statement, and we took the minutes and had her sign them together with other evidence confirming the case. And this woman was released into freedom, after she had been restored to health, though as a wreck.[70]

The question of why he could not intervene against the then camp commander Höß as investigating judge or prosecutor, Morgen answered during the 1st Frankfurt Auschwitz trial:

> Bormann and Höß had done time together in the Rendsburg [sic] jail, as far as I recall, and since then had been good friends. (...) Furthermore I may tell you, honourable counsel for the defence,

these investigations I am describing, which I made against Höß, I did not note in my private diary, but imparted the information to all higher SS authorities and suggested they pressed charges. Yet since Höß belonged to the Central Economic-Administrative Office and Pohl was his judge, only Pohl could press charges. And as long as I was in office, he did not do this.[71]

Morgen's statement that Bormann and Höß did time together in Rendsburg jail is without foundation. Morgen was probably referring to the Parchim vigilante murder, the consequence of which Höß had to serve a prison sentence in Brandenburg and Bormann in Leipzig.

The statement by Eleonore Hodys received by SS investigator Morgen in October 1944 does not only provide an insight into her mind, but more importantly into that of Höß. Although allowances have to be made regarding her trustworthiness, her statement, which will be given here in detail, corresponds by and large to the facts:

The commander soon showed a particular interest in me. At first I myself did not notice this. Yet my fellow prisoners soon directed my attention to the fact that the commander took a noticeable interest in me. He had me called to him every time he visited the camp, or he himself came to my workplace. He spoke about his business, but he laughed in a strange manner while doing this. I responded in the same manner, because I have to admit that I liked him as a man. Besides the frequent daily conversations he did everything to alleviate my imprisonment. In the first room I stayed were three other women. When the commander noticed this, he ordered SS Head Storm Leader Aumeier to establish a special room for me in Block 4. I could furnish this with my own furniture and carpets. On Saturdays I received days off in return for my word of honour, could move freely in the town of Auschwitz and stay away overnight. In these cases I slept in the staff building outside the camp. The commander saw me smoking many times, which prisoners were not allowed to do, but he never said anything about it. If I hid the cigarette, he told me not to worry. I even got a cook and a maid for my personal matters. A witness to this is SS Head Storm Leader Aumeier. On my birthday a party was held in the commander's house. The other prisoners believed at first that I was related to the commander, and they questioned me about this.

The commander expressed his particular feelings for me the first time in May 1942 during the absence of his wife, when I was listening to the radio in his house. Without saying anything he approached me and gave me a kiss. I was surprised and frightened, slipped away from him and locked myself into the toilet. There were too many obstacles between me and him with regards to his position and the fact that he was married. From now on I no longer visited the commander's house. I spread a rumour about myself that I was ill, and attempted to hide from him when he asked for me. Although he managed to find me on these occasions, he did not speak about the kiss. I was only in his house twice before my birthday on his orders. Then once on my birthday. Then he sent SS Head Storm Leader Müller to me, who told me that I would be off on Sunday and that I should bathe, arrange my hair and dress in my best clothes. His wife would call me on Sundays. At the end of September Mrs Höß told me that I no longer needed to come, as her husband was sick in Bielitz and she was staying with him. Two or three days later the female supervisor Drexel took away my work.

A fortnight later I joined the punishment detail. I was told that I had committed an indiscretion in the commander's house. In response I wrote a letter to the commander, his wife and his cook, Sophie Stippel. In this letter I clarified the facts and asked them not to listen to rumours and to help me. As an answer I was delivered the next day at 1:30pm to command arrest. This was on 16 October 1942. That day I should have joined the hospital as a chemist, because a month before the leading SS doctor had visited the camp, presented the prospect of my release and told me that my transfer to a field hospital at the eastern front was intended. I pointed out that owing to my long imprisonment my nerves would not be able to cope. The doctor said that in this case I should work at the SS hospital in Auschwitz. Initially I was to be trained in the prisoners' hospital building before going into quarantine. The same day Spritzenheini appeared at 8:30am to fetch me. I said that I would not work with Jewesses and that I did not require training. Then SS Senior Storm Command Leader Krätzer came and told me that I could spend my quarantine period in the camp, as I was totally healthy. During these four weeks of quarantine I was able to select the prisoner Gertrud Malorny as a children's nurse.

I was committed to the command arrest by the female supervisor Hasse. When she passed the guard she said to him: 'That one won't return!'

Nobody could or would give me the reasons for my arrest. Until the end of January 1943 I was relatively fine in the command arrest. Usually I had a cell equipped with a good bed or a good mattress. I had a desk and chair. I could read, write and smoke. Two or three times I wrote to the commander regarding the reasons for my arrest via the political department (SS Senior Storm Leader Grabner). I never received an answer. During this time SS Head Storm Leader Aumeier, SS Head Storm Leader Schwarz and SS Senior Strom Leader Grabner occasionally looked after me. They told me that my case was being processed directly by the commander. The matter would be cleared up. Then they would laugh.

In my recollection the commander appeared in my cell on 16 December 1942 around 11pm when I was already asleep. I had not heard him opening the cell door and received a terrible scare. It was dark inside the cell. I believed at first that it was an SS man or a prisoner and said: 'What's all this nonsense, I won't have it!' Then I heard 'Psst', a flash light was turned on and it revealed the face of the commander. I said: 'Commander, sir!' Then we were quiet for a long time. When I had pulled myself together again, I believed that something terrible was happening and asked: 'What has happened?' Then Höß spoke his first words: 'You are being released.' I asked in response: 'Immediately?' He said once more 'Shush! Be very quiet, we will talk about it.' Then he sat down on the foot of my bed. I reminded him that I had written to him and asked him why he had not replied to me and why I had been placed under arrest. He did not give me an answer to this, but said that he had done everything to ease my arrest. Then he moved slowly upwards from the foot of the bed and tried to kiss me. I struggled against this and made some noise in the process. As a result he warned me to be quiet as nobody knew that he was in the command arrest area. I asked him how he had entered and whether he had not been seen by anybody. He told me that he had entered through the fence gate and had unlocked it himself.

I was very embittered and told him that my release had been fixed for 16th October and that I was supposed to work for some time at the SS hospital. He told me that my release had been approved, but he did not know that I was intended for work at the SS hospital. He remarked that he wanted to have a look at the files first, as he had been ill, had just returned to the camp and had come directly to me. I then asked him why he came at night and told him that he could see me during the day at the commandant's headquarters. I could not shake the thought of execution. Höß calmed me down by saying that I was under his protection, and he had only come to speak to me in private. He then asked me why I was so restrained. I answered that as commander he was a person of respect for me and that furthermore he was married. He replied to this that I should not be afraid, for he knew what he was doing.

Then he asked me whether I wanted to become his girlfriend. I [sic] tried again to kiss me and became somewhat friendlier. During the entire time I was very scared, listened closely and looked at the open door, for I believed that somebody was outside. The commander was not allowed to enter the camp alone. Therefore I could not believe that he was by himself. I insisted again that he should leave. Finally he turned to leave and told me to think about it, he would come back. I replied: 'But not during the night, please.' He closed the door very quietly and one could hear noise of bricks on the floor in front of Cell 26, in which I was. I did not hear the external gate close. The doors were always locked at night.

Two nights later, again a few minutes after 11pm, as he had said he returned. He asked me if I had considered his offer. I said: 'No, I don't want this. I only have the wish to be released.' He replied that he had made preparations. He had furnished a beautiful room in a beautiful house. To my question of when I would be released he answered that the matter would be cleared up. Then we spoke for two hours about personal matters. He did not talk about himself. He questioned me about personal and family matters that were not evident from my files. Then he became pushy again. I resisted and caused him to be more restrained by telling him that the door was open and that somebody might be outside. He replied that I should not be afraid of this. Yet I did not listen to this and he left in a bad mood.

The next day was a Sunday. During the morning Höß made a bunker inspection. I had to go into a cell that could be opened and closed from the inside. If I recall correctly this was Cell 16. Some days later he returned at night. He asked me if he should leave. I said: 'No.' Then he asked me if I had something to say to him. I replied that he should already know. Then he joined me in bed and we had sexual intercourse. Some days later he came again. This time he undressed completely.

At midnight there was a sudden alarm. I believe a fire had broken out in the camp. Outside in the corridor the light had been turned off. We could hear Gering's steps. Höß hid naked in the corner behind the door, and I concealed his uniform inside the bed. At the moment the light was switched on briefly. Gering looked through the cell door and turned off the light immediately. When things had calmed down again, Höß got dressed and left, but soon returned and said that he could not leave yet as there was too much unrest outside. He stayed with me until 1am. The next time he did not get undressed again. He kept it convenient for himself. In total we had sexual intercourse on four to four [sic] occasions. His interest in me did not seem to abate. Later we had further conversations together. I once more touched upon the matter of my release. He told me to be patient. He had instigated an investigation by the head supervisor Hartmann.

When he came to me the next time, I casually asked what would happen if he was discovered. He told me that he would have to deny the affair, and asked me how I would handle it. I swore silence to him. He then advised me that if I was questioned I should say that a prisoner had come to me. I replied that I did not know any male prisoners. He said he believed that several SS men and a handsome kapo had taken an interest in me.

Then he asked me if I had something going on with Fichtinger. I told him that the latter had written to me and I had answered him that he should not harass me. Then he asked me if I had had an affair with a handsome kapo. I described him as short and not quite to my taste. He advised me to name Fichtinger. I did not want to do this, but he was of the opinion that I should do so without qualms. Nothing would happen to me because of having relations with a prisoner. He tore a page from his notebook and I had to declare in the beam of his flash light that I had relations with Fichtinger. This note he kept in a small leather notebook. Höß gave me nothing, but he once lost a strap of his glove. It was strap with a button on which the word Nappa was written. This strap is with my luggage.

These conversations were the reason why during the night the fire broke out the prisoner SS Man Eduard Lockhauserbaum, who was in a cell near me and heard the noise of bricks scraping the floor, looked out from his cell, but Höß thought him to be SS Head Storm Leader Schwarz.

He spoke to me about him from cell to cell. During his last visit the commander said that he would return. Yet soon after, approximately at the beginning of February, I suffered a severe attack. I believed it was a bout of gall stones. This diagnosis was confirmed by the bunker doctor, Dr Stassel. In the evening I suffered a second attack with intense vomiting. As a consequence the prisoner doctor Dr Doering visited. After the examination he said worriedly: 'You are pregnant.' The next day he returned and examined me thoroughly. He confirmed that I was eight weeks pregnant and he asked me after the father. I replied that I was not allowed to speak of this, and pleaded with him to say nothing of it himself. At the same time I asked him to help me. Therefore the next day a hall guard – I believe it was Teresiak – handed me two medications through the window: I took one of them. When I suffered severe pain as a result I threw away the other. Dr Göring [sic] did not return. After this attempt to abort I was brought into the standing bunker, a small dark hole with only a little air. You can just about stand inside it or squat.

When the next morning Gering [sic] fetched me I was completely naked during washing. When I was done, Gering took me back to the bunker. He only allowed me to wear an apron. A witness to this is SS Band Leader Müller. I had to stay in that cell the whole time. I did not learn the reason for this. While I was incarcerated, I became very scared and started to scream, whereupon Hannes had to throw several tubs of water onto me. I screamed so loudly because a corpse was in my cell, which I could feel in the darkness. I was taken from this cell and came into another standing bunker. When I did not stop screaming, I was drenched with water again.

During the first days I received the regular prisoner food. After that I only received a little bread and coffee and every fourth day a hot meal.

For nine weeks I had no opportunity to wash and during the last 17 days I was not allowed to visit the toilet. I had to relieve myself in my cell. During this period I asked the SS band leader for some clothes, as I was very cold. He gave me the advice of turning to Gering. Gering appeared several times, opened the peep hole and called: 'Old cow, hysterical bitch', when I asked him for some water. He expressed his surprise that I was not dead already. (Remark by the head of interrogation: when Ms H. talks about these matters she becomes very agitated. One can clearly see how much the memories of that affair haunt her.)

As far as I recall, I was in this standing bunker during the winter, as Gering ordered the steam heating for the cell switched off. During that episode SS Senior Storm Leader Grabner and SS Head Storm Leader Aumeier were in front of my cell, too. The cell door was not entirely shut so I could see them. I could also understand what they spoke in front of Herbert Roman's cell, and when Roman begged them for his life, Aumeier replied: 'You dog have to die.' I had to throw up, and felt better as a result.

After my release from this cell I asked my neighbour in the next cell how to perform an abortion. That was around April or May 1943. The prisoner Regenscheidt advised me to organise a long needle and puncture the ovaries with it, then to ingest green soap. The aforementioned Kurt Müller brought me these things, when I told him I needed them for washing. With the aid of a small mirror I tried it with the result that I lost a lot of blood and the puncture marks swelled up. The entire attempt was without success.

I believe it was 26th June when I was released, the same day the Jewesses Zimmersitz were killed. When Aumeier ordered me to step outside, I entered the corridor. When SS Senior Storm Leader Grabner saw me, he only said: 'Oh my god, that is H.', and I was sent back into the cell. To Aumeier he said: 'She will be returned to the camp. The commander had given that order. She is intended as a block chief at Budy [concentration camp outpost].' Instead I came to the punishment detail, where SS Senior Company Leader Tauber received me. He told me that I had been sent here on the order of the commander and would have all privileges. I went to the hospital and got something that caused an abortion. In the punishment detail I was allowed to stay in bed for 10 or 11 days. After my recovery I worked as a surveyor for three months. After that I worked in the kitchen and then had to go to hospital due to bronchitis. Before my release I contracted typhoid. From that time I was in hospital and was waiting for my transfer to Munich.

On 12th July I believed I would travel to Munich, as the entire hospital building was closed down. That was 1944. Only five old Jewesses and I remained. SS Senior Storm Leader Hessler wanted to lock me in the bunker until my transport to Munich. When I refused to go, he received an order from the commander to accommodate me in the new barracks. The civilian clerk, Dr Goebel of Glauberg station [sic][72] gave the order to take me to Birkenau for gassing. Indeed I was placed on a cart with other Jewish women, but at the last moment an SS guard from the Glauberg station [sic] came along and ordered them to return me. (…)

The meeting with the commander in the presence of the SS judge Wiebeck happened as follows: Wiebeck asked me what led me to the conclusion that the commander knew who had been with me inside the bunker. I laughed, and the commander said that this was wholly unclear to him. He was very agitated and clenched his hands around the bed frame for support. He confirmed that my conduct had been very orderly and that I had been committed to the bunker for my own protection. He did not know why I had been locked up in the standing bunker. On the contrary, he complained that I did not say anything to him about it. If I hear now that Höß rejected my release in January 1943 due to very bad conduct, I have no explanation for this. I spoke with my fiancé Fichtinger mentioned above about the dangers attached to my transfer to Munich. He advised me not to give the name of the commander under any circumstances. I was careful enough to place myself under psychiatric supervision for six weeks.[73]

Regarding Hodys' trustworthiness, Hermann Langbein, who from 1941 until 1945 had been imprisoned at the concentration camps in Dachau, Auschwitz and Neuengamme, writes that she originally worked in the property room.[74] She was in charge of the jewellery at Birkenau, as Hugo Breiden, kapo in Birkenau, recalled. This is also alluded to in the nickname she received in the camp: 'brilliant Nora'. According to Grabner's statement she had to fetch jewellery for Höß. When the trade was busted, Höß had her incarcerated and attempted to liquidate her.

Chapter 4

The Cynic

Limitless Contempt for Humankind

Höß' readiness to talk seems to have been unstoppable? With his British interrogators, then as witness before the International Military Tribunal in Nuremberg, in conversations with the American court psychologist Gustave M. Gilbert and later also in Warsaw and Cracow it did not require much in order to get him to talk, or like in his Polish prison, to write.

A person whom he evidently trusted, although he stood virtually on the 'opposite side', was Jan Sehn, Polish judge and member of the central commission for the investigation of Nazi crimes, who led the initial trial against Höß. He prompted Höß to write down his *Autobiographical Notes*. In an introductory work prefacing the Polish edition, the historian Stanislaw Batawia described the mood prevailing during the long conversations with Höß:

> The inhibitions shown by Höß at first decreased gradually, and at the moment when he began to trust his listener the investigation took place in an atmosphere favouring sincere answers. (...) An objection to the sincerity of the statements of the Auschwitz camp commander, the trustworthiness of which could only partially be verified, is of course possible. Yet equally the investigators as well as all those who came into closer contact with Rudolf Höß usually considered his statements to be reliable, in contrast to the statements of the majority of the war criminals. The sincerity with which he discussed many matters of principal importance was sometimes, though unjustly, seen as cynicism characterising a person without any moral sentiments.[1]

Investigating judge Sehn was convinced that Höß had not withheld or concealed anything: 'To no question did he make use of the right to remain silent – of which he was informed during the course of the interrogations – and willingly provided detailed answers to all the questions of the interrogators.'[2]

Höß always seemed trustworthy when he spoke of the mere technology and of the organisation of the mass murder of millions of people. Yet even here allowances have to be made. For instance, Höß had volitionally stated already shortly after his arrest in Schleswig-Holstein that 2.5 million people had been murdered at Auschwitz. This statement was judged as frankness, although it soon came to light that the number of murdered was closer to 1.3 million. Höß had merely echoed what he allegedly learned from Eichmann.

Jadwiga Bezwińska does not rule out that Batawia and Sehn were blinded by Höß and his seeming frankness.[3] Possibly they were deceived by the 'sincerity' of the commander whom they got to talk, and accepted each statement by Höß at face value. If it concerned the set-up of Auschwitz, the procedure and the mass murder, these were largely true. Yet neither Batawia nor Sehn could figure out Höß' personality during these early post-war years, either.

Höß claimed, as mentioned at the beginning, that he had never mistreated or even killed a prisoner. He even went as far as to say that 'these so-called mistreatments and tortures in the concentration camps, news of which was spread everywhere among the population, also later by the prisoners liberated by the occupation, were not, as assumed, methodical, but they were the excesses of individual leaders, junior leaders and men abusing prisoners'.[4] As contrary to the truth this statement is, the following comment made before the Nuremberg Military Tribunal is equally absurd: 'The disastrous situation towards the end of the war had been caused by the fact that by the destruction of the railway network, by the continual bombardment of the works, an orderly supply of these masses – I think of Auschwitz with 140,000 prisoners – could no longer be ensured, although everything was undertaken by the commanders to improve this with improvised measures such as truck convoys and similar things.'[5] Such statements only served to lessen Höß' personal guilt regarding the Holocaust.

It is undisputed that Höß not only organised, managed and to all extent perfected the mass murder at Auschwitz, but previously as adjutant of the camp commander and then leader of the protective custody camp at Sachsenhausen he had people tortured to death. This is documented by extracts from the chronology of the camp senior of Sachsenhausen, Harry Naujoks, who was under Höß' management:

September 1938:
First public execution. Shooting of the Jehovah's Witness August Diekmann.

Political special operation, circa 800 prisoners are committed to the camp. These prisoners had to run in a circle on the parade ground. Among them Erdmann. (…) He hung for one and three quarter hours from the pole. Subsequently he was placed across the stand [translator's note: most likely for further beating]. Then, under constant abuse with the participation of the 'iron one' and Schubert he was chased again and again across the yard. He died in the sick bay.
Circa 1,000 Czech hostages committed.

13th September:
Circa 1,200 Jewish prisoners committed. In three barracks of the new camp (Block 37, 38, 39) all windows were nailed and glued shut. 400 each of these Jewish prisoners came to one block. (They had to sleep on the bare floor.)

November:
Temperature minus 30 degrees Celsius. The undervests of all prisoners had to be handed in. On our intervention the prisoners received their own undervests from the property room. All fur coats of prisoners in the property room were confiscated by the SS. In spite of the terrible cold no coats or gloves were provided for the prisoners, although there were enough in store.

December:
The Jewish prisoners were prohibited by the SS camp command from visiting the sick bay. (…) Installation of 'hunger blocks', e.g. Block 23. All beds are removed. The straw mattresses are placed on the ground. Rations for the prisoners of the hunger block: half a litre of soup, 250 grams of bread, half a portion. The 'standing detail' is set up.
Beginning of December:
Block 42 is occupied with 212 antisos.[6] After one month only 8 are still alive.

18th January 1940:
Camp leader Höß orders that the standing detail should be examined for those fit to work.
Labour duty leader Politsch [sic] carried this out for hours during the most freezing cold. 150 dead.
January/March:
2,000 dead.

April:
Polish Catholic priests in Block 17. As new arrivals the priests were forced into a locker, which was then tipped forward.[7]

About the shooting of an Austrian supervised by Höß, Naujoks writes:

> This was a prisoner who had refused to undertake armament work as a foreigner. He was brought by the Gestapo to Berlin and on 8th May 1939 at 12:40 am shot 'by order'. In his report Höß writes: 'Almost daily I had to set up with my execution detail. These were not objectors or saboteurs. The reason for execution could only be learned from the accompanying Gestapo officials, since it was not given in the execution order.'[8]

In context with a suggestion to set up blocks for the physically weak and mildly ill, Naujok describes:

> When I leave the block, SS Head Storm Leader Höß, who had just become camp leader at that time, passes by. Through the open door he sees those reporting sick and asks me: 'What's the matter with them?' I explain the circumstances to him and mention that these are temporarily ill, but otherwise fit to work, among them important craftsmen. These men could easily catch pneumonia here and then be absent from work for a longer period. He does not respond to my advice, but answers in a quiet tone: 'These are no humans, these are prisoners.' Then he leaves me standing there.[9]

This attitude also corresponds to the experience Kurt Leischow, block chief in Auschwitz, had with Höß. He had been lectured by Höß on how to treat prisoners. The identification of the prisoners was systematised: a red triangle for the political opponents of the National Socialist system, i.e. Social Democrats and Communists, a pink triangle for homosexuals, a purple triangle for Jehovah's Witnesses, a black triangle for the work shy and pimps, the so-called antisocials, a green triangle for criminals, a blue triangle for emigrants, and later the brown triangle for gypsies. According to this, most prisoners were dangerous criminals in the National Socialist view. To the question if it was permitted to kill prisoners, Leischow answered meaningfully: '*In the abstract* it was prohibited.'[10]

Höß and 18 January 1940[11]

From August until September 1939 the number of prisoners in Sachsenhausen had increased from 6,563 to 12,168. For several thousand prisoners there was no work. When frost set in, their situation worsened. Höß had two standing blocks set up in which the prisoners had to keep standing from morning until evening. On the evening of 17 January Höß told the camp senior Naujoks that he had given the order to the block leaders to have the standing details stand on the parade ground the next morning after the departure of the work details. He was of the opinion that the prisoners should be outside for once, since they were doing nothing the whole day. The notification that these were the old and sick he swept aside. If the others had to freeze outside, these 'lazybones' could withstand a day outside, too. At that time the temperature was minus 26 degrees.

After the morning roll call the work details set off – 800 men remained behind, most of them without coats and gloves. Many of them only wore canvas suits. After a short period the first dead were lying on the frozen ground. Naujoks was called to Höß, who forbade those ailing being taken to the sick bay. In the meantime, Höß observed the events on the parade ground from his office and gave further instructions. Finally he set off to personally search the barracks for prisoners. If someone was found, he was driven to the parade ground under blows and kicks. Höß recalled that the Czech students housed in a special block were missing, and they were shooed into the cold, too.

Naujoks described the further dramatic events:

> More and more people collapse. The dying and dead are lying on the ground. Nobody removes the corpses (...) The number of prisoners crawling towards the sick bay despite the prohibition grows ever larger. In the walk-in clinic, in the rooms, in the corridor, everywhere the sick and dying are lying. (...) Höß has the gates closed. After some time he appears personally in the sick bay. (...) In front of the closed gate a convulsing bundle of desperate people crawling on the ground has formed. When Höß leaves the sick bay again, he has to pass through them. He climbs over those lying on the ground. Hands make a grab for his trouser legs, the trim of his coat. Begging hands are raised. They plead for help. He shakes everyone off and tries to continue. Then one of them cries 'Murderer! Murderer!' and once again 'You scallywag, you murderer!'. Höß kicks about himself in order to get away.[12]

Using a mundane camp procedure, Höß had killed hundreds of prisoners. With steely deliberation he had made use of nature and exposed the helpless people to the cold. With this murderous operation he had demonstrated his abilities in his new function as SS camp leader.

Hermann Langbein had had to observe and suffer Höß at close range. Fittingly he speaks of the true fanaticism with which Höß endeavoured 'to have the death machinery run as smoothly and quickly as possible'. Höß took care less of the camp and more of the extermination operation, the mass murder of the Jews. He himself saw that following the escape of a Polish prisoner Höß arranged:

> that the parents of this prisoner were brought to Auschwitz. They were dressed in prisoner garments, shaved and had to sit on stools.

Behind them a sign was affixed: 'These are the parents of Prisoner X who has escaped. Such is the fate of all who flee.' This was meant as deterrent, and underneath was written: 'on the express order of commander Höß'.

In spring '44 – it was at the beginning of May, if I recall correctly – Höß reappeared in Auschwitz. He had already been seen occasionally beforehand. Höß had been transferred to Oranienburg to Office D, I do not know which department thereof. He appeared sometimes, namely to 'organise', as we were able to surmise. Yet at the beginning of May he appeared not for a brief visit, but he took up residence again in his villa, and immediately many rumours sprang up. And soon it came to light that the reason for Höß' reappearance in Auschwitz was the initialisation of the 'Hungarian operation', the SS code word for this event.[13]

The same man who had people killed without scruples under the worst circumstances or rather claimed not to have seen the daily torture, mistreatment and death, then worried about above all things the well-being of lilac bushes in Auschwitz. In 'Special Order 14/43 dated 13 May 1943' he ordered:

> I have noticed and there is justified complaint that SS members rip the blossoms off from the lilac bushes in a virtually incomprehensible and radical manner. This bad habit has already taken extreme forms, and not only prisoner details can be observed, but also SS members who not only drag bouquets, but entire shrubs into the camps or rather the accommodation.
>
> I forbid the prisoners taking even one more bouquet into the camps, and I expect of the SS members that if they wish for lilac, they will cut this to a modest extent and in a sparing manner from the bushes and do not pillage and destroy it in a senseless way. In the general interest, since these lilac bushes ought to serve sooner or later for the decoration of our entire camp, I expect the full understanding of all SS members of this measure.[14]

On another occasion he had noticed 'that SS members have gardens laid out near and in front of their residences randomly and haphazardly'. He prohibited this 'wild gardening' and demanded that before the setting up of a garden appropriate sketches or maps were presented to him for his approval.[15]

Stanislaw Dubiel made a statement on Höß' daily routine before the investigating judge Jan Sehn – and here the rift between pretence and reality becomes evident, too.[16] Dubiel worked in the garden and household and had the opportunity to observe Höß and his family very closely. According to him, Höß very frequently returned to his official villa during the day and spent the least time in his commander's office. Post requiring his signature was brought to his house, where he frequently received 'dignitaries', too.

Praise for the Shooters

Höß had every attempt at escape by prisoners punished without mercy and commended the SS members preventing the flight – even through the escapees' death, as the following examples show:[17] for instance, SS Band Leader Richard Stolten shot a prisoner during his escape attempt in Dworny. He was commended. SS Storm Man Ewald Luwow, 4th SS-Death Head Storm Command, prevented the mass escape of Jews. He received recognition, as did SS Private Wilhelm Danschke, who arrested a fugitive prisoner on 9 August 1941.[18]

SS Private Karl Mathey received two days of extra leave for the prevention of an escape,[19] SS Private Otto Müller arrested a fugitive who was already wearing civilian clothes,[20] and SS Storm Man Reimers managed to shoot a fugitive Russian prisoner of war c.5,400 metres outside the cordon and thus prevented his escape.[21] SS Head Private Franz Rott and SS Private Johann Kamphus were commended after they had arrested a fugitive prisoner near the Sola river,[22] and SS Private Alexander Horschütz foiled the escape of two gypsies on 6 May 1943.[23]

Höß' entirely inhuman attitude is revealed in his following order:[24]

> The SS Band Leader Wilhelm Reichel, 5th SS-Death Head Storm Command, concentration camp Auschwitz, managed to shoot two out of three escapees fleeing together. (...) Reichel has herein shown himself to be wary and with presence of mind. I hereby express my appreciation for his deed.

On the occasion of the murder of SS Band Leader Peter Jarosiewitsch, the head of the Central Office, SS Senior Group Leader and General of the Waffen-SS Pohl cautioned that no prisoner could be trusted and further ordered that:

1. It is the main obligation of the escort duty to keep six strides away from the prisoners.
2. The escort guards of the outside details armed with rifles have to carry a locked and loaded rifle from now on only under the right arm resting on the bullet pouch.[25]

The Orchestra of Auschwitz

While Höß ruled over the concentration camp with an iron fist and took care of the smooth operation of the death machinery, at the same time he authorised that a prisoner orchestra played for the SS and that those doomed to die were further humiliated. Fania Fénèlon, prisoner number 74862, described this in the following manner:

> Immediately after the first bars the spectacle begins. In rank and file a troop enters the ground, a herd of dwarves. From where have they come? How has Mengele got hold of them? Later we learn that it is a Lilliputian circus famed throughout the whole of Europe, coming with the transports from Hungary.
>
> Some of them wear their circus costumes, the others opulent clothes: tailcoats and tuxedos for the men; the women wear evening dresses, of which some have had to be altered from taller women's wardrobes brought along by the optimistic and naive. (…) After the parade around the ground a part of the little people sit down on the steps, the remainder caper and show a little of their acrobatic skills while emitting shrill screams, plus a mundane piece of clownery, while the plump little hands clamp along in a ridiculous manner. It is pitiful. (…) Jammed in a corner, an audience of striped ghosts with hollow eyes is standing unmoving under the scorching sun, with the fear of death in their hearts, and watching this insane display uncomprehendingly. (…) The SS audience is laughing. This laughter, our music, the dwarves and their masquerade finally turn into such a horrible spectacle that the girls are shaking with fear. Enormous mad laughter drowns out our popular tunes. (…) Mengele himself leads the Lilliputian troop into the gas chamber.[26]

In this context let us take a detour. On the website 'Wider das Vergessen' [Against the oblivion] Rena Jacob has published an article with an extensive analysis by the historian Gabriele Knapp, which brings home the perversion of the Auschwitz camp system, its commander Höß and his successor:

> Millions of men, women and children were mistreated, tortured and murdered in the concentration and extermination camps established by the National Socialists during the so-called Third Reich. In spite of this, or for this very reason, an artistic-musical 'scene' developed among the people imprisoned behind barbed wire and guard towers, who made their own stand against the inhuman, abhorrent and perverted machinations of the brown regime. Depressing-realistic, but also humorous and optimistic songs and texts, were thus created under the deathly swastika. Why did singing and music in particular play such an important role in the camps? The former conductor of the camp orchestra at Auschwitz, Adam Kopycinski, said regarding this: 'Music conveys to us the simple knowledge of life's truth. The desires of the human heart look for guidance in the sphere of sounds. Thanks to its might

and suggestive power here music strengthened in its audience that which is most important – the true nature (...) and promoted self-respect in the person, which was so cruelly trampled underfoot during life in the camps.'

The concentration and extermination camp Auschwitz had already in 1941 a men's orchestra on the initiative of the SS. During this initial period Jews were not yet allowed in the orchestra. In the many outlying camps up to six orchestras were gradually set up, among them a 'gypsy band' in the gypsy camp Auschwitz-Birkenau.

The men's orchestras consisted of professional musicians for the most part, in contrast to the girls' orchestra. The girls' orchestra reached a higher degree of fame than the men's orchestra. The orchestras had to play daily in the morning during the departure of the prisoners and in the evening during their arrival.

The girls' orchestra of Auschwitz was assembled in June 1943 in the camp Auschwitz-Birkenau by the Polish music teacher Zofia Czajkowska, who passed herself off as a descendant of Tchaikovsky, also on the orders of the SS. The members were female prisoners who were saved from destruction through labour and from death in the gas chambers by their acceptance into the orchestra. The conductor of the orchestra from 1943 until April 1944 was Alma Rosé, the niece of the famous composer Gustav Mahler. The brutal but music-loving SS head supervisor Maria Mandl, from October 1942 the unofficial head of the women's camp at Auschwitz-Birkenau, was a champion of the orchestra. She supported the establishment of a special barrack (camp section B I b, in immediate vicinity to the barbed wire) for the musicians. The block bore the number 12, from autumn 1943 the number 7. Inside the barrack was wooden flooring and an oven in order to protect the musical instruments from humidity.

Josef Kramer, from May 1944 the camp commander, mainly wanted the work details to march in step, accompanied by the girls' orchestra. Furthermore an orchestra made a good impression when SS dignitaries visited the camp. The musicians had to give private concerts time and again, too. For instance, Josef Mengele, a lover of classical music, requested frequent performances. Anita Lasker-Wallfisch, a cellist, had to play Schumann's Reverie regularly for Mengele, as he loved to hear this piece. On one Sunday the orchestra had to perform together with the so-called 'Lilliput circus'. The little people trusted the SS doctor, who joked with them and afterwards led them personally into the gas chamber. Kramer insisted on special performances, too.

Again and again many musicians fell ill with diarrhoea, oedema, tuberculosis, spotted fever, typhoid, diphtheria, malaria etc. If the illness was not very infectious, the sick girl was not transferred to the prisoner hospital. If a musician was transferred to the hospital, however, she was usually spared the selections by the SS. This women's orchestra was an opportunity to stay alive under bizarre circumstances. Furthermore, there was a kind of competition among the camp commanders. Since the men's camps had each their own men's orchestra, the leaders of the women's camp wanted to show that they could get this off the ground, too. So the SS men first gathered together young women able to play an instrument at all. During the roll calls, when new transports arrived at the camp, it was simply asked who could play an instrument. The musicians of the orchestra were all particularly dependent on each other, a smooth collaboration resulting in a homogeneous orchestral sound was a kind of life insurance.

The historian Dr Gabriele Knapp commented on this subject: 'Around this orchestra block destruction was everywhere. The musicians were basically only granted a respite. They were continually thinking that they "had to go to their death if playing badly". And thus music was on the one hand a chance to live longer, but on the other hand produced with great exertion.'

Everybody playing music knows that one puts one's soul into the music. Yet to have to play this music now in front of one's own murderers made it necessary to dissociate oneself emotionally in a certain way, reports Dr Knapp: 'How the women surmounted this we probably do not know even today. (...) They wanted to survive, and they made every effort. The conductor Alma Rosé, who had experience as a conductor and who established with each woman in the orchestra a very intense relationship, contributed to this very significantly. And she spurred them on again and again by saying they must, otherwise they will perhaps be sent into the gas chambers, too. It is actually confirmed by all contemporary witnesses that Alma Rosé was the driving force.' The conductor Alma Rosé possessed a great psychological ability. On the one hand she was strict if she had to be in order to discipline the women, too. Yet she also showed much sympathy. She kept weak women who did not belong to the musically most gifted in the orchestra out of pity. For the musicians were good in varying degrees. Some who had already begun to study music were a little older, in their mid-twenties. And then there were the gifted girls who joined the orchestra at 17 or 18, having had only private lessons.

Rehearsals mainly dominated the orchestra member's daily life in Auschwitz. Where others departed for forced labour carrying a spade, they held their violins. Dr Gabriele Knapp says: 'Due to the fact that they had to rehearse a lot in order to be able to meet the expectations of the SS members, they were exempted from this straight forced labour, i.e. working in the fields or draining swamps.

Their forced labour consisted in their daily rehearsals of 10–12 hours at least. This sounds easy at first, but everyone who knows what it means to practise an instrument so intensely also knows how exhausting this is. Therefore they had slightly better living and working conditions in that respect that they were not exposed to the extremely difficult conditions outside during any wind and weather such as cold etc. Nevertheless, the camp routine was exhausting. They were outside in the morning and played these marches to which the forced labourers then had to march in step. During the roll call upon their return the musicians learned who had died in between and they then had to play cheerful hiking songs. Many of the surviving women tell that they cannot remember the images without hearing the music they had to play. And if they heard this music after 1945, the images sprung up immediately before their eyes.[27]

The inhuman attitude that Höß had already shown at Sachsenhausen he also kept as commander of Auschwitz. There he informed the Jewish Council of Elders that Jews were no longer permitted to greet the SS men. 'It is not dignified for an SS man to be greeted by one of these scoundrels. Therefore each SS member is once again alerted and admonished not to touch any Jew who refrained from greeting.'[28]

In his function as camp commander Höß issued a series of orders in which he expressed his deep contempt of prisoners and particularly of Jews. He considered it 'absolutely impossible and also not according to SS standards, if detail leaders of work details from the women's concentration camp have the prisoners carry their lunch boxes, tents etc. during departure and arrival'.[29] It was contrary to the honour of an SS man 'to make use of the help of prisoners for the transportation of such equipment'. Höß demanded a 'strict and coolly rational relationship' towards the – in this case – female prisoners and gave notice of the strictest punishment of even the slightest relaxation. Female prisoners did not exist to provide the guard personnel with any kind of easements, but had to work productively. On 24 October 1942 Höß threatened the strictest punishments to all those SS men who continued to have the prisoners fetch their 'lunch, supper, coffee etc'.[30] Later he pointed out once more 'with all urgency that under no circumstances are prisoners allowed to be entrusted with the delivery, the cleaning etc. of bicycles and motor bikes'.[31] Some SS members had kept a shred of humanity and occasionally gave a tip to the prisoners working in the barbershops. With command order 29/44 this was strictly prohibited.[32] At the same time it was declared that violations of this order were viewed and punished as facilitation to escape.

Aside from the fact that in many respects Höß did not act as a role model himself, the orders he issued show that the SS members had made themselves at home in the concentration camp and knew how to obtain amenities.

Although the Reich Leader SS Himmler demanded certain standards of behaviour from the members of the 'elite order SS', those in Auschwitz were a long way from the rule makers. Let us just recall the embezzlement of dental gold that had finally brought the SS judiciary to the scene.

In an order dated 16 November 1943, Arthur Liebehenschel, of whom it was said that under his command of the camp there had been relief for prisoners, drew attention to the fact that SS members recklessly misappropriated prisoners' possessions.[33] This property – clothes, gold and other valuables, food and other personal items – had to remain untouched, he declared in Garrison Order 51/43. This order declared that the state would decide on its use, and he who embezzled state property turned himself into a criminal and by his own volition barred himself from the ranks of the SS. It went on: 'I expect of every clean, decent SS member – and this will be the majority – that he assists with open eyes in removing potential scallywags as quickly as possible so that our ranks remain pristine.' This order shows the state of discipline among the SS at Auschwitz. According to these guidelines, Höß would also have had to be removed from the SS as a 'scallywag', for his wife and he continually misappropriated prisoners' property.

That discipline was not in the best shape is further documented by an order by SS Head Storm Leader Heinrich Schwarz, commander of Auschwitz III. He criticised the fact that time and time again men were reading the newspaper while on duty. The same was also true for conversations with women. 'The individual man commits a serious offence against guard duty by this means and could plunge himself as well as his family into disaster by his untoward behaviour,' Schwarz warned.[34]

As a rule such violations did not lead to imminent dismissal, but to rather mild punishments. For example, SS Under Company Leader Herbert Pritzokleit of the 2nd Headquarters Company and SS Storm Man Alfred Schütter of the 7th SS-Death Head Storm Command. On 1 October 1943 they were prohibited from entering the 'House of the Waffen-SS' for three months due to undisciplined behaviour.[35]

Chapter 5

Höß and his Fellow Perpetrators

Sketches from Polish Imprisonment

During his stay in the Cracow prison between the end of 1946 and the beginning of 1947, with his execution in sight, besides the *Autobiographical Notes* Höß also wrote about numerous people whom he had encountered in the course of his SS career and especially as commander of Auschwitz or as head of department in Oranienburg. Among those was first and foremost the Reich Leader SS, Heinrich Himmler, whose description is widely known and reproduced in the appendix of the German edition of the *Notes*. Therefore this is only summarily discussed here.

Beyond the autobiography thirty-four individual portraits are recorded, which were developed between interrogations from October 1946 until January 1947. Copies of these are kept, among other places, in the archive of the Federal Commissioner for the Records of the State Security Service of the former GDR (BstU).

The historian Martin Broszat, who from 1972 until his death in 1989 was head of the Institute for Contemporary History in Munich, writes in his introduction to the initial publication of the *Notes* in 1958 that Höß wanted to provide as detailed and accurate information as possible on people and matters known to him. Höß wrote down these personal descriptions between the individual interrogations, and Broszat attested that they 'by no means represent dubious products of talkative or wordy pomposity, but despite some distortion and whitewashing are on the whole chilling especially because of their accounting-like brevity and exact dispassion'.[1] This view has to be vehemently opposed.

If we took Höß' statements literally, then it would have been the deficiencies of superiors and subordinates in equal measure that prevented him establishing and managing the 'perfect' concentration camp. The recurring description of his impotence is remarkable. Whoever reads the descriptions gets the impression that Höß had not been able to influence the selection and behaviour of SS personnel either as concentration camp commander or as garrison commander. He describes the intrigues, barbarism and bloodlust, the sadism and the greed, the lack of professional skills – of course exclusively of third persons – as well as the inadequate external circumstances and had allegedly not been able to undertake anything against it.

By speaking of real and supposed weaknesses of others against which, in his own words, he fought in vain, Höß wants to shirk his own responsibility and at the same time admits his own failure: in the characterisations of superiors and subordinates he stresses again and again in the individual sketches that these people did not inform him and deceived him, that his superiors forced wholly incompetent people upon him who were only pursuing their own interest and were brutal and corrupt. These were alcoholics, sadists and drug addicts unqualified and unreliable in every respect with nothing more on their minds than to deceive him. The few whom he initially trusted had let him down.

In contrast to this he described the task of a camp commander, hence his own, in the following manner: 'The camp commander is in every aspect fully responsible for the entire area of the camp. To ensure the security of the camp at all times is his foremost duty. He has to be always available. Every important occurrence in the camp has to be reported to him immediately.'[2] In fact, important occurrences were rarely reported to him, preferably not at all, as he himself admitted. If the commander was absent, he had to hand over his responsibilities to his deputy, who ought always to be the protective custody camp leader. After his return the latter was supposed to report all important events to him – that evidently did not happen, either.

Höß went on that the commander must be on constant standby and able to cope with every situation. His decisions must be clear and carefully considered, since their effects were often of great consequence. With 'continual instructions' he was supposed to train the men subordinate to him in their duties and tasks, especially in camp security and their conduct with prisoners.

Höß did carry out 'instructions' in how to deal with prisoners in person, as Kurt Leischow, former block leader in Auschwitz, confirmed. According to him, Höß brought it home to his subordinates 'that the largest part of the prisoners, for example those with the green triangle, were all dangerous criminals, those with the red triangle political opponents of the National Socialist system, with the black triangle work shy with no appetite for labour, and pimps.'[3]

He maintained that he had wanted to establish a 'model concentration camp' at Auschwitz – with sufficient accommodation for the prisoners, with the necessary sanitary installations, a hygienic minimum standard as well as honest SS members who neither tortured prisoners, misappropriated their property or showed themselves to be corrupt. Instead external circumstances, the cramped situation and overcrowding of the camp as well as the lack of understanding by his superiors led to catastrophic conditions, in the face of which he had been powerless. If he had had his way, so he suggests, the hundreds of thousands of Auschwitz prisoners would have performed slave labour for the National Socialists being well-fed and decently dressed.

Höß only envisaged such a concept for the non-Jewish prisoners. In his conviction the Jews were only fit for mass extermination. This was for him merely a component of his 'work' that he wanted to perform as perfectly as possible in accordance with his superiors' wishes – in a concentration camp with well-kept gardens in which not human beings but lilac bushes were under his protection.

In this context it should be mentioned that Joachim Caesar frequently made critical remarks on the conditions in the camp – the food and the overcrowding – and he therefore got into conflict with Höß again and again. Himmler paid a visit to the camp on 17 June 1942, the schedule of which is noted accurately in his official diary:

12.45 setting off from Lötzen
15.15 arrival Katowice
Pick up of Regional Leader Bracht, Senior Group Leader Schmauser and Storm Command Leader Höß
15.15 Regional Leader [Gauleiter] Bracht
SS Senior Group Leader Schmauser
SS Storm Command Leader Caesar
SS Senior Storm Command Leader Vogel
SS Storm Command Leader Höß
Drive to Auschwitz
Tea at the Leaders' Residence
Meeting with Storm Command Leader Caesar and Senior Storm Command Leader Vogel, Storm Command Leader Höß
Visit to the agricultural enterprises
Visit of the prisoner camp and female prisoner campaign
Dinner at the Leaders' Residence
Drive Auschwitz – Katowice to the residence of Regional Leader Bracht
Evening with Regional Leader Bracht[4]

During this visit Caesar, who was also special commissioner of the Reich Leader SS for plant-based rubber, was 'cautioned with the threat of the severest punishment'.[5] He was told that he ought not to worry about these problems as they were the commander's concern. Caesar had primarily criticised the conditions in the women's camp at Birkenau. Due to overcrowding there was too little water and too few washing facilities. Furthermore, there was a lack of clothing and means of transport to get to work. In any case, Caesar had criticised Höß for the selection of the location at Birkenau and the occupancy of Auschwitz II several times. There were neither trails nor clean water; all wells were infested with E.coli, there was not a single puddle without anopheles mosquitoes, the carriers of malaria. Originally Oswald Pohl, head of the Central Economic-Administrative Office, was supposed to accompany the Reich Leader SS, too, but in his stead came SS Brigade Leader Hans Kammler as head of the budget and construction department. Kammler wrote a detailed report on the building projects approved by Himmler. Primarily it dealt with drainage and large-scale water supply, the expansion of agriculture and the 'Russian camp' at Birkenau.

According to Höß, Himmler visited the farmyards, the improvement works and the dam construction and showed himself to be especially interested in the laboratories and the rubber plant breeding programme. On this occasion he approved the construction of an underwater power station. In Birkenau, Himmler, together with Bracht, Schmauser and others, received a demonstration of the entire 'extermination' process: the 'selection' of those fit to work from a transport just arrived from the Netherlands, the murder of several hundred Jews inside the gas chambers as well as the concluding 'clearance' of the bunker. According to Höß, Himmler ordered shortly after that all the mass graves used so far should be dug up and the corpses burned. Himmler showed himself to be so satisfied with Höß that he promoted him to SS Senior Storm Command Leader.

The head supervisor of the women's concentration camp, Johanna Langefeld, complained on that occasion about the protective custody camp leader Hans Aumeier and Höß' adjutant, Robert Mulka. In March 1942 she received an order from the chief inspector of the concentration camps, Richard Glücks, to establish a women's concentration camp within the main camp of Auschwitz with ten supervisors and a hundred prisoner functionaries from the Ravensbrück camp. This women's camp was relocated to Birkenau in summer 1942. Since then a conflict with Höß had been rumbling on. In Höß' opinion Langefeld had previously led a 'quiet, cosy and comfortable life'[6] at Ravensbrück and was not equal to her new tasks at Auschwitz. As a result he gave the management of the women's camp to Aumeier because the 'sloppy work could not continue like this'. 'Yet as the head supervisor thought herself to be an independent camp leader, she complained about being subordinated to one of equal rank. And indeed I had to retract her subordination.'[7]

During the visit by the Reich Leader SS, Höß presented his grievances to Himmler in the presence of the head supervisor and requested that he be allowed to continue to subordinate Langefeld to the protective custody camp leader. Himmler rejected Höß' request with the argument that a women's camp should be led by a woman and suggested he assigned an SS leader to Langefeld for assistance, which was not implemented. In agreement with Oswald Pohl, Langefeld returned to Ravensbrück at the beginning of October 1942 and took over the post as head supervisor from Maria Mandl, who in turn took Langefeld's place in Auschwitz. Furthermore, Himmler now forbade men in principle to enter the women's camp. On 24 October 1942 Glücks then ordered that in the Auschwitz, Ravensbrück and Lublin camps the protective custody camp leaders on duty in the women's camps were to be replaced with female head supervisors. However, this rule was rescinded after just one year.

In regarding to Himmler's visit, Mulka, Höß' adjutant, recounted the following episode: Höß accompanied the Reich Leader SS through the camp, during which Mulka had the opportunity to speak with Himmler, too. As Mulka recalled, they talked about the 'exceptional behaviour' of SS leaders:

> During the meal in the Leaders' Residence one under storm leader had put both forearms on the table. I sent an orderly to him and let him be asked whether he wished to have a chaise longue. Himmler had heard that and said: 'Brilliant, I want to have my leaders like that! They should not only be brave at the front, but able to move in polished boots in every salon.'[8]

Even though the individual portraits that Höß wrote in prison raise many questions concerning the truthfulness of their content, they are nevertheless an important historical source. The passages quoted in what follows will be given in accordance with the original manuscript for the sake of authenticity.

The public has so far remained largely deprived of these sketches. Beyond the people described, the characterisations mainly shed light on the character of Rudolf Höß. The following sketches are presented:

- Heinrich Himmler, Reich Leader SS
- Heinrich Müller, SS Group Leader, head of Office IV in the Reich Security Main Office (RSHA)

- Oswald Pohl, SS Senior Group Leader, head of the SS Central Economic-Administrative Office (WVHA)
- Theodor Eicke, SS Senior Group Leader and General of the Waffen-SS, inspector of concentration camps
- Richard Glücks, SS Senior Group Leader, inspector of the concentration camps
- Bruno Streckenbach, SS Brigade Leader, commander of the security police and security service in Cracow, head of Office I (Organisation, Administration and Law) of the Reich Security Main Office
- Hans Kammler, SS Senior Group Leader, head of Office Group C at the WVHA, responsible for the construction of gas chambers and crematoria
- Karl Bischoff, SS Storm Command Leader, head of the central construction department in Auschwitz
- Odilo Globocnik, SS Group Leader, regional leader [Gauleiter] of Vienna, SS and police leader in Lublin district
- Robert Mulka, SS Head Storm Leader, Höß's adjutant
- Arthur Liebehenschel, SS Senior Storm Command Leader, commander and camp senior of Auschwitz, main camp
- Maximilian Grabner, SS Senior Storm Leader, head of the Political Department in Auschwitz
- Karl Möckel, SS Senior Storm Command Leader, head of the general premises administration Auschwitz
- Ernst-Robert Grawitz, SS Senior Group Leader, Reich Physician SS
- Joachim Mrugowsky, SS Senior Storm Leader and head of the Hygienic Institute of the Waffen-SS
- Enno Lolling, SS Standard Leader, head of Office D III: medical corps organisation and camp hygiene
- Karl Fritzsch, SS Head Storm Leader, first protective custody camp leader of the concentration camp Auschwitz
- Hans Aumeier, SS Storm Command Leader, protective custody camp leader at the main camp Auschwitz
- Gerhard Maurer, SS Standard Leader, Head of Department D II in the WVHA
- Friedrich Hartjenstein, SS Senior Storm Command Leader, commander of Auschwitz III

- Richard Baer, SS Storm Command Leader, commander of the concentration camp Auschwitz, main camp
- Gerhard Palitzsch, SS Head Company Leader, report leader concentration camp Auschwitz
- Heinrich Schwarz, SS Head Storm Leader, commander of camp Auschwitz III
- Maximilian Sell, SS Senior Storm Leader, head of the work details in Auschwitz concentration camp
- Eduard Wirths, SS garrison doctor in Auschwitz

Reich Leader SS, Heinrich Himmler[9]

Höß called Himmler 'probably the most faithful, selfless follower of Adolf Hitler'. He never heard, not even from his worst enemies, that he was accused of personal enrichment or that he abused his position of power for personal purposes. 'He himself was personally clean, was living a simple and modest life and was always busy, always full of new ideas and improvements in the service of the National Socialist idea. Every other school of thought or world view he rejected as damaging or corrupting for the German people. In this manner he also wanted to educate the SS as his creation.'

Of his encounters with Himmler, Höß wrote among other things that in June 1934 the former had asked him during his visit to the Pomeranian SS in Szczecin if he wanted to join the SS and serve in a concentration camp. Only after intensive discussions with his wife Hedwig, with whom he actually intended to become a settler with the Artaman League, he decided to follow Himmler's invitation and resume active duty as a soldier. It is telling that Höß considered the work in a concentration camp – the organisation of mass murder – to be that of a 'soldier'. On 1 November 1934 he was called to Dachau by the inspector of concentration camps, Theodor Eicke. The next meeting with Himmler took place on 8 May 1936. The Reich Leader SS visited all the SS installations at Dachau including the concentration camp. In his retinue were all the Nazi regional leaders and Reich leaders, and all the SS and SS group leaders. Höß remembered this day in his Cracow cell thus:

> I am at that time report leader and deputise for the absent protective custody camp leader. H. is in the best of moods because the entire visit goes smoothly. In the concentration camp Dachau everything is in order at that time, too. The prisoners are well-fed, dressed and accommodated well and cleanly, for the most part employed in

workshops and the sickness absence rate is negligible. The entire occupation is c.2,500 in ten residential barracks. The hygiene of the camp is adequate. There is enough water. The underwear is changed weekly, the bedding monthly. A third are political prisoners, two-thirds prisoners in police preventative detention, antisocials and prisoners sentenced to forced labour, homosexuals and c.2,000 Jews.

During the visit Himmler approaches me together with Bormann and asks me if I am satisfied with my position and how my family are. Shortly afterwards I am promoted to Under Storm Leader. During this visit, H. – as it was his habit – singled out a few prisoners and asked them for the reason of their imprisonment in front of all the guests. There were some Communist leaders who admitted quite frankly that they continued to be Communists and would remain so. Some professional criminals played down their list of crimes significantly; the quickly consulted prisoner files had to refresh their memories regarding their crimes. This incident was typical of the Reich Leader, and I have experienced this several times. H. punished those who had lied with several Sundays of penal labour. Further, some antisocials who had always drunk away their wages and abandoned their families to public welfare. Then a former Social Democrat minister from Braunschweig, Dr Jasper, and some Jewish emigrants who had returned from Palestine and who answered the questions posed to them from all sides with the ready wit inherent in Jews.

Höß and Himmler met once more in Sachsenhausen camp, when in the summer of 1938 Reich Minister for the Interior Wilhelm Frick visited a concentration camp for the first time. In his company were all the senior and district presidents, plus the police chiefs of the larger cities. Höß gave a guided tour through the camp and provided explanations. He was at that time adjutant of the camp commander. He always remained close to Himmler during the tour and thus could observe him very closely:

He is in the best of moods and really pleased that he finally can show the minister of the interior and the gentlemen of the internal administration of the Reich one of the most mysterious, notorious concentration camps. He is bombarded with questions, he answers all of them calmly and courteously, but often sarcastically. Questions inconvenient to him, regarding the numbers of prisoners or similar, he answers evasively, but all the more courteously. (All numerical data of the concentration camps had to be treated as top secret according to the order by the Reich Leader SS.) I believe, the Sachsenhausen concentration camp had at that time 4,000 inmates, mostly professional criminals who were accommodated in clean wooden barracks, separated in sleeping and daytime quarters. The food was good and sufficient for general acceptance. Clothing was sufficient and always clean, since a very modern laundry existed in the camp. The sick bays with the treatment rooms were exemplary, absence due to sickness minor. Apart from the cell block, which was not allowed to be shown to outsiders in any camp as most of the time special prisoners of the Reich Security Main Office were incarcerated there, all the installations of the camp were shown. Certainly nothing was kept from the critical eyes of these old government and police officials. Frick showed himself to be very interested and declared during the meal that it was quite shameful of him that only now, in 1938, he was seeing a concentration camp!

Despite the limited time, and although he was continually pressed with questions, H. found the opportunity to speak to me personally and in particular to ask after my wife. This he never neglected to do on any occasion and I felt that this did not just happen out of politeness.

However, the inconsistency in Himmler's orders that was criticised by Höß finds particular expression in the following passage:

Himmler's attitude toward the concentration camps, his view on the treatment of prisoners, was never clearly discernible and changed several times, too. Principal guidelines on the treatment of prisoners and all questions related to that were never provided. There were significant contradictions in his orders throughout all the years. Also, during his camp visits the commanders could never receive from him clear, precedent-setting instructions regarding the treatment of prisoners. One time the strictest treatment with no consideration – another time gentle treatment, taking the state of health into account, attempting to educate with the possibility of release. One time: increasing the working hours to 12 and the most severe punishment for idlers, another time: an increase of bonuses and the establishment of brothels for a voluntary increase in efficiency.

After a meeting in January 1940 Höß was ordered in November of the same year to report to Himmler on the set-up of the Auschwitz concentration camp. He claimed again and again to have described the situation 'extensively and starkly, depicting all grievances that seemed at that time probably quite significant, but were minor compared to the catastrophic conditions of later years'. Himmler hardly responded to this and only said 'that as commander I above all would have to find a remedy, how it was my problem. Furthermore we were at war, and much had to be improvised. Likewise we in the concentration camps must stop living according to the peacetime modus.' The soldier at the front was lacking much, why not the prisoners? Höß's warning over the eruption of epidemics in view of inadequate hygienic installations Himmler dismissed with the words: 'You are too pessimistic.'

Later Höß lamented in his cell:

> No help from any side! I went to work with gritted teeth. No SS man was spared, no prisoner. The possibilities available had to be used to the last. I was almost constantly on the move to buy materials of any kind, to steal, to confiscate. I was supposed to help myself after all – and I did this most thoroughly! Thanks to my good relations to the industry I managed to snatch considerable amounts of materials.

Höß accused Himmler 'that thousands upon thousands of non-Jews who were supposed to remain alive had to die of epidemics and illnesses caused by the deficient accommodation, insufficient food, inadequate clothing and the lack of hygienic installations – the blame for this falls solely on Himmler, who refuted all reports on these conditions given to him incessantly by all leading offices – did not put a stop to the causes and did not provide any remedies'.

This sympathy, it has to be emphasized, was extended only to the non-Jews. Yet it is a fact that again and again epidemics erupted from which mainly both the prisoners and their torturers suffered. For example, the wife of Storm Command Leader Caesar died of typhoid, and Caesar himself was infected by it a little later, too. In the 'special order 15/43' dated 7 July 1943 Höß referred to the fact that in the previous days two SS members on duty in gypsy camp B I had caught spotted fever.[10] As there had been additional cases of spotted fever, Höß imposed an absolute camp lockout. Further, he ordered that the SS members on duty in gypsy camps B I to III had to be housed separately from the others. After duty hours they had to bathe and were examined for lice.

Camp leader Aumeier believed it would be possible to fight the spotted fever epidemic by ordering the hospital personnel to carry out consecutive lice controls in all blocks. On this Wieslaw Kielar remarked: 'When it did not rain, the lice control usually took place in the yard regardless of the season. The prisoners stripped down to their hips had to pull down their trousers. We examined their underwear simply crawling with insects. (...) The most infested with lice were the Musulmen[11] of course. The lice literally ate them alive.'[12]

Himmler absconded to Flensburg shortly before the end of the war. He was recognised and arrested by the British, committing suicide on 23 May 1945.

Heinrich Müller, SS Group Leader, Head Office IV in the RSHA, Deputy Chief Security Police and Security Service [SD][13]

From 1929 Müller was charged with combatting Communist organisations in the Munich Political Police. After Heydrich's appointment to head of office of the Secret State Police (Gestapo) in April 1934 he took several of his co-workers from the Bavarian Political Police along with him to Berlin. In 1936 Müller became deputy chief of the Political Police office in the central office of the security police, with which the Gestapo was merged. In 1939 Müller became head of Office IV, i.e. of the infamous Secret State Police, in short the Gestapo.

Müller only visited the concentration camps a few times and not all of them, wrote Höß. Nevertheless, he had been informed on all the events in the concentration camps, after all the heads of the respective political department belonged to his office and thus he was their superior. Müller's personal views on the prisoners and their treatment could never be deduced, as he always hid behind the Reich Leader SS:

> I had to deal with him very frequently as adjutant of the Sachsenhausen concentration camp, as camp commander in Auschwitz and later as head of department D I. Here I never experienced that he said even once: I decide in such way, I order this, I want that. He always took cover behind the Reich Leader SS or the chief of the security police and security service. However, every insider knew that he made the decisions and that the Reich Leader SS or Kaltenbrunner relied completely on him in all questions concerning the prisoners! All the commitments were ordered by him as well as the releases. Among other things the executions, as far as they were decided within the RSHA, were only decided by him, i.e. in important cases he submitted the execution orders to the Reich Leader SS for signature.
>
> The wide and very sensitive area of the special prisoners was on his mind. He knew the exact data for all those numerous prisoners, knew all their locations and their weaknesses.
>
> Müller was an incredibly versatile and tenacious worker. He only went on a few official trips, yet he could be reached at any time, day or night, Sundays and holidays, either at his office or at home.
>
> (...) From Eichmann and Günther, who had even more extensive dealings with him than me, I know that he also supervised the most important features of the Jewish operations, although he then gave Eichmann virtually free rein. As I detail above, he was informed thoroughly on all concentration camps, hence also on Auschwitz, which he never visited himself. Yet he knew all the details, whether these were Birkenau or the crematoria or the numbers of prisoners or of deaths, to my frequent astonishment.

My personal interventions with him in an attempt to slow down the operations in order to take care of the grievances were always without success, since he hid behind the strict order by the Reich Leader SS 'to carry out the operations ordered without regard!' In this respect I tried everything with him – yet in vain. Although I otherwise achieved much with him, of which others were not capable. Especially later, at D I, he valued my judgement highly. Today I believe that they did not want to change the conditions in Auschwitz in order to increase the effect of the operations in this indirect way.

Müller would have had the power to stop or to slow down operations, he would have also been able to convince the Reich Leader SS. He did not do so, although he knew the precise consequences – because it was not wanted – that is my opinion today. At that time I could not recognise the reasons for the Reich Leader's behaviour.

Müller told us repeatedly: the RL SS is of the opinion that the release of political prisoners during the war must be refused for security police considerations. Therefore requests for release should be restricted to a minimum and only to be presented in exceptional cases. The RL SS has ordered that all prisoners of foreign nations were not to be released for the duration of the war in principle. The RL SS wishes that execution shall be requested even for minor acts of sabotage by foreign prisoners – as a deterrent.

It is no longer difficult to guess – considering everything mentioned above – who stood behind these orders and wishes. (...)

Personally, Müller was very proper, but obliging and companionable. He never let the superior or rank shine through, but one could not establish a personal connection. This was confirmed to me again and again by his subordinates who had been working for him for many years.

Müller was a cold-blooded executioner or organiser of all the measures considered necessary by the RL SS for the security of the Reich.[14]

In his description of Müller, Höß omits an important aspect with regards to the release of prisoners. Even after the incorporation of the 'inspection concentration camps' into the Central Economic-Administrative Office ordered by Himmler, effective 3 March 1942, the Reich Security Main Office was solely responsible for commitments, releases and the treatment of prisoners. However, the head of Office Group D or his representative as head of Office D I were to be the liaison for the RSHA – and that was according to Liebehenschel Rudolf Höß![15]

Müller is believed to be still missing. According to information from Johannes Tuchel, the director of the Memorial for the German Resistance, however, he died shortly before the end of the war: his corpse was supposedly found in a provisional grave near the former Reich Aviation Ministry, today the seat of the Federal Ministry for Finance, definitely identified and subsequently buried in Berlin in a mass grave in the former Jewish cemetery at Große Hamburger Straße that was dissolved in 1943 on the Gestapo's orders.

Oswald Pohl, SS Senior Group Leader, Head of the SS Central Economic-Administrative Office[16]

Oswald Pohl was among the most influential people at the head of the SS. He enjoyed Himmler's trust and took care of the finances of the SS and its widespread activities – including the construction and maintenance of the concentration camps.

According to the former prisoner Stanislaw Dubiel, the SS Group Leader Ernst-Heinrich Schmauser was a frequent guest at the Höß villa in Auschwitz and SS Senior Group Leader Pohl also visited several times.[17] Höß and Pohl were friends and during his visits a cordial atmosphere prevailed.

Höß said Pohl came from Kiel – however Duisburg is correct – and had been paymaster at the navy SA, from where Himmler recruited him in 1934 and made him head of the administration for the Reich Leadership SS (SS Central Office).

While this department had hardly played any role under his predecessors, Pohl knew how to make himself indispensable to Himmler in the shortest time and his department 'all-powerful'. For instance, his auditors – chosen by him and responsible only to him – were feared by the administrative heads of all SS offices. Pohl saw to it that, in Höß' assessment, the SS administration 'worked cleanly and dependably and that all dirty, unreliable administrative heads were caught and dismissed'.

The fact that Pohl provided Himmler with financial means of an almost unlimited amount made him practically untouchable:

> Under Pohl's predecessors the higher unit leaders of the SS had been quite independent in financial matters and acted as they saw fit. Pohl secured an agreement with the Reich Leader SS (RL SS) that all financial outgoings of the entire SS required his approval and were subject to his review. That caused much bad blood and agitation, but Pohl prevailed with his typical energy and thus gained an immense influence on all units of the SS. Even the most stubborn pigheads among the higher SS leaders like Sepp Dietrich and Eicke had to give in and ask Pohl for money if these were extra-budgetary means.

Each unit of the SS had an exactly calculated annual budget, which had to be kept to absolutely. Pohl's bloodhounds, the auditors, found each penny that was listed above or below this total.

Pohl's main task from the beginning, however, was to gradually render the SS financially independent of state and party by economic enterprises owned by the SS in order to guarantee the necessary freedom of action for the RL SS in all his plans.[18]

This was a task with a far-reaching goal of whose feasibility Pohl was totally convinced, however, and towards the achievement of which he was working incessantly. Almost all the economic enterprises of the SS sprung up on his initiative.

Höß lists here among others the Deutsche Ausrüstungswerke (DAW = German Equipment Works), the porcelain manufacturer Allach, the quarries and clinker production plants combined under the Deutsche Erd und Steinwerke (DEST = German Earth and Stone Works Company), brickyards and cement factories, clothing factories, bread factories, grocery outlets and canteens, numerous spa enterprises, agricultural and forestry enterprises as well as printing companies and publishing houses.

Pohl stood without reservation behind the 'Jewish extermination operation'. The efforts that Höß claimed he made for prisoners only concerned non-Jews and only had the goal of exploiting their labour for the SS or the war economy.

In addition, according to Höß' claims, Pohl allegedly demanded the release of prisoners known to him if he was of the opinion that they were unjustly imprisoned or that the length of the sentence was unjustified. 'Thus he entered into an irreconcilable antagonism with Eicke, to the RSHA and later to Kaltenbrunner. Pohl did not shy away from personally intervening in particularly extreme cases with the RL SS, which he usually avoided. This was mostly without success, for the RL SS stuck in principle to the assessments by the RSHA.'

> During my time as D I I had the task of enforcing or constantly counselling in person Pohl's demands for release with the RL SS. He always set short deadlines and became very annoyed if the demanded releases had not been carried out by these dates. He did not relent even in the case of the most hopeless demands for release. Yet in some cases he achieved a so-called conditional release, i.e. the former prisoner had to work as a voluntary civilian employee under supervision by the concentration camp in one of the SS enterprises associated with the camp.
>
> (…) As long as I knew Pohl and until the downfall he always had the same attitude to all questions regarding prisoners. He held the opinion that a prisoner who was accommodated well and

warm, was adequately fed and clothed would work diligently by his own accord, hence punishments must only be applied in the most extreme cases.

(…) In 1941 the concentration camps were incorporated into the WVHA as part of Office Group D and put under Pohl's command. Pohl was well informed on all camps through the economic enterprises linked to all camps, through their managers, through the temporary inspector of these enterprises, through the heads of the office groups and through the heads of departments. (…) Pohl's principal demands were:

Decent treatment of prisoners, elimination of all whimsical treatment by subordinate SS members, improvement of the catering facilities, creation of warm clothing for the cold season, adequate accommodation and improvement of all hygienic installations. All these improvements ought to have the purpose of keeping the prisoners in a physical state that allowed them to fulfil the required work performance.

To conclude from this narration that Pohl had even a small amount of pity for the prisoners would be totally amiss. His aim was exclusively to achieve the maximum work performance from the prisoners, which they could only achieve with good nutrition. Yet due to continued rationing the food situation became worse and inadequate, and the creation of the position of food inspector did not help at all. This role was taken by SS Senior Storm Command Leader Ernst Günther Schenck. About him Höß states the following:

This Professor Schenck cannot increase the rations despite his extensive knowledge and abilities. Minor improvements through improved cooking methods, in part additions of raw food and wild vegetables, did increase the number of calories in theory. Yet the next shortening of rations rendered all his efforts to nothing.

The textile shortage equally brings one shortening after another for the prisoners' allocations. The clothing quota can no longer be kept by 1940. Even the textiles and shoes accruing from the Jewish extermination operations cannot improve the clothing crises significantly.

The creation of sufficient accommodation comes to nothing due to the unstoppable cramming of all camps, the lack of building materials – finally there is even the halting of all construction plans for accommodation. Even the best construction manager would not have been able to keep up with the pace of the numerical increase of the camps with his construction activities, not to mention creating accommodation in reserve. The improvement and extension of the hygienic facilities was wholly impossible.

Pohl inspected the concentration labour camps often and on most occasions unannounced:

> He did not let himself be guided, he wished to explore everything by himself. Without regard for time, people, food etc. he hurried from one point to another. He had a fabulous memory. He never forgot any numbers once mentioned. Furthermore, incidents and matters he had criticised during previous inspections were always on his mind. He always remembered orders and instructions he had given. There arose bad situations for those caught by him at misconduct and neglect.

The way such a visit to Auschwitz went is described by Johann Paul Kremer in his diary. The medical officer had arrived on 20 August 1942 without being a fixed member of the camp personnel. Among his tasks was, among others, to determine and certify the death of prisoners. On Pohl's visit on 23 September 1942 Kremer reported:

> In the morning Senior Group Leader Pohl arrived with his retinue at the residence of the Waffen-SS. In front of the door a guard was standing presenting his rifle to me. In the evening around 8pm, dinner with Senior Group Leader Pohl in the Leaders' Residence, a true feast. There was roast pike as much as anybody wanted, real coffee, excellent beer and sandwiches.[19]

Outside the door people starved to death and died in the gas chambers, while Pohl, Höß and others feasted to their hearts' content!

Besides Dachau – as Höß continued with his notes – Pohl kept an especially close eye on Auschwitz and campaigned for the establishment and extension of this mass extermination complex with the greatest vigour:

> Kammler often said to me that Pohl begins all construction meetings in Berlin with the question of how matters have progressed in Auschwitz. The SS raw material department had an extensive file with Pohl's requests, reminders and angry letters concerning Auschwitz. I was probably the only SS leader in the entire SS who had such an extensive carte blanche for the acquisition of all that was required in Auschwitz.
>
> Later, as D I, he chased me time and again about the concentration and labour camps where he had encountered grievances that he could not clear up, so that I should look for the guilty parties and possibly put an end to the worst matters. As the fundamental cause was not rooted out by Himmler, all efforts to improve the conditions were futile from the beginning!

Pohl was on the one hand the cold, sober calculator; a numbers person demanding the most of his subordinates in sense of duty and performance, who often punished misconduct and neglect most inhumanly and severely, who brutally got his will and his wishes. Woe betide him who dared to cross his path, as he did not rest until he had sidelined or destroyed his opponent.

On the other hand, he was very companionable, and helped everyone who suffered hardship through no fault of his own. He was very soft, indulgent and considerate, especially to women. He placed special importance on treating the female supervisors, communications officers and other female civilian employees with consideration and preference. He was most especially concerned with the surviving dependants of fallen or deceased SS members and supported them to the greatest extent. They could turn to him at any time. The SS leader of this area who missed or even grossly neglected something in this respect was finished forever.

He never overlooked diligent, thoughtful work. He was always grateful for all suggestions, improvements or references to matters to be improved or halted by him. Who had distinguished himself in his eyes through good performance could approach him at any time with issues and requests; then he always helped as far as it was in his power to do so.

Pohl was very capricious and often went from one extreme to the other. To contradict him in a bad mood was inadvisable and led to angry rebukes. In a good mood one could say anything to him, even the most disgusting and unpleasant things, and he took no offence whatsoever. It was not easy to be in his immediate environment for a longer period. His adjutants changed frequently and very suddenly.

Pohl loved to represent and to display his position of power. His uniform was ostentatiously simple and he wore no decorations at all until he was forced by the RL SS to wear the German Cross and the Knight's Cross to the War Merit Cross when he received these honours.

In spite of his age – he was more than fifty years old – he was extremely energetic and lively and immensely tenacious. It was no unadulterated joy to have to go on an official tour with him.

His relationship to the RL SS was peculiar. For Himmler Pohl meant everything; each letter, each telegram was signed: your faithful H. Himmler, and yet Pohl only went to the RL SS when he was called.

For Pohl all wishes of the RL SS – and these were more than a few – were his commands!

I have never heard or never experienced that Pohl hesitated with an order by the RL SS or even spoke disparagingly of it.

An order by the RL SS was for him something fixed, a fact and to be executed regardless of the consequences. In addition he did not like it if one puzzled over orders by the RL SS – which were often very obscure – or if their impracticality was mentioned. Kammler and Glücks, who both had a very loose tongue and who took quite a few liberties with Pohl, were often often rebuked in unequivocal terms.

Pohl was, despite his violent nature, the most willing and obedient executioner of all the wishes and plans of the RL SS Heinrich Himmler.[20]

Pohl's first marriage ended in divorce in Dachau and it was rumoured that his wife could not cope with his ascent. This marriage had produced a son and two daughters. The son served with the Waffen-SS, was wounded several times and was considered an able troop leader. Both daughters were married to SS leaders and had several children. The second time Pohl tied the knot it was with an officer's widow whose husband had fallen as a regiment commander. This marriage also produced two children. He lived on an estate near Ravensbrück, did not enrich himself personally according to Höß, but in every respect made use of the advantages brought by his position.

In mid-April 1945, with the impending strangulation of the Reich and its division into two parts, on Himmler's orders Pohl went with the remaining staff of WVHA to Dachau. Only a few liaison officers remained in Berlin. His family had already travelled long before to the estate owned by his wife in the Bavarian Alps.

The Office Group D still maintain radio communications with the head of the Central Office until the evacuation of Oranienburg. Höß: 'After that I heard nothing more of him.'

Pohl was by no means the 'good person', as Höß described him. During his interrogation on 13 September 1946 the Gestapo chief Ernst Kaltenbrunner made it plain that it was solely Pohl who decided if and when prisoners were released.[21] According to him, the state police had a right of proposal, Pohl the power of decision, if we disregard Himmler. Pohl, however, was the principal interested party in the concentration camp workshops continuing their operations. Therefore he had no interest at all, for example, in releasing specialists who were important to the armament industry. In such matters there arose frequent differences between Pohl as head of the WVHA and the state police, Kaltenbrunner claimed. Incidentally, it was Pohl who ordered that in all concentration camps 'human hair is consigned to further processing': 'human hair is made into industrial felt and spun into thread. From cut and combed women's hair thread footlets for submarine crews and felt socks for the Reich railway are manufactured.'[22]

Höß' description of how much importance Pohl placed on the work performance of the prisoner is substantiated by the following order dated 15 April 1942. He prohibited work on Sundays in the camps, but not for humanitarian reasons. He was solely concerned with deploying the prisoner even more inhumanly and exploiting them all the more:

> It is intended that in future Sunday labour will be cancelled in all concentration camps and women's concentration camps. This order is now effective immediately. For Sunday labour in general the work detail administration can in future only take into consideration the enterprises of vital importance, among others such as cattle and horse stables and kitchen operations etc. Further only for the execution of essential repairs of installations necessary for maintaining operations. As a result of this it is necessary, and this is hereby ordered with immediate effect, that the work detail leaders must be trained so thoroughly that they are capable of achieving the prescribed weekly workload under all circumstances with the aid of the prisoners' work performance within the fully available six working days.
>
> In this context it must be mentioned that it has been shown that the Sunday labour so far has not advanced the work status by anything, but that the Sunday occupation in its entirety has only brought about setbacks and disadvantages in widespread areas.
>
> If a full working capacity is to be achieved by the prisoner, it is necessary that the latter approaches the respective workload sufficiently invigorated, rested and prepared. For this reason he needs the Sunday for rest. In this regard care has to be taken that the prisoners will in future have an obligatory bath once a week and that the Sunday rest is used specifically to repair clothes and all other items of daily personal use by the prisoner. Only after achieving the goals hereby defined can full capacity with respect to the work performance of the prisoners be assured.[23]

Kaltenbrunner also speculated in the aforementioned interrogation about Höß' role within the complex web of the SS. When the question was discussed who produced the statistics on the extermination of the Jews, Kaltenbrunner thought that this must have been Office Group D in the WVHA, certainly with the knowledge of the Jews Section [Judenreferat] headed by Eichmann in the Reich Security Main Office and of 'Gestapo-Müller'. It was not certain that Pohl had known the statistics, too, because it is wholly conceivable that only Glücks had been involved. Kaltenbrunner said during his interrogation: 'There were people who were directly answerable to Himmler under threat of death regardless of their actual superiors.' As an example he mentioned

Höß: 'Höß had been subordinated to Himmler personally. It would thus be possible that Höß in his sector at the Auschwitz camp was not even accountable to Glücks.'[24]

Pohl hid near Flensburg after the war but was caught and sentenced to death on 3 November 1947. He was executed on 8 June 1951 in Landsberg.

Theodor Eicke, SS Senior Group Leader, 1st inspector of the concentration camps[25]

Eicke originated from Alsace-Lorraine and was one of the early followers of Hitler. In 1929 he established the first SS units in the Rhenish Palatinate. In 1932 he was sentenced to two years in prison for bomb making in Pirmasens, but received a suspended sentence. On 21 March 1933 he was placed under protective custody by the then regional leader Josef Bückel and his mental condition was examined in Würzburg. Three months later he was commander of the Dachau concentration camp. So much for the reality, but in Höß' notes his biography reads completely differently. He turned Eicke into an early resistance fighter against the French occupation of the Rhineland and a fierce defender of National Socialism. According to him, Eicke had been sentenced to death in absence by a French military court for murder. He fled to Italy, returned in 1928 and joined the NSDAP and the SS.

In 1933 Himmler promoted him to standard leader and appointed him commander of Dachau, which Höß claims he immediately remodelled according to his own ideas. 'Eicke is a stubborn old Nazi of the combat period,' he wrote. 'All his doing proceeds from the thought: National Socialism has seized power at great cost and in a long battle; now we must use this power against all enemies of this state. So he views the concentration camps, too. The prisoners are for him all enemy of the state in general, who have to be securely detained, harshly treated and destroyed in case of resistance.'

In 1934 Eicke became the first inspector of the concentration camps. He began 'with all eagerness' to reshape the existing camps at Esterwegen, Sachsenburg, Lichtenberg and Columbia after the 'Dachau model'. Dachau leaders and men were constantly transferred to the other camps in order to spread the military–Prussian 'Dachau spirit'. Himmler gave him free rein, for he knew that he could not entrust the concentration camps to any 'man more suitable'. The Reich Leader SS stressed this on several occasions. He agreed with Eicke's views on the concentration camps and of the 'enemies of the state' and concurred with him completely.

When Eicke was first appointed commander the largest part of the guard details came from the Bavarian state police, who had also occupied most of the leading positions. For Eicke these policemen were a red rag, since they had made life difficult for the National Socialists during the 'combat period'. In a very short period he replaced them with SS men and dismissed the 'Laponese', as the state policeman were called in camp slang. Höß wrote:

> Under Eicke the prisoners were treated strictly and harshly, the most minor offences he punished with beatings, which he had carried out in front of the gathered guard details – at least two companies, in order to harden the men, as he expressed it. The political prisoners in particular had to watch these beatings regularly.

According to Höß, Eicke's instructions could be summarised as follows:

> There beyond the wire the enemy is lying in wait and observes all your doing in order to make use of your weaknesses for his purposes. Do not show any vulnerability, show these enemies of the state your teeth. Anyone who shows only the faintest trace of pity has to vanish from our midst. I can only use hard SS men ready for anything. Weaklings have no place among us.

He formed a hard, brutish team from the guard detail, which was quick with the rifle, if an 'enemy of the state' attempted to flee.

Höß described in great detail the differences between Pohl and Eicke, which resulted from the fact that Eicke wanted to decide on how the concentration camps were set up. When, for example, a women's camp was to be constructed near Ravensbrück, Pohl wanted a capacity of 10,000 prisoners, but Eicke insisted on 2,000 and prevailed. Later the camp had to be constantly extended. While Eicke showed restraint in the financing and construction of concentration camps, he saw in the expansion of SS Death Head Units his life's work. According to Höß: 'The newly constructed barracks could never be big enough for him, never spacious enough, the furniture never comfortable enough. What space he saved in the concentration camps, the troop received tenfold. In order to obtain the necessary funds for the troop, he even made peace with Pohl.'

Apparently Eicke and Höß only got on to a limited extent, for Höß conceded that he was 'no expert in human nature'. Eicke was often deceived by impostors, sweet talkers and people who knew how to conduct themselves deftly and adroitly, and trusted those people too much. His assessments were subject to chance and mood swings, too. If an SS leader had incurred his disfavour, or if he did not like him for some reason, so it was best for the person concerned to let himself be transferred out of Eicke's official sphere of influence:

> Leader or junior leader – he hoped to transfer the men who in his view were unsuited for duty with the troop – he either shunted them out of his duty area, or he transferred them to the concentration camp, after in 1937 troop and concentration camp had been separated on his instigation. By this means the command staffs were gradually full of leaders and junior leaders incapable of anything, whom Eicke nonetheless did not want to drop entirely due to their party membership or their long membership of the SS. The camp commanders could worry about them. They were constantly transferred in order to find a suitable position for them after all, and most of them ended up in the course of time in Auschwitz, which had gradually become the dumping ground for personnel of the concentration camp inspection! If Eicke had dismissed all these duds completely, much unpleasantness and inhumanity would have later been spared the concentration camps.

Eicke's instructions and orders regarding prisoner issues in later times were described by Höß as 'viewed from the desk'; they were based on his Dachau experiences and views. Höß attested that Eicke did not bring 'anything new, anything revolutionary' any more:

> In spite of his indefatigable work and elasticity and his eternal thrust for improvements and innovations, he did not bring anything more to the concentration camps: his vigour was dedicated to the troop. His office of the concentration camp inspection was merely the framework now (...) Eicke lived very simply and reclusively in happy marriage with his excellent wife. They had a son and a daughter. In his representative villa – built generously by Pohl – in Oranienburg he never felt at home. He would rather have remained in his modest apartment in Berlin-Frohnau.
>
> Eicke was hard – brutally so – in his orders and when these were not followed.
>
> Many an SS man – even some leaders – were degraded before the troop and, dressed in prisoner attire, they received 25 blows with a stick. He even treated his own cousin in that manner. He showed no human empathy for the prisoners as a whole – they were enemies of the state – although he has interceded for some individuals he knew more closely. For his SS men he did everything – whether because of comradeship or also for reasons of expediency I cannot judge. Personally he was clean and untouchable.

In spring 1943 Eicke was shot down while undertaking a reconnaissance flight near Kharkov, looking for the tank battalion led by his son-in-law. Only part of his uniform with the Knight's Cross and Oak Leaves was found.

Richard Glücks, SS Group Leader, second inspector of the concentration camps[26]

Richard Glücks joined the party and the SS early. In the SS first worked as staff leader at the Higher Section West, then led a standard of the General SS in Schneidemühle. In 1936 he came to Eicke as staff leader in the concentration camp inspection.

Höß describes him as a:

> typical paper pusher without any sense for practical matters. He believed he was able to direct everything from his desk. Under Eicke he made hardly an appearance at the concentration camps. Even though he occasionally visited the individual camps in the company of Eicke, this did not have any practical significance; he never saw anything and did not learn to do so, either. As staff leader he had hardly any influence on Eicke, as Eicke got these matters done himself, mostly in person during his camp inspections with the commander. Eicke had a high opinion of him, though, and in matters of personnel Glücks was almost the decisive factor, to the disadvantage of the command staffs. Various commanders tried repeatedly to sideline Glücks, but his position with Eicke could not be unsettled.

Himmler supposedly never trusted Glücks much and had wanted to transfer him on several occasions, but Eicke and Pohl championed him 'time and again in the most vigorous manner'.

> Glücks was always of the opinion that nothing must be changed of Eicke's arrangements, orders and instructions, even if these were evidently outdated. Firstly for reasons of tradition, secondly in order not to have to apply for changes with the RL SS. Furthermore, he believed that he would only fill the post of inspector temporarily. He did not consider himself qualified to make even the slightest change in the existing order of the concentration camps without the approval of the RL SS. He rejected or answered evasively every suggestion for alterations by the commanders. During my entire term of office he had an almost unbelievable fear of the RL SS. A call by the latter made him confused; if he had to go to the RL SS in person, he was of no use days before the appointment. Reports and comments requested by the RL SS made him lose his otherwise unflappable cool.

According to this, Glücks did not take incidents in the camps seriously if they did not need to be reported to Himmler. On the other hand, the escape of prisoners gave him no rest either day or night. His first question when entering the office was: 'How many have bunked off?' Auschwitz caused him the greatest concern in this respect. The constant fear of Himmler defined his whole attitude to the concentration camps in line with the motto: 'Do what you want. It just must not reach the RL SS.' When he was made subordinate to Pohl, he breathed a sigh of relief. Someone stronger became an intermediary and absorbed the blows.

Glücks only visited camps if it was necessary for important reasons, or if Himmler or Pohl urged him to do so. During the tours he saw nothing – as he himself said time and again, too – and was glad when the commander did not 'drag' him through the camp for too long. He preferred to sit inside the leaders' residence at the camp and talk about all kinds of topics, just not about the commander's worries.

Glücks had a solid Rhenish humour and saw everything from the bright side. Even the most serious matters he turned into ridicule, joked about them, did not remember anything and did not decide anything, either. He never took Höß seriously, either, as the commander of Auschwitz wrote:

> He considered my constant concerns and hardships regarding Auschwitz wildly exaggerated and was astonished when he heard the confirmation of my views from Pohl or Kammler: he never helped me in any manner, although he could have provided essential help to me, e.g. in matters of personnel by the transfer of untenable leaders and junior leaders from Auschwitz. Yet he did not want to do this for the sake of the other commanders. Don't rock the boat! And Auschwitz always rocked the boat and brought unrest to the sacred peace of the concentration camp inspection.

Höß calls Glücks' visits to Auschwitz 'virtually pointless and always without any success'. Auschwitz had been too extensive and confusing for him and caused him too much trouble. In addition, Höß constantly expressed too many requests and complaints as far as Glücks was concerned:

> Twice Glücks wanted to relieve me or rather to confront me with a higher ranking leader as my superior, only he did not dare to do so because of the RL SS. (...) He wanted nothing to do with the extermination operation of the Jews, and did not like to hear about it, either. That the catastrophic conditions of the later period were also linked to it, he could not understand. He was, after all,

clueless in the face of all difficult situations in every camp and left it to the camp commanders to cope with them. 'Do not ask me so much,' was often the answer in command meetings. 'You know the situation much better than me.'

(...) Glücks was too soft and did not want to hurt any subordinate. He was too indulgent, especially towards the old commanders and SS leaders he favoured. Out of good heartedness he kept on leaders who had long since belonged in front of an SS court or at least should have been removed from the concentration camp sphere. Due to his good nature he also overlooked the many misdemeanours of the staff members of the concentration camp inspection. When, after Liebehenschel's departure from Auschwitz, Maurer became Glücks' deputy and I at the same time head of D I, we cleaned house quite rigorously among the all-too-many junior leaders and staff men who had been indispensable so far. Rather hefty arguments took place with Glücks because of this. Maurer finally threatened to bring in Pohl and Glücks gave in with a heavy heart.

Finally, Höß wrote about Glücks as a private person:

In private he lived very modestly and reclusively – he invited nobody to his house, either. His wife was similar to him, too. They had no children. I He was extremely soft-hearted and generous towards prisoners he encountered, such as hairdressers, gardeners, craftsmen etc. He never observed an execution or a beating. He usually left the approval of beatings to his deputies. Glücks was a contrast to Eicke in everything. Both were extremes that turned the development of the concentration camps into tragedy.

Glücks committed suicide on 10 May 1945 in the navy field hospital at Flensburg-Mürwik.

Bruno Streckenbach, SS Brigade Leader, commander of the security police and security service in Cracow, head of Office I (Organisation, Administration and Law) of the Reich Security Main Office[27]

Höß had met the commander of the security police and the security service (Befehlshaber der Sicherheitspolizei und des SD = BdS) for the entire General Government during his time as adjutant of the camp commander of Sachsenhausen, SS Senior Leader Hermann Baranowski. Streckenbach and Baranowski were free corps men and old SS leaders from Hamburg. Streckenbach visited Sachsenhausen twice and was considered a 'diligent worker'. After the occupation of Poland occupation he became BdS in Cracow and then for the entire

General Government. He subsequently joined the RSHA and according to Höß it was generally assumed that he would become the successor to Security Police and Security Service Chief Heydrich. Yet instead Streckenbach was assigned to duty at the front and began his career in the Waffen-SS as SS Head Storm Leader of a SS cavalry division. He was considered a good troop leader, was promoted rapidly and early on received a number of decorations.

Höß judged him in the following way:

> Streckenbach was a suave, energetic man with varied interests, but an old stubborn Nazi and SS leader for whom every order by the RL SS was sacred. My commander often said that Streckenbach would be the most suitable successor for Eicke as inspector of the concentration camps. He would be even harder, but also more approachable.

Streckenbach was arrested on 10 May 1945 by the Red Army and sentenced to twenty-five years of reform and labour camp. He returned to the Federal Republic of Germany under the final prisoner release on 10 October 1955 and worked as a procurator in an iron works. A first German judicial inquiry was closed in September 1956. In a second one in 1974 the Hanseatic Higher Regional Court rejected the opening of the main trial on the basis of an evaluation by the court medical service of the Hamburg Health Authority.

Hans Kammler, SS Senior Group Leader, head of Office Group C[28]

Kammler was a member of the Free Corps Roßbach and later of a cavalry regiment of the Reichswehr. In the emerging Luftwaffe he became head of construction; from there Himmler, who had known him for a long time, called him to the WVHA. The architect became the director of construction and armament projects in the German Reich, SS Senior Group Leader and general in the Waffen-SS. Primarily, however, he was responsible for all concentration camp construction, including gas chambers and crematoria.

Höß says about him:

> Soon after my appointment Kammler appeared at Auschwitz, the pressing extension of which the RL SS had pointed out to him. My then head of construction, Schlachter,[29] was a good lad, but of unsurpassed narrow-mindedness. In peacetime he had been an architect in the countryside near Würzburg and he lacked any generosity. Kammler realised this immediately and promised me a more suitable man from the Luftwaffe, who then appeared on 1st October 1941 in the person of Bischoff.[30] Kammler now began

to draw up the general building plan for Auschwitz-Birkenau in accordance with the expansion order by the RL SS dated 1st August 1941. This was definitely generous, Kammler incorporated all my experience therein and also took the sequence of the building projects into consideration. On the most important issue, the accelerated extension of drainage and irrigation, he had the greatest appreciation and immediately brought along a water expert. Furthermore, Kammler put at my disposal contingents needed immediately. He did everything to help me, but the effects of the war were already felt quite keenly even then.

The most urgently needed building materials could just not be procured in the amounts required despite being top priority. Building in Auschwitz was always an ordeal. When I thought we were finally making progress in one place, then the building project would certainly be abandoned due to the lack of material, because what was missing was the thing that was needed the most. Kammler always helped me wherever he could; he curtailed many other equally important construction projects in order to advance Auschwitz. Yet it was a drop in the ocean, it was never enough. The events got the better of us. Kammler also saw the miserable conditions in the camp during the later period, improvised and improved in a makeshift fashion, brought specialists and experts from all areas of construction.

(...) Kammler certainly did not neglect anything in trying to improve the building situation at Auschwitz-Birkenau. He understood everything, helped where he could, but in the end was as powerless in face of this development as I myself.

(...) Kammler knew exactly that only healthy, fully fit and capable prisoners were useful to the armament industry; what is more, for the strenuous work below ground later directed by him. Kammler often spoke with me about all pending prisoners issues. He also spoke several times with the RL SS, when the occasion arose. But the latter rebuffed him, as this was not his problem, although Kammler told him repeatedly that he would not produce a single V weapon with half-dead men.

Kammler was supposed to build, build, build, for the armament industry, for the troops, for the police (whose special construction department K. had to take on likewise), for the concentration camps, for the special purposes of the RL SS and once again armament and moving underground. A numerically significant workforce was not provided to him by Labour Minister Saucke, but again predominantly prisoners and in such a state. With them Kammler was supposed to achieve the extraordinary and unprecedented, as the RL SS demanded. The V weapons were supposed to be produced in enormous amounts, largely by prisoners!

K. was certainly not easily defeated, but in the face of such demands even his courage failed occasionally. He managed, managed, used up innumerable project managers and subordinates. It was not easy to work under him, he demanded too much work. He encountered enormous difficulties during the underground projects, had his own state police sites with special courts, which took the strictest action against each deliberate delay, regardless of whether the person concerned was a director, engineer, project manager, German specialist worker, foreign assistant worker or prisoner. The RL SS demanded the keeping of the schedules he had reported to the Führer. K. was often in dire straits, but thanks to his incredible tenacity and his energy he managed to just about keep up with the underground construction, although almost two years had been wasted.

(…) On Kammler's demand the railway construction brigades were formed – these were prisoner work details of up to 500 men in specially furnished freight trains driven to the respective railway installations destroyed by bombs in order to make these operative for traffic again as soon as possible. The railway construction brigades had special equipment and achieved remarkable feats. The prisoners were specially selected and had a much better life on these trains than in the camp. Yet they were continuously exposed to aerial attacks and suffered considerable losses, likewise also the accompanying guard details. The war had really become *total*!

The construction brigades also owed their creation to Kammler. These prisoner details – up to 1,200 men strong – were deployed to the larger cities in the west and to Berlin in order to remove bomb damage at essential installations as quickly as possible, likewise after large-scale attacks on major traffic routes.

At the beginning of 1944 Kammler was commissioned to construct the Führer's headquarters inside the rocky slopes of the military training area of Ohrdruf in Thuringia with such tight deadlines that even the planning was barely completed in that time frame. The RL SS had ordered that only prisoners were to be used for the construction for reasons of secrecy. Circa 30,000 men were to be assigned. The first few could be gathered – mainly from Auschwitz. (…) Most of them arrived there already in a totally rundown state. The accommodation in tents, mud huts, makeshift barracks and similar did not improve their condition and after they had actually spent a few days on arduous work, or a few weeks, they died.

This assignment of prisoners ordered and repeatedly inspected by the RL SS cost thousands upon thousands of lives without achieving anything essential. The construction project was not completed. Kammler was burdened with it – he did what he could in order to eliminate the worst deficiencies. The blame was with the RL SS and his unachievable promises and his unwillingness to acknowledge the occurring difficulties.

The entrance gate to Auschwitz I with its infamous 'Arbeit Macht Frei'
('Work Sets You Free') sign. (Caminoel/Shutterstock)

Three SS officers in the grounds of the SS retreat outside of Auschwitz in 1944.
From left to right they are Richard Baer, Dr. Josef Mengele, and Rudolf Höss.
(All images Public Domain unless stated otherwise)

Rudolf Höss, the first commandant of Auschwitz.

The commandant's and administration building at Auschwitz I.
(Courtesy of Dawid Galus)

The commandant's and administration building at Auschwitz I as pictured from the air in 1977. (Polish National Archives)

Ukrainian Jews arrive at Auschwitz and make their way along the ramp in close proximity to the gas chambers. The chimneys in the background belong to Crematoria II and III on the left and right respectively.

Himmler, surrounded by SS officers and camp personnel, is pictured during his visit to Auschwitz on 17-18 July 1942. According to one prisoner, Rudolf Vrba, "the camp put on a show for Himmler because Rudolf Höss wanted to impress him. The prisoners were allowed to wash and have clean clothes. A band played, and people lined up at the gates to greet Himmler."

Hungarian Jews on the ramp soon after their arrival at Auschwitz during May or June 1944.

Jewish women and children waiting in a grove near gas chamber No.4 prior to their extermination, 27 May 1944. It is believed that these people are Hungarian Jews from the Tet Ghetto.

A group of children pictured at Auschwitz following the concentration camp's liberation at about 15.00 hours on 27 January 1945. This image is in fact a still taken from footage shot by the film unit of the 1st Ukrainian Front.

Höss pictured soon after his capture at the end of the war.

Höss listening to the proceedings, through an interpreter, during his trial in Warsaw in 1947. (Polska Agencja Prasowa)

Höss being escorted to the gallows, which were located near to the crematorium at Auschwitz, on 16 April 1947.

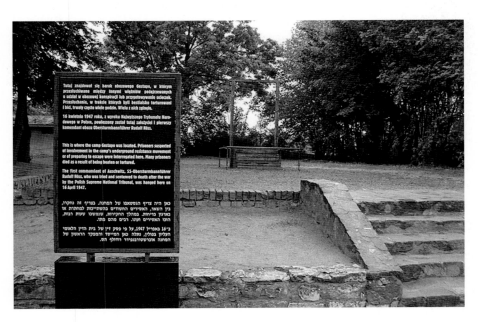

The site where Höss was executed on 16 April 1947. (Courtesy of Jorge Láscar)

7 THE COMMANDANT OF AUSCHWITZ

The gatehouse of Auschwitz II-Birkenau pictured from the air in 1977.
(Polish National Archives)

Another aerial photograph taken in 1977, this image shows a number of barracks
huts, guard towers and a length of the camp fence at Auschwitz-Birkenau.
(Polish National Archives)

Kammler is believed to have died near Prague and was declared dead on 9 May 1945 by the district court in Berlin-Charlottenburg.

Karl Bischoff, SS Storm Command Leader, head of the central construction department[31]

Karl Bischoff worked from 1935 in the Central Office Administration for Construction of the Luftwaffe and after the beginning of the war was instrumental in building airfields in Belgium and northern France. When his superior, Hans Kammler, became head of the SS Central Office Finances and Constructions (SS-HHB), he offered Karl Bischoff a rapid rise to the rank of an SS Head Storm Leader. He then assigned him the leadership role in the special construction management (later central construction management), effective 1 October 1941, to set up a camp for prisoners of war at Auschwitz, which later became the extermination camp under the name Auschwitz-Birkenau.

Höß conceded that Bischoff was a good construction specialist, though 'stubborn and wilful':

> He gave everything only from the viewpoint of a building specialist. He was a workhorse and demanded full commitment from all his subordinates, too. From a technical point of view Bischoff was equal to any situation. He was a great organiser, but even better at procuring building material of all kinds. What could be scraped up in the region of Germany and the occupied countries, Bischoff supplied. He had several buyers on the go all the time. Right from the beginning Bischoff recognised correctly the difficult situation of Auschwitz and also always threw his whole person into the fray, often to the limit, in order to spur on the Auschwitz construction projects.
>
> There were repeated sharp disputes between Bischoff and me because he did not want to accept the necessity to change the sequence of the construction projects – to which I was often forced by newly emerging events – or because he saw the situation differently to me for technical reasons. Or he wanted to have the prisoners deployed at a different site, which I had to reject for security reasons. A further sore point between us was the allocation of the civilian workforce, without whom Bischoff thought he could not cope, but which I had to reject because of the high number and the related risk of confusion for the guard details. So there was always friction between us, which could often only be terminated by Kammler's rebuke of Bischoff. Yet nevertheless Bischoff worked incessantly on the expansion of Auschwitz. For some time he was provisionally assigned to the setting up of Mittelbau [Central Block = sub-camp of Buchenwald] and he did not rest until he

could return to Auschwitz, although he had great opportunities for advancement at Mittelbau.

As much as Bischoff organised legally, but most often illegally, in terms of building materials, and moved around in co-operation with I.G. Farben Industries, it was not enough to put an end to the Auschwitz calamities. All the offices cursed him because they thought that he put their offices last of all the construction. He was continually at war with everybody. He could never cope with the prisoners' labour, he was of the opinion that the prisoners worked far too little – he could never be convinced otherwise. Furthermore, he demanded much too much work performance. In his opinion too few prisoners were always assigned. He apportioned a large amount of blame for the lack of progress at the construction sites to the inadequate and faulty work of the prisoners, so he had a reason for not keeping to the set schedules. He did whatever was in his power for Auschwitz. Nobody else could have achieved more.

Bischoff's range of duties can be gleaned from a communication by Kammler to Höß. He had informed him on 11 October 1921 that Bischoff was responsible for all construction at Auschwitz, in particular the building support for the agricultural testing sites. At that time some buildings had still to be completed or constructed:

> Six prisoner accommodation buildings, a provisional laundry barrack in the old protective custody camp, fifteen new buildings for prisoners, five prisoner back-up workshops, a laundry and a registration building with delousing facility and prisoner bathroom, three residential barracks for leaders, the command building and the command residence, the entrance building, the service building, accommodation for one battalion, a residential quarter, stable yards in Auschwitz, Babitz and Budy, two laboratories in Raisko as well as stores and delivery buildings.[32]

Twenty-four prisoners were assigned to the building work in autumn 1941 besides the SS members. In the light of these building projects, to which numerous others were added – construction of the gassing complexes and crematoria, railway sidings etc. – Höß had been forced in February 1941 to request in writing an appointment with the inspector of the concentration camps at Oranienburg in order to receive further funds for the establishment of Auschwitz.[33] This letter stated that Bischoff managed the extension of the rail tracks towards the Auschwitz crematoria in order to speed up the mass extermination.

Bischoff lived in West Germany after the war and died in Bremen in 1950.

Odilo Globocnik, SS Group Leader, SS and Police Leader in Lublin district[34]

Globocnik was regional leader in Vienna for some months after the annexation of Austria, then SS and police leader in the Lublin district. Here he directed Operation Reinhardt for the extermination of the Jews within the General Government. The extermination camps at Belzec, Sobibor and Treblinka were under his control. In 1943 he was appointed Higher SS and Police Leader in the Adriatic Coastal Region operational zone, where he organised the battle against partisans and the deportation of Jews to Auschwitz-Birkenau. Höß claimed he was unsettled by Globocnik's views: 'G. was a grandstander who knew how to push himself into the foreground and to represent his phantasms of plans as if they had already been realised for the largest part. He only he wanted to do everything by himself and in the best way. Whether this concerned the extermination of Jews or the resettlement of Poles or the processing of the confiscated valuables.' Himmler stood by him until he became untenable and was relieved.

The second time Höß encountered Globocnik was in spring 1943 in Lublin. He needed to discuss with him the machines and tools delivered by him from the German Equipment Works there to Auschwitz. Globocnik had 'thereby called the oldest junk modern machines' and ordered these fiddles personally. Globocnik did not elaborate on the incidents, but presented Höß with 'truly modernised used machines for the German Equipment Works at Auschwitz 5'.

Globocnik founded a series of workshops in which Jews had to work and produce the 'most impossible everyday objects'. These ranged from brushes to door mats, 'but all at a quality which had to be called rubbish'. In truth the Jews had organised everything and duped Globocnik. They created for themselves as many indispensable supervisory posts as possible and pursued their own businesses.

According to Höß, Globocnik did not stick to the instructions of the RSHA, but carried out his police operations as he liked. He executed people on his own initiative and at his own discretion: 'He established prisoner labour camps wherever it seemed suitable to him without any regard for Pohl or D II, for these were "his camps", "his" prisoners. He also viewed "his" extermination sites Sobibor, Belcyk and Treblinka in such a manner.'

> Eichmann, who knew Globocnik from their illegal SS activities before the annexation of Austria, had got his hands full with him.

While I constantly grappled with Eichmann in order to slow down the Jew transports to Auschwitz, Globocnik could not get enough of them. He wanted to be on top at all costs with 'his' exterminations and 'his' numbers accrued during these.

(...) In summer 43 Globocnik came to Auschwitz to look at the crematoria and the extermination on the orders of the RL SS. He did not find all this very special, though. His locations worked much more rapidly and he began to throw numbers around (...) He exaggerated shamelessly at every possible occasion.

In and of himself he was a good-natured fellow. The evil he did only happened through swagger, throwing his weight around and self-importance, in my opinion.

Globocnik was arrested in Carinthia and committed suicide on 31 May 1945.

Robert Mulka, SS Head Storm Leader, Höß' adjutant[35]

According to the camp regulations written down by Höß in October 1946, the adjutant was the first assistant to the camp commander. A special relationship of trust ought to exist between them. Ultimately the adjutant was supposed to have responsibility for the entire procedure within a concentration camp, but not the slightest trace of this could be found in Höß' relationship to his adjutant, SS Head Storm Leader Robert Mulka.

In context of the German Equipment Works Auschwitz, a statement by the head of W IV Economic Department at the WVHA, Kurt May, is hereby of importance.[36] When May inspected the works at Auschwitz, Mulka approached him during the walk through the halls and said that everything 'sucked' and if May could have him transferred. He had already discussed this with Höß, but the latter had cut him short and said that this was out of the question. When May said his farewells to Höß the following day, he asked him if he did not want to take over the position as director of the work, after SS Senior Group Leader Pohl had mandated that camp commanders should become union directors of the respective German Equipment Works – and Höß thus the Auschwitz economic manager. May wrote to Pohl regarding this on 25 November 1943:

Now Höß seems to me – I myself came from the economic sector – not exactly to be the prototype of a manager, and Mulka had said to me that he is from Hamburg and had worked there as an export merchant. I asked him whether this office could not be assigned to Mulka, if he could not delegate his post to Mulka in practical terms. And then he said that we could speak about this, as he himself was no desk jockey. This writing and records were not his thing any way. And Mulka, he is no real SS leader. He came from the Wehrmacht, that is a reactionary.[37]

It should be mentioned as an aside that Höß, as managing director of the economic enterprises owned by the SS, would have been entitled to an additional monthly allowance, but he passed this up.

For the aforementioned view by May that Höß was no 'manager' and that Mulka should have taken on the task of economic manager instead, the number of Auschwitz outposts is of importance. In managing all these enterprises Höß would have been hopelessly overextended:[38]

1. Monowitz-Buna, Buna Work, synthetic fuel, rubber

2. Fürstengrube [Princes Pit] near Chelmek, I.G. Farben, coal

3. Günthergrube near Myslowice, I.G. Farben, coal

4. Janinagrube near Chelmek, I.G. Farben, coal

5. Blechhammer (Heydebreck), Upper Silesian Hydrogenation Plant, synthetic fuel

6. Laurahütte (Siemianowice), Upper Silesian Equipment Engineering GmbH, navy equipment

7. Jaworzno (Neudachs), Energy Supply AG/OS, electricity and coal

8. Lagisza, Energy Supply AG/OS large power station 'Walter', electricity

9. Swietochlowice, Ost-Maschinenbau AG, Wehrmacht equipment

10. Sosnowice, Ost-Maschinenbau GmbH (Berghütte AG), main product anti-aircraft cannon

11. Gliwice I, Radial-Axial Rolling Mill, radial-axial rolling mill

12. Gliwice II, Deutsche Gasrußwerke, industrial exhaust heat for synthetic rubber

13. Gliwice III, Army Building Administration, construction of military barracks

14. Gliwice IV, Army Building Administration, construction of military barracks

15. Brno, SS Building Administration, construction of police barracks

16. Bonbrek, Siemens-Schuckert Works AG, electrotechnical assembly plant

17. Tezebionka, Vacuum Company AG, oil drilling

18. Czechowice, Vacuum Company AG, oil refinery
19. Zabrze (Hindenburg), Oberhütten AG, smelters and foundries
20. Jawiszoiwice, Hermann-Göring-Works, coal
21. Gute Hoffnungshütte [good hope smelter], Haniel, smelters and foundries
22. Rydultowy and Rybnika, Haniel, pits
23. Bruntal (Moravia), WVHA-SS Central Administration, vitamin and mineral water
24. Goleszwo, WVHA-SD-DEST (German Earth and Stone Works), cement factory
25. Kobiór near Auschwitz, WVHA-SS Central Administration W, forestry

The relationship between Höß and Mulka was extremely tense. This was mentioned during the 1st Frankfurt Auschwitz Trial by the representative of the accessory prosecution when he examined Joachim Caesar as a witness. Caesar had been director of the agricultural enterprises in Auschwitz from February 1942 until 17 January 1945, or – as he himself said – commissioner for agricultural special tasks. He pointed out that Mulka 'allegedly did not enjoy Höß' trust at all and as a consequence was almost always overlooked in an official capacity'. He practically divested him of all functions and did not employ him as an adjutant at all.

Witness Erich Rönisch, SS Under Company Leader and head of the SS leaders' residence in Auschwitz, also confirmed the ambiguous relationship of Höß and his adjutant.[39] Mulka had had difficulties of a 'political kind'. The latter had once unburdened his heart to him at the leader's residence and said again and again: 'I am fed up with all of this stuff.' He evidently did not have the political attitude expected of an SS leader. He often let it show that he had certain reservations and that he was depressed.

The statement by the former dentist Elise Heinisch-Utner, who had a practice in Auschwitz town, is further instructive on the men's relationship.[40] She had received a request to treat SS members and wanted to inform Höß personally that this was out of the question. She set off to the commandant's headquarters, yet did not meet Höß there but Mulka. In contrast with other officers, he made a 'genteel' impression on her. Mulka evidently registered her astonished expression and remarked: 'You are surprised. I only joined the SS by chance,' and to the question 'Why do you stress this?' he answered: 'Because it is no honour to wear this uniform.' In the further course of the conversation Mulka opened a window and women could be seen who were probably being led to their meal. Then Mulka said: 'Look at that. A large part of these women are Polish prisoners. The kapo is a child murderer.' He wanted to reveal the nastiness of the system making criminals the superiors of relatively decent people. Mulka spoke about the fact that people were gassed in Auschwitz and that he was probably the only SS officer in the camp who considered Germany's defeat. At that time the conflicts with Höß had apparently escalated and Mulka thought it possible that a listening device had been installed in his office.

His wife, Erna Mulka, stated on 22 October 1964 that she had visited her husband in Auschwitz for the first time on her birthday, 26 May 1942. He said there to her: 'Mami, if I could only leave here again. People are murdered here.' He was not allowed to tell her any details, and told her that if she mentioned one word of this he could lose his head. He was unhappy, everything was different to the Wehrmacht, and he could no longer endure being in Auschwitz. In the summer of 1942 she returned once more to Auschwitz and her husband confirmed that he could not remain there.

She visited Auschwitz for a third time around February or March 1943. They had debated that she should call Höß and tell him that her husband had developed a severe attack of colic and could not assume his duty. She did that, and Höß had been very brusque: 'Why, Mrs Mulka, your husband was totally hale just yesterday.' 'Well, such colic attacks occur very suddenly.'

When she was back in Hamburg, she received a postcard of her husband from prison. 'His own commander Höß had had him arrested in Auschwitz. At that time it was said: subversion of the war effort, Treachery Act.'

To the question of whether her husband, as the commander's adjutant, could have not done anything about the situation at Auschwitz Erna Mulka answered: 'I believe he probably did not have the power to do so. The commander was very closed off, very aloof. And I have to say that I sometimes mustered the courage when I spoke with him, I said then: "Mr Höß I think you should not view everything through rose-tinted glasses. The war is probably lost anyway."'[41]

Adolf Trowitz, at that time artillery commander, called Mulka's wife during a stay in Hamburg. He met her at Altona station and Erna implored him to visit her husband when he was in Berlin. Her husband was in the SS field hospital at Zehlendorf and had broken down completely – and Trowitz did so together with Mulka's wife. Trowitz told the 1st Frankfurt Auschwitz Trial: 'We sat down on a bench, and an assistant went to fetch him. And there he was approaching us outside. I do not believe I would have recognised him if I had seen him suddenly on the street. He was so changed in his entire appearance.'[42] Mulka reported that he had experienced terrible things and could no longer take part in them. Trowitz thought at that time: 'What must the fellow have experienced to break down emotionally in such a manner.'

Mulka was arrested for a short period, and during the 1st Frankfurt Trial it came to light that it was the wife of Storm Command Leader Karl Bischoff – not Höß, as initially assumed – who had denounced Mulka to Pohl.[43] Mulka had called Goebbels an idiot who had done great damage to the German people with his Sportpalast speech. In Frankfurt Hildegard Bischoff admitted that her husband had prompted her to this denouncement, which could have led to a death sentence for Mulka. Bischoff, who held the construction management of the Waffen-SS and police at Auschwitz, had wanted to take revenge because in his view Mulka led a 'boozy life' in the middle of the war.

The case against Mulka under the Treachery Act was dropped at the beginning of 1944, though. According to files from the Nazi period, until 19 January 1944 he was allocated to SS Central Economic-Administrative Office (Office Group D – concentration camps) and subsequently to the SS Central Personnel Office until the end of August 1944. From the beginning of September 1944 until 19 January 1945 he was supposedly working at the SS school at Rajsko[44] and afterwards with the SS pioneer and training reserve battalion in Dresden.

It has to be mentioned that in Rajsko, near Auschwitz, an agricultural trial station with about 300 female prisoners was located as an outpost of the concentration camp managed by Joachim Caesar. Caesar gave a few statements regarding Höß and his character, as he had experienced him. He said he was a stickler for discipline: 'He was stubborn, in my opinion a totally bullheaded recipient of orders and – let's say – brutal.'[45] Apparently there had been considerable dissonance between Höß and Caesar. For instance, Mrs Caesar had accused Höß of blocking a promotion for her husband.[46]

During the 1st Frankfurt Auschwitz Trial Mulka was sentenced to fourteen years in prison for the 'joint abetting of joint murder in at least four cases of at least 750 people each'. Mulka survived a suicide attempt in the Kassel penitentiary. In 1968 he was released early, being severely ill and unfit for prison, and died the following year.

Arthur Liebehenschel, SS garrison commander and commander of the main camp at Auschwitz[47]

Höß first met Liebehenschel during his time in Dachau. Later they were neighbours for two years in the SS settlement at Sachsenhausen. They met frequently, wrote Höß, but did not become close on a personal level as their natures were too different. Liebehenschel was a creature of habit who 'did not like to have his quiet daily grind disrupted and preferred to take things as they came'. Höß describes the SS leader as calm, quiet and good-natured, and furthermore he had to take his state of health into consideration – he had a serious heart condition. Some attested that under Liebehenschel things were slightly 'more humane' in Auschwitz than under his predecessor Höß, who thought very little of the latter in a professional respect:

> Under Eicke, Liebehenschel had experienced the whole set-up of the concentration camps, though from his desk. He knew the nature and the entire organisation of the concentration camps from the official correspondence, orders and decrees of Eicke, who processed the most important goings on himself after all. Later, under Glücks, Liebehenschel became more independent and handled the largest part of the correspondence on his own initiative, including the orders and decrees for the camp commanders, though with Glücks signing them off.
>
> He hardly knew the camps in person, although he visited this or that camp on some occasions. Once in a while Glücks wanted to send him to the camps as a stand-in, but he copped out every time. He was in Auschwitz once before his transfer. This was the reason for neither Glücks nor Liebehenschel knowing the harsh reality of the camps so that the orders and instructions for the camps – often with far-reaching consequences – emerged from a desk perspective. Further, all the hardships and worries of the camps were seen from the unrealistic vantage point of the desk. L., who was also Glücks' deputy, was presented daily with the entire incoming mail of the inspection of concentration camps, and equally he saw the largest part of the documents to be signed by Glücks. So he observed from the correspondence everything that came from and went to the camps, and directed much himself, for Glücks was easily influenced. L. never cared much for Auschwitz because it fell entirely outside the usual business routine of the other camps and brought too much unrest. In Auschwitz something was going on all the time, and the commander wanted too much help and improvement. Furthermore, the RL SS attended to Auschwitz too much. L. could have done many things for Auschwitz. Later he regretted this, when he had to grasp the nettle himself and became commander of Auschwitz.

Yet his divorce threw him completely off his quiet path of life. He had not had a good life with his wife, who was very cantankerous and fussy, for years. In Glücks' receptionist he finally found a woman who understood and humoured him in his peculiarities. The divorce took place and L. could no longer stay at the inspection, hence his transfer to Auschwitz; he himself would have much preferred a different camp. Soon after taking up his post in Auschwitz he married again and had another child. The first marriage had produced four children. With the divorce, custody of the oldest son was given to him and he accompanied him to Auschwitz, and then later during the evacuation fell into the hands of the Russians and is probably dead.

With his transfer to Auschwitz as a consequence of the breakdown of his marriage L. believed he had been treated badly by his superiors Glücks and Pohl. Further, he expected that with his transfer he would be promoted to standard leader.

During his stay at Auschwitz he had fallen out with all and sundry and also showed quite a physical decline. Pohl determined that L. should become garrison commander and commander of the main camp at Auschwitz, which at that time held circa 18,000 prisoners. Once again L. felt slighted, since he had received the numerically smallest camp.

In addition he suffered financial cuts, as Pohl had the allowance for economic management cancelled. Then L. lost his allowance as head of department and his ministerial allowance received by all members of the WVHA. Since he had to maintain his first wife and the three children remaining with her, being the guilty party in the divorce, and had now entered into a second marriage, these financial worries did not rest easy with him.

It has to be added that Liebehenschel's second wife, Anneliese Hüttemann, who was fifteen years younger, had broken the Nuremberg Racial Laws in 1935 by entering into an affair with a Jew and consequently had been sentenced to a short period of imprisonment in a concentration camp.[48] Pohl sent his adjutant Baer to Auschwitz to sort out the matter, but Liebehenschel did not want to separate from Hüttemann. When she became pregnant, finally even Himmler gave the marriage his blessing.

In the aforementioned state he now assumed his duties at Auschwitz. As he had been at a senior department for years, he believed it would be easy for him to play the camp commander. In his view I had basically done everything wrong in Auschwitz, and he began to arrange everything differently than it had been previously. His adjutant, Zoller, whom he was allowed to bring in from Mauthausen, showed him the mistakes made previously.

At that time the special commission of the SS court officially appeared on the scene, too, in order to search for SS members who had misappropriated effects from Operation Reinhardt. Furthermore, Grabner was arrested at that time, because he was suspected of having executed prisoners of his own volition and high-handedly.

For L. these investigations were welcome in so far that he believed he would be able to prove in this way how wrongly Auschwitz had been managed so far. However, he could not change a thing regarding the state described in his report either.

As protective custody camp leader he had appointed SS Head Storm Leader Hofmann, who was no match for the seasoned old prisoners of the Auschwitz camp who were familiar with all matters. In a short time he was 'run over' and did what the prisoners wanted! L., who had no idea of the stark situation in a protective custody camp, let Hofmann do as he liked and was popular with the prisoners. He even gave speeches to the prisoners, promising them that from now on everything would get better and he would turn the murder camp into a proper concentration camp.

He gave the prisoners his word of honour that furthermore no prisoners would be selected and brought to be gassed. When then one day a truck with 'chosen' drove from the hospital to Birkenau, the saying was coined that there drives the commander's word of honour! He made such blunders constantly without him becoming aware of them.

Yet he soon realised that a concentration camp – especially Auschwitz – looks different in reality than from Oranienburg, despite the fact that Sachsenhausen was on the doorstep. Yet from the superior office and from the desk everything looks different after all, mostly better!

In Auschwitz L. spent most of his time in his office and dictated one order after another, and held meetings with the garrison commander for hours, until the camp slipped further and further in its general state. Yet he did not see this. Meanwhile, he had married again, and it came to light that his second wife had been accused by the SA of having had a sexual affair with a Jew for some time, even after the Nuremberg Racial Laws. This fact soon became known at Auschwitz, too, and L. was then no longer tenable. He was unceremoniously transferred by Pohl to Lublin in June 1944. He did not like that at all. As his second wife was living in Auschwitz town, L. spent more time on official trips to Auschwitz than in Lublin. With the evacuation of Lublin he avoided another transfer, which would have certainly followed due to his behaviour. From Lublin he left the sphere of the WVHA once and for all and went to the Higher SS and Police Leader Globocnik at Trieste in order to fight partisans – L. who could not hurt a fly.

Liebehenschel's order dated 14 February 1944 should be mentioned here, in which he ordered some easements to improve the work performance of the prisoners:

> Special order regarding the decrease of the prisoner work details at all departments of Auschwitz garrison.
>
> Every German person, especially the SS man, knows what is now at stake during the 5th year of war. *All manpower and all working hours belong to armament and hence victory.*[49] The execution of this demand has top priority over the solution of all other, ever so necessary tasks. We finally have to *act* like this; enough has been spoken about it. In our camp household we have already started with this immediately. If here in Auschwitz more than 12,000 of roughly 41,000 prisoners are assigned to the maintenance of the camp operations etc., then this peacetime attitude wasting manpower can no longer be tolerated. Through longer-term personal observation I have determined that in all workplaces – except the armament works – too many prisoners are employed who are not made use of, who are idle and are even trained to be lazy by wrong work management and inadequate supervision. While outside at the armament works etc., with the workforce being constantly reduced the work performances are increased daily; the SS ranks responsible here on concentration camp duty have not understood this aspect yet. Henceforth I am putting an end to this. As SS leader responsible for the entire work management at Auschwitz garrison I will determine the necessary number of workers for the individual workplaces myself, starting with the camp operations. With these numbers the current workload must not just be achieved, but further increased. Junior leaders not managing this ought to report this to me; I will then take over the respective work detail myself for a few days and show them that the working target ordered by me can be achieved in any event with the allocated prisoners. I ask the camp commanders II and III to likewise act in this way for their area of responsibility. In all future assessments for promotion the functional achievements in this respect will be highlighted and evaluated accordingly. We know that for an improvement of the work performances by the prisoners closer supervision by the SS ranks is necessary, but we also know that no additional SS supervision ranks are available, because they are doing their duty at the front or with us in other important functions. We will thus have to help ourselves. To this end I order:
>
> (...) The supervision of the workplaces has to ensure that every prisoner works continuously during working hours. Prisoners

not working or not knowing what they have to do have to be registered by name by the monitoring bodies and to be reported to my department IIIa – Central Work Management. They will no longer deploy the following day and will be collectively allocated to an armament works. On the other hand, as repeatedly ordered, everything has to be done to maintain the ability and strength of the prisoners to work. This requires that the prisoner is treated decently after work well done. The most important issues shall be listed once more:

1. As before, there is only *one* roll call per day, which does not last longer than 10–15 minutes.

2. Leisure time serves the restoration of spent working strength; this includes sufficient sleep. Unnecessary or even bullying encroachment on the prisoners' leisure time will cease. Violations of this will be severely punished.

3. Food has to become a top priority, i.e. each prisoner has to actually receive his due (including allowances for heavy and taxing work). The delivery of packages plays an equally important role here. At Auschwitz during the course of 2½ months more than a million packages have arrived. Many packages containing perishable goods that the recipients cannot consume by themselves, as I have convinced myself, will after appropriate instruction be handed to other prisoners in a worse position in this respect, if this is not done voluntarily.

4. The condition of the clothing has to be monitored constantly, especially of shoes.

5. Sick prisoners have to be pulled out in time. Rather a short stint in the hospital with the appropriate medical treatment and then back to work than a long time left at the workplace without achieving the workload.

6. For the diligent prisoner easements of any kind are possible, in the best case scenario even release; for the lazy, incorrigible prisoner the severity of any punishment is possible under the regulations.[50]

Incidentally, Höß had already given orders meant to improve the prisoners' performance. On 17 April 1942 he had fixed the working hours in the morning from 6am to 11am and in the afternoon from 1pm to 7pm.[51] The prisoners had to use the lunch break for rest. Höß hereby placed importance on the fact 'that after lunch the prisoners rest lying on their beds in order to achieve the best absorption of the meals as possible to strengthen their work performance'.

127

SS Head Storm Leader Heinrich Schwarz, camp commander of Auschwitz-Monowitz, added on 22 February 1944:

> It has occurred at an outpost that prisoners were beaten and partly mistreated by civilians with whom they were sharing their workplace, so that they had to be temporarily committed to the hospital. (...) On this occasion I once more want to point expressly to the existing order that no SS man ought to raise a hand against a prisoner. In the 5th year of war no effort is to be spared to preserve the working power of the prisoners.
>
> Prisoners coming from night shifts are not to be assigned to other work. In order to preserve the strength of these prisoners care has to be taken that they have 7–8 hours of rest in order to resume their work rested.[52]

Regarding the note that SS members misappropriated the possessions of the Jews murdered during Operation Reinhardt, the following records are interesting, as they show the extent to which murder and plunder took place:

> The entire movable property of the Jews at a value of more than one hundred million Reichsmark was brought with c.2,000 transports into the 'Reich' – from feather duvets and cushions to combs, handbags and silver cutlery. Everything was meticulously noted. Until 30th April 1943
> 93,000 men's watches
> 33,000 women's watches
> 25,000 fountain pens
> were requisitioned.
> The confiscated hard currencies and precious metals had a total value of 60 million Reichsmark.[53]

During an interrogation of Pohl the following numbers were mentioned: one million individual pieces of clothing, 25,000 sets and 175,000 pairs of shoes were taken from the murdered Jews and – as far as possible – distributed among other prisoners or civilians.[54]

On 22 December 1947 the Supreme People's Tribunal of Poland sentenced Liebehenschel to death. He was executed on 24 January 1948 in Cracow.

Maximilian Grabner, SS Under Storm Leader, head of the political department at Auschwitz[55]

Maximilian Grabner came from Vienna and had been active in the illegal SS in Austria. During the setting up of the concentration camp at Auschwitz Grabner was made available by his office, the State Police headquarters at Katowice, to be head of the political department. In this he conformed with the requirements at least in one aspect, for the head of this department ought always to be a member of the Gestapo or the Reich Criminal Police Office.

Höß wrote quite disparagingly about him:

> Grabner had no clue of concentration camps, even less of the affairs of a political department. Most of the time I had my hands full with him. Gr. was very nervous and touchy. In addition, he always felt slighted if one drew his attention to a mistake he had made – and he made many and serious mistakes during his first time in Auschwitz, so I asked the state police headquarters in Katowice for a replacement several times. The chief at the headquarters was at that time Standard Leader Dr Schäfer, who could not provide us with a better official, though. And thus he stayed. Gradually he got the hang of things, especially since I was able to provide him bit by bit with junior leaders who had already worked in the political departments of other camps.
>
> Grabner was a diligent worker, but distracted and without any steadiness. His greatest flaw, however, was his forgiving behaviour toward comrades. Out of misplaced loyalty he did *not*[56] report innumerable, often wild, incidents and excesses by SS leaders and men in order to save the persons concerned from punishment. With this short-sighted behaviour Grabner contributed much to the fact that these excesses won the upper hand. He in particular had the duty to report all violations of the existing rules and camp regulations to the camp commander.

Although Höß apparently did not think much of Grabner's qualifications, he defended him when officers of the SS court had Grabner in their sights for murder. The charge read that Grabner had 2,000 people shot who were being held in the so-called command arrest. The shootings always took place when the area was overcrowded, and Grabner created space for additional prisoners with the aid of murder. The murders were covered up by compiling fake sickness reports for the prisoners and the doctors certifying natural causes of death. Among the investigating SS officers was Werner Hansen, who gave a witness statement during the 1st Frankfurt Auschwitz Trial in 1964.[57] Grabner's trial had taken place in Weimar and Höß had been heard as a witness, when he was no longer commander, but working in Oranienburg at the WVHA. Grabner's trial lasted two days and Höß must have left a lasting impression because Hansen could only recall him. According to him, Höß attempted to exonerate Grabner:

He 'swooped in' in a rather condescending manner, threw himself into a pose and asked something like this: 'What is actually happening here?' Höß described the 'transports', and deflected time and again from the actual charge, so that Hansen had to make it clear to him: 'That which you are stating here is no excuse for the 2,000 murders that are the subject of this case.' Without doubt, Höß wanted to insinuate to the court: 'Entire transports of people have been killed here, in this case to what do the deaths of these 2,000 people amount?'

Höß then incurred a reprimand during a recess, according to Hansen:

> As cockily as Höß had entered, so sheepishly he then left the courtroom again. Later I had a further clash with him, when I observed that he stood with Grabner during the recess, shook his hand and made some kind of remarks, disparaging remarks about the court.

As a consequence, Hansen took him to task 'rather rudely'. Höß did not want to take on the responsibility for Grabner's actions, incidentally: 'This he shifted away from himself' and invoked orders 'from above', said Hansen.

Grabner declared before the Supreme People's Tribunal of Poland that he participated in the murder of more than 3 million people only in defence of his family. He was never an anti-Semite. On 22 December 1947 Grabner was sentenced to death and executed.

Karl Möckel, SS Senior Storm Command Leader, head of the general premises administration Auschwitz[58]

Born in 1901, Möckel was a member of the SA from 1924, and on 25 November 1925 he joined the NSDAP. In 1926 he switched to the SS and there he rose until in 1939 he became SS Senior Leader. He received the Golden Party Badge, in 1933 became a full-time employee of the SS at the SS Administrative Office and from 1935 belonged to the staff of Reich Leader SS Himmler. After several roles, on 20 April 1943 he became the last head of the general premises administration of the Auschwitz camp.

Höß noted:

> Möckel came from Saxonia. He was a very old party member and had a really low SS number. Early on, long before the advent to power, he had joined the SS administration full time. (...) In 1933 he came to Munich to the head of the SS administration and in this office – later the WVHA – he held various posts until 1941. When Pohl established the W offices, Möckel became head of Office W III, where all food production and similar enterprises were merged.

His special task was the takeover and extension of the mineral spring operations, which had an unexpected boom during the war.

Möckel became an expert in his area and carried out the rapid takeover and establishment of bread and meat factories.

'Of his own initiative', in Höß' assessment, 'M. never achieved anything remarkable. That was not his nature. He liked to drift along, although he was very industrious.'

M. was a quiet, somewhat easy-going person who took everything as it came at first and only then began to work against it. Yet he was also very obstinate and did not like it when one meddled in his business.

Therefore he did not get along very well with Pohl, for whom M. worked too slowly and listlessly. At the beginning of the war M. wished for a deployment to the front or an assignment with any department of the Waffen-SS. The W enterprises were managed by leaders of the General SS. Yet Pohl always refused him. After a serious argument, Pohl permitted his transfer to the Waffen-SS. Möckel had to give up the rank of SS senior leader and make a fresh start as a simple SS man, though. In spring 1943 he finally came to Auschwitz.

M. had already been familiar with the concentration camps through the food enterprises, but the management of a concentration camp, especially with the dimensions of Auschwitz, was not easy for him. Also, his slowness in tackling new tasks meant that it took a very long time until he learned the ropes at Auschwitz. He scraped along in his post, trying as best as he could to meet every requirement. Yet the conditions in Auschwitz demanded more. I assisted him wherever I could for comradeship's sake, as he himself was a really good comrade. Yet Möckel made no progress. Besides a few good existing staff members he received help from his ever increasing pool of staff. As he himself noticed little, he was deceived and cheated in any which way.

M. had a young wife and did not have a good marriage. He thus began to drink more and more, often for days on end, and was, of course, then no use to anybody any more. This increased under Liebehenschel, as the two tried to drown their sorrows in alcohol together. Most of the work was done by his deputy, Head Storm Leader Polenz, as well as he could. Nothing essential or even improvements on the more and more untenable conditions of Auschwitz were achieved by Möckel's administration. When the general premises administration became independent and turned into the central administration, M. saw it as his special duty that the interests and independence of 'his' office were preserved at any cost! Yet he had no overview over his entire – now very wide-ranging – area of responsibility. His subordinates muddled along at their own discretion and were very happy to have such a good boss.

After his arrest Möckel was detained and later extradited to Poland. There he was prosecuted together with further defendants in the Cracow Auschwitz Trial and on 22 December 1947 sentenced to death by the Supreme People's Tribunal. He was executed on 24 January 1948.

Ernst-Robert von Grawitz, SS Senior Group Leader, Reich Physician SS and head of the SS Central Medical Office[59]

Grawitz was managing director of the German Red Cross, SS Senior Group Leader and general in the Waffen-SS. As Reich Physician SS and Police (RP SS) he was jointly responsible for the mass murder of disabled people and for medical experiments on prisoners.

Höß wrote about him:

> The RP SS had already been known to me since 1938. During my time in Sachsenhausen he visited the camp several times. Since the sick bay of the camp was furnished with medical equipment and also the rest of the sick bay was in an exemplary state, the RP SS liked to show it to medical commissions and other delegations meeting in Berlin; furthermore, at all times to the trainees of the Army Medical Academy.

The RP SS was a lively, energetic man with versatile practical knowledge. He took an interest in everything. According to my observations in Sachsenhausen and later in Auschwitz, he had a good eye, too. He was able to assess his doctors correctly and was not to be deceived, either. Twice he was in Auschwitz, when exactly I no longer recall. He wanted to see *everything*[60] and it was shown to him. I even showed him the worst deficiencies, the overcrowded sick bays, the post-mortem rooms – including the more than provisional sewage works in Birkenau. He observed closely the entire procedure of the extermination of the Jews including the burning in the pits or in the crematoria. He saw the lack of SS medical supervision as well as the inadequate treatment of the sick and the general state of health of all prisoners. He promised during both visits to do his utmost to provide redress – nothing ever came of it. He could not help, either.

The entire medical organisation of the SS was incorporated in the Central Medical Office that he had created and was under his control.

On 22 April 1945 Grawitz detonated a hand grenade inside his apartment in Babelsberg and thus killed himself and his family.

Joachim Mrugowsky, SS Senior Storm Leader and head of the Hygienic Institute of the Waffen-SS[61]

After his A-Levels in 1923 Mrugowsky had completed an apprenticeship at a bank and subsequently studied medicine and biology, specialising in botany. In 1937 he received a commission from Himmler to set up the so-called Hygienic Institute of the SS. Numerous prisoners fell victim to him, among other means by being shot with poisoned ammunition, while he took meticulous notes on their suffering and dying. According to Höß, in 1942 Zyklon B was ordered centrally by Mrugowsky from the Reich Leader SS for all SS organisations and installations. Mrugowsky himself was then responsible for distributing the deliveries. Höß writes about him:

> His principal areas of responsibility were the concentration camps during the war. His 'problem child' was and remained Auschwitz. From 1940 onward he visited the camp repeatedly.
>
> He saw the whole development, wrote angry reports to the RP SS and the RL SS and rejected any kind of responsibility – if the camp was not given relief and the stream of arrivals was not stopped. It was of no use – everything remained the same. M. provided the construction management with much good advice and brought many practical improvisations, but this was not enough to create fundamental change.
>
> (...) If I recall correctly, the gas Zyklon B required for the disinfection and extermination of Jews was supplied until 1942 to the administration of the Auschwitz camp by the company Tesch and Stabenow, Hamburg. From 1942 the poisonous gas supply for the entire Waffen-SS was regulated centrally by the SH[62] of the Waffen-SS, since the contingents were only made available to him. Therefore he had to continually procure the gas for the extermination of the Jews. Until 1943 the company T. & Stab.[63] was able to deliver the requested amounts on schedule by train. Due to the aerial offensive intensifying at that time this was often no longer possible after that.
>
> So Auschwitz was forced several times to fetch the gas from the production site at Dessau with trucks. As was said to me by the English prosecutor in Minden – who charged the owners of Tesch and Stabenow over supplying the gas to Auschwitz – it had been deduced with the aid of the company's books that in total 19,000kg of Zyklon B gas had been delivered to Auschwitz.

Furthermore, the Hauptsanitätslager (HSL) [Principal Medical Store] was in the Central Medical Office. The head was the medical quartermaster SS Group Leader Dr [Karl] Blumenreuther. The dental gold from the extermination of the Jews had to be delivered to this department continually every month. What was done there with the gold, I have never been able to learn. Likewise, the most valuable medications brought in by the Jewish transports had to be handed in at this department.

The RP SS and president of the German Red Cross was very well informed on these goings on in my opinion. Especially since he had seen the removal of the gold teeth from those gassed in Auschwitz and the melting down by the dentist.

The medical vehicles were at the disposal of the garrison doctor, and he was also authorised to issue the travel orders for their use. As there was always a lack of vehicles in Auschwitz, the garrison doctor could not be provided with a different vehicle for the supply runs into the individual camps. It gradually became the custom to carry out every journey necessary for the office of the garrison doctor with MVs.[64] Not only the sick were driven from camp to camp, but often also the dead. Bandages, equipment and medications were transported with them. The doctors and MOs[65] drove in them to the individual camps and to their duties at the ramp and at the extermination sites. The Jews no longer able to walk from the ramp were driven to the crematoria; if there was no truck nearby at that moment, they simply took the medical vehicle at hand. And since the MOs inserting the gas most often had no other means of transport in order to reach the extermination sites with their gas tins, they just used the MV going there anyway with the doctor.

In the course of time the MVs were used for transport purposes of all kinds – because often no other vehicle was available, nobody spared a thought for the fact that with the journeys to the extermination camps, with the people to be exterminated and with the gas the symbol of the Red Cross was profaned. No doctor ever took offence at this. Even Dr Wirth, very sensitive in these matters, has never spoken to me about this. And I myself have never thought of it, either.

Mrugowsky was sentenced to death in the so-called Nuremberg Doctors' Trial and on 2 June 1948 he was executed in Landsberg.

Enno Lolling, SS Standard Leader, Head of Department D III in the WVHA[66]

Lolling had begun his SS career at the Dachau concentration camp and then continued it at Sachsenhausen. On 3 March 1942 he was appointed head of the Department D III of the SS Central Economic-Administrative Office for Medical Organisation and Camp Hygiene with his base in Oranienburg, and thus senior physician of the concentration camps, i.e. superior of all camp doctors.

In Höß' opinion he was not capable of administering his office, especially since he was apparently addicted to morphine:

> Dr Lolling was already an elderly gentleman, tired and jaded, was addicted to morphine and drank a lot. He never did anything significant of his own volition during his entire period in office. He always drifted along with the events, and undertook many inspection journeys to all the camps. Yet he had no eye for the necessities. He also never properly realised the state of health, in general the overall sanitary–hygienic conditions in the camps. Only when epidemics or failings had already occurred, to which he was alerted by Pohl, did he wake up and – wrote reports. He was not capable of doing more.
>
> Pohl and Glücks tried repeatedly to get rid of him, especially at the beginning of his appointment. Furthermore, he was on leave for a long period of time with the aim to dismiss him because of his morphine addiction, which had come to light. Yet since the Reich Physician SS could not replace him with a better doctor – all suitable doctors were at the front or at SS field hospitals, and the lack of doctors had already been a constant worry before the war – he continued in his job. Finally they resigned themselves to him and his 'quirks'. He was not taken seriously in the WVHA nor at Office Group D, much less by the doctors of his area of responsibility. He often attempted to play the strict superior, but only embarrassed himself in the process. His orders were only followed in so far as it was deemed right. After all, he was easy to deceive during his visits, too, especially when he had been plied with alcohol, which frequently occurred.
>
> He was probably most often in Auschwitz, but I never had the experience that anything was undertaken by him on the basis of his extended tours. What happened in Auschwitz with respect to sanitary or medical improvements was undertaken by the camp doctors of their own volition. Dr Wirths often complained bitterly to me that he had absolutely no help and understanding from Lolling. (…) His position in particular ought to have been filled by a man full of energy with vision, knowledge and skills. However, the highest echelons did not see this necessity. Much could have been prevented with this!

Lolling was arrested on 27 May 1945 in Flensburg, where on the same day he committed suicide in his cell.

Karl Fritzsch, SS Head Storm Leader, first protective custody camp leader of Auschwitz concentration camp [67]

Fritzsch came from Regensburg and joined the NSDAP and SS early on. In 1934 he was deployed as company leader with the 1st SS Death Head Regiment Upper Bavaria at Dachau concentration camp. At the beginning of September 1939 he switched to the camp commandant's headquarters in Dachau and was head of the postal censorship office. In 1940 he became Höß' deputy at Auschwitz. In August 1941 he ordered that Russian prisoners of war be gassed with Zyklon B. About him Höß writes:

> Although Fr. had spent more than seven years in a concentration camp, the essentials had not dawned on him yet. Although he felt experienced enough in all concentration camp matters, the old professional criminals ran him *over*[68] within the first eight days. Fr. was limited, but very obstinate and quarrelsome. He had to be right in all matters. He especially liked to parade his role as superior. The fact that at Auschwitz he was now the deputy of the commander made him particularly proud. I raised objections against Fr. with the concentration camps inspection right from the beginning, since I knew him well enough from Dachau. His stupidity, narrow mindedness and obstinacy did not bode well. Yet Glücks refused, saying I should try him for a while for now! Later major objections on my part had no success, either. Fr. was good enough for Auschwitz!
>
> In principle Fr. did everything the way how *he* liked it. He followed my orders and my instructions only in so far as these corresponded with his views. He was never guilty of explicit insubordination because he feared the consequences. However, he knew quite well how to blur instructions issued by him – contradicting my orders – or even to cover them up. If his behaviour came to light, then he claimed he had not understood the order correctly – or his subordinates had deceived *him*.
>
> (...) He did not know how to deal with prisoners. He still had Eicke's instructions and views in his head: the enemies of the state must be treated harshly. And this he did, or rather trained his block leaders accordingly. Prisoners who were popular with him could do what they wanted, he protected them. But woe the prisoner who had incurred his displeasure! Fr. was also the protector of the kapos and block chiefs in his mould. He let them get away with anything; those who did not do as he wanted, let alone had closer contact with the commander, were moved to the punishment detail for a crime 'committed', or they were shunted to the sick bay, where they died of spotted fever or typhoid.

When I suspected something, I confronted Fr., but he always denied everything, felt insulted and could not be exposed. He was clever enough after all to cover his tracks. If an incident was actually reported, one of his subordinates had to take the fall.

With this behaviour he taught his SS men dishonesty, especially toward me. The prisoners knew that bypassing him had terrible consequences. Therefore no prisoner dared to turn to me. Even if I tried to learn something from the prisoners, I encountered reluctance and evasive answers. The terror deliberately created and inflicted by Fritzsch could never be ousted from Auschwitz again. It was inherited from report leader to report leader, from block leader to block leader, from kapo to kapo, and so on. An evil inheritance with horrible effects. Fritzsch, however, did not realise its consequences. He only wanted to rule himself. He viewed Auschwitz as his camp! Everything created and done was 'his work', were 'his ideas'.

It was difficult to work with Fritzsch. I repeatedly tried to resolve the matter in good faith, pointing out his impossible behaviour to him. It was of no use. I became very strict with him on a professional level and reprimanded him. It was of no use, on the contrary. He then became even more obstinate and stubborn. In my absence he permitted himself arbitrary acts that I could not condone. He gave instructions and orders in my name that were exactly opposite to my views. I could never fully catch him, however, moreover I did not have the time to deal with these disgusting matters.

I repeatedly described his conduct in great detail to the concentration camp inspection and pointed out the sheer impossibility of continuing to work like this – without success. Fr. remained at Auschwitz and did his work as he saw fit. The protective custody camp – and everything immediately related to it – he considered his very own sphere of responsibility in which he let nobody else meddle. He did not want to listen to reason, even from me.

As Höß lamented, he had to constantly smooth frictions and all heads of department complained about the 'devious and malicious' behaviour of Fritzsch. And yet off duty Fritzsch 'liked to show himself as the best of comrades' and spoke much about comradeship. Höß no longer remembered which incident led to Fritzsch' transfer, but at the end of 1941 Glücks realised that Fritzsch could no longer remain at Auschwitz. Instead of removing him entirely from the sphere of the concentration camps, however, as Höß had 'bluntly' recommended in his assessment, Fritzsch was transferred to Flossenbürg.

In October 1944 Fritzsch was deployed to the front, where he presumably fell during the battle of Berlin in spring 1945.

Hans Aumeier, SS Head Storm Leader, protective custody camp leader[69]

Aumeier came from Munich, had joined the NSDAP early, had worked full-time at the 'Brown House' before the Nazi seizure of power and belonged to the staff of Reich Leader SS Himmler. When Dachau concentration camp was built at the beginning of 1933, he was one of the first SS men commanded thereto.

Due to his low SS number, 2700, he soon became SS leader and despite his 'origin' – he had previously received military training from the State Police – he was also appointed head of special training at Dachau. Here Höß rubbed shoulders with Aumeier for the first time for half a year. In 1935 Aumeier was transferred as troop company leader to Esterwegen, then to Lichtenburg and finally to Buchenwald. In 1937 Eicke wanted to first send him to the General SS as leader of a storm command, before he ordered him to be the protective custody camp leader at Flossenbürg and then in January 1942 sent him to Auschwitz. There he inevitably came into close contact with Höß, who in his Cracow prison wrote the following about Aumeier:

> Aumeier was in many respects the exact opposite of [his predecessor] Fritzsch. He was lively, almost mercurial, easy to influence, good-natured, zealous and willing to execute any order given. However, he had an – inexplicable – fear of being reprimanded by me. And he had the principal fault of being too comradely without a firm will of his own. Furthermore, his range of vision was blinkered, he easily lost track. Foresight and forethought were not his forte. He often acted quickly without thinking of the consequences and the further effects. Also, he was not independent and showed no initiative. He always had to be pushed. The RL SS, who had known Aumeier since 1928, told me during his visit in 1942 that he believed his brain was too small.
>
> Aumeier had taken on an evil heritage from Fritzsch in the protective custody camp. From the beginning I had pointed out all the grievances to him, explained Fritzsch' entire conduct and asked him in a spirit of comradeship to assist me in eliminating these conditions created by Fritzsch and to be a real co-worker to me. I am firmly convinced that Aumeier was willing to do so. Yet he was not strong enough to go up against the now established rut and he did not want to immediately fight the report leaders and block leaders too harshly. Soon he succumbed to the suggestions by 'good' comrades not to change anything in the existing routine. His mistaken comradeship soon brought him so far as to continue the use of Fritzsch' watchword 'don't let the old man learn of this', on the one hand out of fear of being rebuked by me for mistakes

discovered, and on the other hand out of an aversion to report misconduct by subordinates so that they would not be punished. So little by little, though for other reasons, he got onto the same track as Fritzsch. They continued to cover up even the worst violations. Once he set off along this path he could no longer leave, with his mentality. And this path led farther and farther astray. He became more and more distant to me – out of fear and a guilty conscience and out of comradeship.

At first Aumeier did nothing wrong, but:

In later times he did quite a lot of things in my name, without my knowledge or approval. Also, Aumeier continued to live according to Eicke's views regarding the treatment of prisoners. For him all of them were 'Russians' (a Buchenwald expression for prisoners without differentiation). Aumeier was more cunning than Fritzsch and was not so easily 'run over'. However, he granted the kapos and block chiefs etc. even more power. In the meantime, the camp had rapidly grown, too, as the women's camp, Birkenau and the extermination operation of Jews had been added, which for Aumeier's range of vision had long since been too wide and large. He became nervous and more erratic, smoked and drank more and more and became more reckless, 'run over' by the operation he could no longer steer. He was floundering and was carried away by the events. He[70] could not master, not eradicate, the bad conditions: everything will be alright, may the commander see how to deal with all these matters!

The *nefarious* deeds of the kapos and block chiefs were in full blossom and experienced their heyday. The rapid expansion of the camps brought an enormous confusion with it. The daily increasing numbers of prisoners required daily new block chiefs, new kapos. The most evil creatures were employed for this. To cap it all, Aumeier did not have the slightest knowledge of human nature, either. Everybody could win him over with an assertive attitude. (…) Also, the leaders assigned to him (…) could not oversee the whole affair. So everybody muddled along as well and as much as he could. Only I had to stay on top of things and take stock of everything.

Most of the leaders had their hands full concealing their mistakes and neglect from me. (…) I often spoke with Aumeier plainly and, in a spirit of friendship, told him openly how I was being deceived by him and the other 'comrades'. He denied this most of the time and said that I was too pessimistic and trusted nobody, that I was very strict with the leaders on a professional level and demanded more of them. The cover-ups only increased.

Several attempts to persuade Glücks to get rid of Aumeier in an amenable way failed, as well as the later transfer request that included a ruthless representation of the reasons, until finally – instigated by Maurer – Glücks had to give in. He did not remove him from the concentration camp sphere, however, but appointed him commander of Vaivara in Estonia. In Glücks' view, out there he could not spoil anything. It was far away, there the RL SS would certainly not visit and furthermore there were only Jewish prisoners! After the dissolution of the camps in the Baltic states, Aumeier came to Oranienburg and was initially commissioned with the labour camps in Landsberg. In January 1945 he again became a commander, of the newly set up concentration camp Grini near Oslo in Norway. Aumeier was useful in a subordinate position with easily manageable conditions under close supervision – but he was no protective custody camp leader for a concentration camp and much less one with the dimensions of Auschwitz.

Aumeier was arrested by the British Army in Norway on 11 June 1945. During interrogation he at first denied any knowledge of the gas chambers at Auschwitz, but later revised his statement. After his extradition to Poland, Aumeier was sentenced to death in the Cracow Auschwitz trial and executed on 24 January 1948.

Gerhard Maurer, SS Standard Leader, Head of Department D II in the WVHA[71]

In 1934 Maurer had joined the SS administration in Munich, where Pohl employed him for audit tasks and then for the establishment of the Central Administration of SS economic organisations. Maurer became inspector of the economic enterprises and thus got to know the concentration camps more closely. He was particularly interested in the work deployment of prisoners.

Höß wrote about him:

> He sees neither the quirks of the commanders and of the protective custody camp leaders, nor their hostile stance toward the enterprises: most of the old commanders and protective custody camp leaders actually believed that the prisoners were treated too well in the economic enterprises and that the managers learned too much about the goings on in the camp from the prisoners. They played many a prank on the managers by suddenly transferring efficient specialist workers from the enterprises to outdoor labour or by holding them back in the camp, or by assigning prisoners unsuitable for the enterprises.

In 1947 Maurer was arrested in Nuremberg, extradited to Poland, sentenced to death on 22 December 1947 and executed on 2 April 1953 in Cracow.

Friedrich Hartjenstein, SS Senior Storm Command Leader, commander of Auschwitz III – Birkenau[72]

The son of a cobbler worked as a farm hand on an agricultural estate and studied agriculture in Hanover. From 1926 onward he was a professional soldier in the Reichswehr and in 1938 switched to the Waffen-SS. There he met Höß, who in his individual character studies expanded on the latter's personality during Cracow imprisonment thus:

> He was first platoon leader, then company leader in Sachsenhausen. In 1939 he became detail leader of the labour camp for some time. In 1940 he then joined the Death Head Division, where he was assigned to various posts until 1942. Eicke no longer had use for him, as he had failed repeatedly as unit leader, and so he came – as was custom in such cases – to the concentration camps. Glücks sent him as an outstanding chief guard to Auschwitz, where his predecessor, Storm Command Leader Gebhardt, had rendered himself untenable.
>
> Hartjenstein immediately began to exploit and incorporate his front experience into the wildly cobbled together guard storm command of Auschwitz. He wanted to approach everything in a strictly military manner – especially the training and instructions of the leaders.
>
> The principal task, guarding the prisoners and securing the camp, were trifles to him, which he thought he would manage effortlessly. He commenced so grandiloquently and pompously and it remained thus. All the grand talking paled in the light of the harsh reality of the Auschwitz state of emergency. The number of guards was always too low, never sufficient to be able to carry out an orderly, scheduled deployment of prisoners to the outdoor works. And now Hartjenstein wanted in addition to have whole companies freed of guard duties for parading and training. He never saw the necessity to fully deploy the entire guard storm command. (...) He could never understand that securing the camp and adequate guarding of the prisoners took precedent over military training. I was constantly accused by him that I had no sympathy for the military concerns of the guard storm command.
>
> Another constant bone of contention was the disciplinary authority. If I caught a leader or SS man showing misconduct regarding the guard duties or other transgressions of the security and order of the camp, I punished the man concerned myself, if in my opinion H.'s authority to punish did not suffice, or I handed him over to the SS court. H. always fought against this, as he always told the SS men concerned in a high-handed manner that the punishment was too severe and that he would reverse it.

141

The commander had no heart for the soldiers! So he systematically drove a wedge between the troop and me. Any remonstrance on my part to desist bore no fruit. He wanted to play the independent regiment commander. I aimed at forming fewer, but strong companies, in order to pare down the functional staff, which is the same in a company whether it has 150 or 250 men, and to free them up for guard detail. He wanted to have 12 companies at any cost in order to be able to underline the necessity of the regiment and its division into battalions. In spite of my contrary notion and other arguments he pushed the regiment through with Glücks. He also received some additional leaders, something Glücks had always denied me for the camp.

H. trained his leaders in such a manner that they served primarily the regiment. The camp came second. I actually had need of the leaders of the troop for the supervision of the far spread work details, the numerous cordons and other special details. They were only available one drop at a time, as they were needed more urgently for the actual troop duty. He had made a 'comradely' agreement with the protective custody camp leader that all reports of transgressions by the leaders or men of the troop went first to him, and he then reported them to me, if he deemed it necessary, and they should proceed vice versa concerning the transgressions of members of the commandant's headquarters. With such an attitude it is self-evident that most of the incidents were swept under the carpet.

H. liked to party with the leaders very often. Since I had little time and also no particular desire to do so, he used this fact to convert most of the leaders of all the departments to his views and to turn them against me, all in the 'best spirit of comradeship'! That the entire range of duties suffered from these machinations is all too understandable.

Constant quarrels arose because of construction matters. He only saw the interests and requirements of the troop. He did not appreciate that it was much more important to improve the general state of the camp – mostly in hygienic respects – with construction. That it was even necessary to eliminate the catastrophic conditions in the protective custody camps with accelerated and preferential construction activities penetrated his skull even less. Later, as commander of Buchenwald, he got a taste of the effects of his attitude.

H. was too short-sighted and too narrow-minded, pig-headed and dishonest. He worked behind my back against my orders and instructions again and again. I told this to Glücks in plain terms and even proved it on occasions, to no avail. Glücks always held the opinion that it was my fault that I did not get on with any leader.

He did not meet my invariant demands to instruct the guards *constantly*[73] with the aid of examples on the treatment of prisoners either. He always excused his detail leaders on the grounds that they never had enough men. Further, the men could not be expected to attend training after 14–16 hours of duty. That the most important issues could be pointed out in a few minutes *daily before* deploying to duty was not to the leaders' liking, because then they would have to assemble too early. After all, they were too often involved in regiment or battalion parties at night in order to raise the level of comradeship!

From the troop's side there was no appreciation of the dire conditions of the entire camp, although I pointed out the conditions plainly enough in the leadership meetings. There was only the odd leader who actually took his duties and tasks seriously and also attempted to instruct and train the men properly. H. frowned upon those, however, and got rid of them at the earliest opportunity. I will remain silent on his activities as commander of Buchenwald, since I did not observe him in person there. He barely concerned himself with the camp proper. He had enough to do during the six months to create a sufficiently large command staff. After Birkenau he went as commander to Natzweiler, and subsequently Pohl cleared him for front duty.

Hartjenstein was sentenced to death by a British military court, but committed to French custody for further trials. French military courts in Rastatt (1947) and Metz (2 July 1954) likewise sentenced him to death. He died of heart failure in a Paris prison before the sentence could be carried out.

Richard Baer, SS Storm Command Leader, last commander of the main camp Auschwitz[74]

Baer had joined the guard detail of the Dachau concentration camp in 1933, the SS Death Head Division in 1939 and transferred to the concentration camp Neuengamme. He became Pohl's adjutant and enjoyed the latter's special trust. On 3 November 1942 he became Höß' adjutant and in 1943 relieved the too-lenient Liebehenschel. On this matter Höß wrote:

> He had a hold over Pohl and knew expertly how to influence him and to persuade him of his wishes and views until the latter saw them as his own! Baer was suave, knew how to talk and knew how to assert himself. He treated heads of office group and heads of department as if they were his subordinates, but always in a clever way so as not to offend. As the status Baer enjoyed with Pohl soon got about, everyone who wanted to get something from Pohl attempted to ingratiate himself with Baer regardless of official rank.

Baer thus became spoilt beyond all measure, power hungry and extravagant. Further, he began to spin his own webs. Pohl, however, had complete confidence in him and called him his friend! Attempts to draw Pohl's attention to Baer's machinations were deflected, and even fell back on the well-intentioned whistle-blower. Glücks and Maurer later bitterly regretted suggesting Baer as adjutant and then even as successor of Liebehenschel.

When Liebehenschel had to leave Auschwitz, Baer was appointed his successor. Baer probably realised that – if he continued like this – a falling out with Pohl had to occur. Hence he preferred to retreat in good time to a post that at the same time would mean opportunities for promotion and advancement. He was indeed made storm command leader at the same time, something Pohl would have refused another given the short period of time and his age.

Incidentally, Baer had behaved extremely tactlessly towards Liebehenschel and his wife at the latter's transfer. Another man than Liebehenschel would have brought Baer to account.

In June 1944 Baer commenced his duties as garrison commander and camp commander at Auschwitz I. I had the honour of inducting and training him. Yet in his opinion that was not necessary in his case, since he had enough concentration camp experience. I had little opportunity to acquaint him with all the almost implausible conditions. He had already seen everything himself and would cope with it. During the almost three months I was at Auschwitz in 1944, he did not improve anything and did not even make an effort to do so. He had other interests, went hunting or fishing a lot and took leisurely drives. Baer believed that he had worked enough as adjutant with Pohl and now needed rest. He had become very haughty and also unfriendly. The Jewish operation was not of any concern to him; he left that to me.

He did not concern himself much with the transportation of those fit to work, either; only on occasion if Pohl made himself heard more urgently. I had to intercede with the directorship of the Reich Railways several times in order to get the stalled provision of railway cars going again. In any case, it was all in all an unpleasant collaboration. His two other camp commanders, Krause and Schwarz, barely saw him. They heard from him mostly through the garrison orders.

He took very little care of the prisoners, he not have time for this. As he was very moody, his views on this matter changed constantly. The protective custody camp leader and the report leader were responsible for the prisoners. He only took note of all orders and instructions of Office Group D in so far as they were of interest to him. He could afford failures without thinking twice. Glücks undertook nothing against him, and if he did finally do something, on several occasions he left off after he had experienced serious rebuffs by Pohl.

The 'evacuation' of Auschwitz had to be prepared thoroughly on Pohl's orders. I had to write down for Pohl the exact issues that had to be observed. Baer had two months to make the necessary preparations. He did nothing. The 'state discovered' is the best proof of this. When the evacuation order by Schmauser arrived, Baer climbed onto the best and largest vehicle and absconded to Groß Rosen in order to make preparations from there! He left the evacuation and transportation to Krause and Hößler; they could see how they managed. During a planned and well-conceived evacuation the conditions would have not arisen that I later saw on the Silesian and Sudeten roads and railway tracks four days later. I had been ordered there by Pohl in order to be able to intervene if. B. could not cope with the difficulties and because Pohl did not receive a report from Baer. I was no longer able to intervene – only to observe!

On my return I gave an unsparing and realistic report to Pohl. Furthermore, I castigated Baer's own behaviour ruthlessly. Pohl became thoughtful, but did not say anything. A few days later Baer was appointed commander of Mittelbau and Schwarz, who had been intended for that post, was honoured with the disgusting dregs of Natzweiler. When it became uncomfortable at Mittelbau and the aerial attacks there increased in intensity, Baer sprained his ankle and retreated to Styria to recover.

After the war Baer went into hiding under a false name and was only arrested in 1960. He died on 17 June 1963 in Frankfurt/Main while in custody.

Gerhard Palitzsch, SS Head Company Leader, report leader concentration camp Auschwitz[75]

Palitzsch, a farmer by profession, was one of the most evil creatures that were let loose among the prisoners of Sachsenhausen and then Auschwitz. From mid-March 1933 he was a member of the NSDAP (membership number 1965727) and SS (number 79466). From 1933 he served initially as a member of the SS Death Head Division in the guard details of the Oranienburg and Lichtenburg concentration camps. From 1936 he was block leader at Sachsenhausen and later report leader. In this position he met Höß, when the latter became adjutant at Sachsenhausen in 1938. On 20 May 1940 Palitzsch arrived with thirty 'Reich German' criminal prisoners from Sachsenhausen at the newly created Auschwitz camp. These 'tried and tested' prisoners with the numbers 1 to 30 later served as prisoner functionaries.

Palitzsch never drew Höß' particular attention while in the command staff. He did his duty to general satisfaction:

> Yet I could never shake the feeling that he secretly bullied the prisoners. I tailed him frequently, and further quizzed people on this matter, but did not find a solid reason to intervene. It was strange to me that the prisoners did not like to talk about him and always tried to answer evasively. However, the Sachsenhausen block and detail leaders including the report leader were – apart from very few outsiders – a sworn community of concentration camp old-timers who had served under Eicke, Loritz and Koch. (…)
>
> I do not know, and never heard either, that Palitzsch was involved in any scandals during his time in Sachsenhausen. I do not doubt that he beat prisoners. At any rate, at Sachsenhausen he was already cunning enough not to be caught. He had received outstanding training under the above mentioned.
>
> During the setting up of Auschwitz he was allocated to me by the concentration camp inspection on Loritz' suggestion – and thirty professional criminals were chosen by him. On the one hand I was glad, since in Palitzsch I got an experienced report leader who had at least an idea of the protective custody camp and who was furthermore zealous and knew how to treat the prisoners. Yet on the other hand I always had the feeling – from the start – that Palitzsch was not honest and played both sides. My feeling did not deceive me. He was soon in agreement with Fritzsch and the second protective custody camp leader Meier, and busily involved in their machinations.
>
> From Meier he learned the last touches of how to cover up all kinds of misdeeds. Meier had equally been 'heartily recommended' to me by Glücks, because he could not stay an hour longer in Buchenwald due to his disgusting behaviour. He was one of Koch's creatures who performed every dirty trick, a real gangster. In Auschwitz he only stayed a few months until I could convict him of serious racketeering and handed him to the SS court. Glücks was very mad with me about this because he thought he had to answer to the RL SS. You see, Meier had passed himself off as an associate of the RL SS and thus deterred many superiors from stepping in against him. With this Meier and the professional criminal of the same name, a tailor, P. carried out gross racketeering with money, valuables and clothes through illegal confiscation.

In this context belongs the following garrison order by Höß dated 16 November 1943:

> I have cause to point out for the final time that the property of the prisoners, regardless of its nature (clothing, gold, valuables, food

or other personal effects) and regardless where it is found, remains untouched. The state decides on the disposition of the prisoners' property. In special cases this property becomes state property. Who misappropriates state property marks himself as a criminal and is excluded from the ranks of the SS by his own doing. I will hand over SS members who besmirch themselves with such a foul deed to the SS court for sentencing without regard. I expect of every clean, decent SS member – and this will be the majority – that he assists with open eyes in the rapid removal of possibly existing scoundrels and thus in keeping our ranks clean.[76]

And Höß writes further:

I learned all this, however, only in 1944 when P. had been caught by the SS court with the aid of the recaptured prisoner Meyer. Palitzsch and two junior leaders of the administration aided this prisoner M. in his escape because they feared their racketeering would be discovered, since the prisoner M. threatened them with exposure if they did not let him 'go'. A thrilling gangster novel could be written about the trio of Meier, Palitzsch and Meyer.

Meier's successor became Seidler. Seidler had known Palitzsch at Sachsenhausen, and they had spent several years there together. Though Seidler was not a creature in the mould of his predecessor he shared the same line of thought with Fritzsch and Palitzsch with regards to the treatment of prisoners and was great at hiding detrimental occurrences from me.

P. was not to be surpassed in zeal. He was always at his post and to be encountered everywhere. He knew everything, much better than the protective custody camp leaders, and one could give him the most difficult tasks. He had absolute control over the prisoners – monitoring them with his cunning espionage system of kapos and block chiefs by playing one against the other. The most notorious functionaries always stood under his protection – if their activities drew too much attention sometimes, they had to suffer some time in the punishment detail, too.

P. got them out of there on time. Those who knew too much or even dared not to 'play along' any longer suffered workplace accidents with fatal results or died of spotted fever. The immortal camp senior Brodniewicz[77] was the conducting master on Palitzsch' orders. P. was cunning enough, however, to not show any weakness. He had learned and experienced enough. Furthermore, he was covered by Fritzsch and Seidler at any time. After the Meyer affair I was after him like the devil. He knew and suspected this – he trod all the more carefully. I could not catch him in three and half years, although I did much and risked much to do so. Learning something about P. from the prisoners was completely hopeless – this was not possible even from those transferred to other camps. The fear of the consequences was too great. The recaptured prisoner Meyer only talked when he knew for certain that Palitzsch was doing time, too.

For outsiders the events described are inconceivable, but those who had been a prisoner in Auschwitz themselves or otherwise knew of the circumstances knew what power Palitzsch had and which role he had played.

Palitzsch was always present during executions; he executed the most killings by a shot in the neck. I observed him many times, but could never detect the slightest stirring of emotion. He performed his horrible work calmly and collectedly, without any haste and with an impassive face. Also, during his duty at the gas chambers I could never detect a trace of sadism in him. His face was always closed off and impassive. He was probably so emotionally hardened that he could kill incessantly without sparing a single thought on his actions.

P. was the only one of the men who were immediately involved in the exterminations who did not once approach me in a quiet moment and unburden his heart on the horrific procedure. With the death of his wife – she died of typhoid – he lost the last inner stability, the last inhibitions. He began to drink without constraint and constantly had sexual affairs. Women, mostly supervisors, went in and out of his apartment. I had never previously heard anything about him in this respect. This probably led to the affair with the Latvian Jewess in Birkenau, where he was finally caught. I had long since warned Schwarzhuber[78] of Palitzsch' activities and drawn his attention to his weaknesses. Schwarzhuber had already been after him for a long time. After P.'s arrest his misdeeds all gradually came to light. In 1940 he had embezzled an enormous amount of money, valuables, cloths, clothing etc. from Jews in Auschwitz and from the new Polish arrivals. Later, during the Jewish operation, he practised this to excess. He had then become fussy, however, and only took the most valuable things!

No details of his activities in the camp, his mistreatment of prisoners, could be learned even after his arrest. The prisoners were no use because they feared the kapos and block chiefs. It could not be determined whether P. personally killed prisoners of his own volition at his whim and by his judgement, but this had to be assumed. Again he had been careful enough not to create any inconvenient accessories. After all, he did not need to abuse and kill in person. He had enough creatures submissive to him among the prisoners at hand, who hastened to take care of this in order to gain advantages for themselves at their fellow prisoners' cost.

What was the life, the health of their comrades, as long as they were doing well!

Palitzsch is primarily to blame that these wild excesses, these inhumane abuses of the prisoners, took place. As report leader he could have prevented most of it – but on the contrary he wanted this to indulge in his lust for power. In addition, the dreadful state of affairs regarding the kapos etc. at Auschwitz in the main have to be ascribed to him. This system was along his lines, and with it he wanted to rule everything. He often enough bragged while under the influence of alcohol that he[79] was the most powerful man inside the Auschwitz camp and that *he* alone had everything in his hands.

How far Fritzsch, Seidler and Aumeier had become dependent on him – by transgressions of any kind – is not known to me, but it is possible that Palitzsch played them 'deliberately' into his own hands. He stopped at nothing to strengthen his position of power!

He also behaved in this manner towards his comrades. Those subordinate to him he did not approve of or who were even obstacles to his plans, he let 'stumble' at the earliest convenience and removed them from his sphere.

I tried to get rid of him several times by presenting my suspicions to Glücks. He paid no heed to them. He would not transfer him until I had flagrant evidence at hand. I was supposed to watch him more closely, after all I was supposed to be able to cope with junior leaders!

Palitzsch was the most cunning and sly creature I ever met and experienced during the long, varied years of duty at several concentration camps. He literally walked over dead bodies in order to satisfy his lust for power!

Emil de Martini, prisoner and scribe at the infirmary, made the following statement regarding Palitzsch on 4 June 1964 during the 1st Frankfurt Auschwitz Trial:

> The shootings in the neck were as a rule executed by the former head company leader Palitzsch, of whom I heard that he is no longer alive today. We inside the camp called him 'William Tell'. And when he was walking along the camp road with his small calibre rifle, we knew exactly that executions were now scheduled.[80]

Pery Broad, otherwise not always reliable in his accounts, described Palitzsch – together with Head Company Leader Moll – as one of 'the greatest butchers of the past war'.[81] His relationship to a Jewess did not come to light, but his love affair with the Latvian protective custody prisoner Vera Lukans and his widespread custom in Auschwitz of putting aside some of the valuables taken from the prisoners upon arrival as savings for the twilight years brought Palitzsch a prison sentence of several years.

It is barely conceivable that Höß supposedly knew nothing of this. It is breathtaking how Höß commits untruths to paper and omits truths. His remarks on Palitzsch and Bruno Brodniewicz are examples of this like no other. Höß had got to know both of the men well enough at Sachsenhausen and had brought them to Auschwitz. Brodniewicz was known as a brutal thug, hated all Poles and everything Polish and not only tortured them, but preyed on them in any way possible. He could always feel secure in the light of Höß' backing. He was a leading player in all the acts of violence and became the first camp senior of the newly founded main camp at Auschwitz. He hid gold and other valuables inside his stove, which were found after a tip-off by the prisoner Otto Küsel. As a consequence, Brodniewicz was brought to the bunker and relieved as camp senior. His SS career was not over by any means: he was camp senior in the gypsy camp at Auschwitz, then at an outpost of Auschwitz, Neu-Dachs, at the Eintrachtshütte outpost from April 1944 and finally at the Bismarckhütte outpost.

Küsel, a Reich German in the parlance of the time, had been committed to Sachsenhausen and belonged to the first thirty prisoners who had been transferred to Auschwitz. There he was responsible for the work details as a prisoner functionary and had a certain room for manoeuvre, for example to help prisoners by assigning them easier work. On 29 December 1942 Otto Küsel, together with three Poles, fled from Auschwitz. Küsel left a letter behind, in which he pointed to Brodniewicz' machinations. Küsel played an active part in a Polish resistance group and was then arrested by the Gestapo and brought to Auschwitz again. After the appointment of the new camp commander, Arthur Liebehenschel, he was released from the bunker.

In the context of the 1st Frankfurt Auschwitz Trial, Küsel stated that if Höß had not been ordered to Berlin on the same day that he was brought to Auschwitz again after his renewed arrest, he would no longer be alive: 'If that commander had still been there and the old camp leader, I would not be here today. That I know!'[82]

The behaviour of some members of the Frankfurt State Court was distressing. They reproached Küsel more or less for the fact that he had not been killed after his escape and renewed arrest. The supplemental judge Hummerich in particular gave Küsel a raw deal: he considered the fact that Küsel had shared a cell with the Polish prime minister Cyrankiewicz to be evidence for Küsel having been an informer.

Palitzsch was expelled from the SS in November 1944 and was killed on 7 December 1944 in Hungary.

Heinrich Schwarz, SS Head Storm Leader, work detail leader in Auschwitz[83]

Höß wrote down the following character study of Schwarz, who came to Auschwitz in 1941 as work detail leader:

Schwarz, the choleric type, thin-skinned and quick-tempered.

Yet he never acted impulsively. He was honestly diligent and reliable. He carried out orders he received word for word until the last consequence. He followed my instructions particularly willingly and attentively. I never had the slightest suspicion that he led me on or even deceived me. The other leaders of the camp often laughed about him because of his diligence towards me. He was not very popular due to his strict sense of duty, either. He combatted inefficiency ruthlessly. Schwarz was an indefatigable worker, no job was too much for him. He was always energetic and eager. I could hand even the most difficult tasks to Schwarz without compunction. He carried everything out thoroughly and thoughtfully.

As work detail leader he already had a difficult position in itself. His subordination to D II – Maurer – was not easy, and the latter badgered him badly. New orders and transfer decisions came in continuously – often contradicting the previous ones completely. Schwarz was responsible for every prisoner selected for work deployment, for his actual profession and the appropriate assignment. The prisoners frequently changed their professions depending on the prospect of achieving a better position, or for other reasons important to them.

Transfers to other camps always caused Schwarz particular problems. The final number was never correct, since quite a few prisoners became ill or were held back at the last minute by the protective custody camp for whatever reasons. The prisoners provided to supplement the most recently absent had other professions than those requested and so on. If the transport finally set off, then the complaints of the commander or work detail leader of the receiving camp began. The prisoners were not hale enough, could not perform the intended labour or did not have the slightest knowledge of the stated profession. The letters that Schwarz received from D II on the basis of such complaints were devastating, teeming with accusations of incapability and negligence. Maurer did this on purpose to cheer up the work detail leaders, as he called it. Schwarz, in his diligence, often felt desperate because of it. Although I told him repeatedly that D II did not mean this seriously, he was not convinced. And he did not lose the aversion to Maurer's letters to the last, although he was robust enough otherwise.

Schwarz did not develop a cordial relationship with his subordinates as he –incessantly at work – demanded the same of them. Furthermore, Schwarz had many useless, even incapable men. An exchange was impossible, since most of the time nothing better arrived.

Schwarz had a sense of comradely behaviour, but did deal with misconduct or neglect. He got into constant conflict over this with the protective custody camp and the troop. They were as wary of him as of me. Towards prisoners he was very strict, and demanded much work, but I had the impression that he was just. He did not tolerate arbitrariness.

He did a lot of work with the outpost camps, their set-up and supervision. There was much trouble with the enterprises themselves, until the operation went relatively smoothly when the enterprises knew how to handle the prisoners. Then there was the constant vexation with the detail leaders – they had to be changed often. There were constant incidents with the guards details assigned both by us and the army, navy and Luftwaffe. In spite of the variety of tasks Schwarz oversaw he was always informed about everything. If he was deceived by subordinates, if his instructions were not followed correctly, this was only possible because of the almost unachievable constant supervision needed and the lack of reliable people. Schwarz did his utmost to prevent nasty conditions and to eliminate arising grievances.

In Schwarz I had a faithful assistant who took much essential work off me. Also for the Jewish extermination operation. If Schwarz was on duty there I could rest easy. Nothing slipped his attention easily. I further believe that Schwarz never committed arbitrary acts or gave any instructions without my consent in my name.

As the leader of all the work details he tried to do justice to the prisoner requests of the individual outpost administrations according to the level of importance of the work projects, either by his own assessment or by seeking my decision when in doubt. He often had bitter altercations in this regard with the regional leader and also the agricultural enterprises.

When Schwarz became commander of Auschwitz III, nothing much actually changed regarding his area of responsibility, only that he got rid of the work details, but now had to constantly set up new labour camps instead. The difficulties with the enterprises increased, since he only occasionally encountered a good manager and other leading staff with a good understanding of prisoner matters in the individual enterprises of the armament industry. Schwarz always demanded doggedly and tenaciously that the prisoners had to be treated decently, fed well and housed adequately. On receiving complaints he acted harshly and often brutally against the persons responsible and gave no rest until the grievances were eradicated. In the face of the general difficulties he was powerless, too, but he tried to achieve essential improvements in the food provisions by increasing the allowances.

(...) On the whole Schwarz was one of the few really useful leaders of the Auschwitz concentration camp.

Schwarz was sentenced to death by a French military court on 20 March 1947 and executed in Sandweiher near Baden-Baden.

Maximilian Sell, SS Senior Storm Leader, work detail leader in the concentration camp Auschwitz[84]

From February 1942 Maximilian Sell was general work detail leader at Ravensbrück concentration camp and at the end of 1942 was transferred from there to Auschwitz. He was mainly supposed to process the written communication, the work detail files and the registration in order to take the pressure off Schwarz. About him Höß noted:

I could never quite make out Sell. He was tired and slow, dull and very sloppy in all his work to the constant vexation of Schwarz. Schwarz could never rely on him and had to double-check everything. Furthermore, Sell left most of the work to prisoners, even matters classified as 'Secret Affair of the Reich'. Further, on many issues he worked against Schwarz and tried time and again to direct work assignments according to his assessment. He made promises to many companies, which could never be fulfilled. I also have a suspicion that he accepted bribes. During the Jewish operations he did his 24-hour day like the other leaders of the protective custody camps. There he was involved in constant quarrels with the doctors on duty, as he always attempted 'to select' on his own account. I always suspected Sell of appropriating Jewish effects for himself and watched him particularly closely, but could never catch him in the act. The special commission of the SS court also put him under observation, without success. He treated the prisoners subject to whim. His work detail prisoners working for him were under his special protection and could carry out the worst racketeering.

These rackets became exceedingly excessive when he himself became general work detail leader after the division of Auschwitz into three camps. With money and valuables a canny prisoner could obtain any work assignment agreeable to him. Schwarz often attempted to put a stop to these activities, but Sell then set up the 'black labour market' again in secret. He had a special liking for the women's camp, i.e. the compliant supervisors and the female prisoners to whom he took a fancy. The latter were openly

153

favoured by him and assigned to elevated positions. He hardly concerned himself with the main body and their assignment, which he graciously left to his incapable supervisors or to the prisoners themselves. Although Maurer later put him in personal charge of the transports to the labour camps in the Reich, he had made little effort in that respect.

Maurer had wanted to relieve him during my time and his successor had already travelled to Auschwitz. Yet I had to arrest the latter after a few days when I caught him in misappropriating Jewish effects from Canada II.[85] He was sentenced to death. After this incident Sell stayed, since Maurer had no other leader available. However, Maurer kept an eye on him constantly and also treated him very harshly. Sell was thick-skinned, though, and was not bothered by this. When not on duty Sell led a rather easy life – many women and even more alcohol! Of course, this took its toll on his duty, too. None of his subordinates respected him. Through pandering, he tried to make himself popular with his comrades. The decent and reasonable among them rejected him! Sell brought more damage to Auschwitz than benefit.

On the mentioned 'misappropriation' of effects a further remark is required: according to camp regulations the respective administrative head was in control of the 'prisoner property management'. On this it was written: 'Clothing is to be stored in a clean state and free of vermin, the valuables securely inside safes. Exact documentation of all effects is to be kept. In case of death the entire effects of the deceased prisoner have to be sent to the next of kin.'

Nobody dreamed of obeying these regulations. SS members as well as kapos or block chiefs helped themselves just like the commander's wife, Hedwig. Primarily, however, it was the Nazi regime that was known not only to confiscate the victim's property, but further sinned against him or her by body stripping.

After the evacuation of Auschwitz in February 1945 Sell became work detail leader at the Mittelbau camp. He disappeared in April 1945.

Eduard Wirths, SS garrison doctor in Auschwitz[86]

Before the war Wirths was a country doctor in the Baden region and then joined the Waffen-SS. Due to a heart condition he came to the concentration camp inspection and later to Auschwitz.

Höß drew the following character profile of him:

> Wirths was a diligent doctor with a strongly developed sense of duty and extremely conscientious and cautious. He had extensive

knowledge in all medical areas and always strove to expand his medical skills and knowledge. Yet he was very soft and good-natured and needed strong back-up for his support. He followed all orders and instructions given to him with extraordinary care. When in doubt he always made sure of their correctness.

For instance, he always had the orders of the political department from Grabner regarding concealed executions confirmed by me personally before he carried them out. This was to the constant vexation of Grabner, who resented him very much for this. Wirths often complained to me that he could not square these killings demanded from him with his conscience as a doctor and was suffering much from it. He asked Lolling and the Reich Physician for another medical assignment again and again, but in vain. I had to raise his morale time and again with reference to the harsh necessity of the orders given by the RL SS. In addition, the entire extermination campaign of the Jews caused him scruples, which he revealed to me as his confidant.

In his thoroughness and carefulness he would perform all the experiments with Zyklon B himself – the manufacture of the hydrogen cyanide solution for injections and trials with only the compound for mass delousing. These experiments caused him some damage several times, until I forbade him to continue.

He found no particular help from the doctors and medical personnel subordinate to him apart from a few exceptions. The number of doctors was much too low for Auschwitz, and they were often useless, often untenable, due to their conduct or their flaws. The lack of personnel was – as with all Auschwitz departments – chronic. Almost the entire medical care of the prisoners was in the hands of the prisoner doctors, carrying out their medical practice under the 'supervision' of the few SS doctors. In part this was outstanding and valuable, but often also disastrous. The activities of the kapos and block chiefs found their crowning in the infirmary. The multitude and complexity of the prisoner infirmaries made their supervision unachievable. Furthermore, it was hardly possible to keep undercover informants in a hospital. The prisoners in the know preferred to remain silent. Wirths often reported to me on his attempts to clear up this condition and their miserable failure. It was not possible to prove any misdeed of the prisoner doctors and nursing staff, especially not with the mass mortality during the epidemics.

Wirths' efforts to find out the perpetrators from prisoners injured by beatings and committed to the infirmary yielded no results. The fear of the omnipotence of the *true*[87] camp authority was too great.

Wirths considered it his duty to constantly monitor and improve all hygienic installations and to campaign by all available means for the elimination of the bad hygienic and sanitary state of affairs. W. was at constant war with the building management, because he constantly urged the improvement and new establishment of these installations and because he did not rest until errors that came to his knowledge were dealt with.

In his monthly medical reports to D III and to the Reich Physician SS, Wirths described in great detail the exact state of health, the state of the entire hygienic and sanitary installations and the grievances that had arisen in a clear manner and with ruthless openness. In these reports Wirths asked every time for assistance in eradicating the stark, later to be called horrific, general state of the camp.

Everybody reading these reports could gain a realistic picture of these conditions. During his oral reports to D III or the RP SS W. also showed no regard and reported bluntly. For example, Wirth wrote the special reports requested by Pohl via D III in case of epidemics – when the high number of fatalities caused concern – so frankly by emphasising and underlining first and foremost the causes leading to all these deficiencies that the reports often seemed exaggerated even to me. Noticeable relief never got to Auschwitz as a result of all these medical reports. Yet no influential, superior department was left in the dark over the catastrophic conditions in the Auschwitz concentration camp and no superior – including the RSHA – could ever claim not to have learned anything of it.

Wirths was often desperate because of this unwillingness to listen by the higher departments, but he still believed that one day decisive intervention from above would happen! I left him in his belief, I no longer expected anything after the visit by the RL SS in 1942.

Wirths did everything in his power to stop the worst abuses; he had good and also practical ideas – but by the time they could be carried out, they had become outdated and irrelevant due to further overcrowding.

Wirths was a good, faithful assistant to me, a good advisor in all matters of his area of responsibility.

Even Lolling admitted – which he was not keen on doing – that W. was the best doctor of all the concentration camps. In my ten years of duty in concentration camps I never met a better one.

In his conduct with prisoners he was correct and tried to do justice to them. In my opinion he was often too good-hearted and most of all too trusting. His good nature was abused to his disadvantage by the prisoners, especially the females. He favoured the prisoner doctors in particular. I often had the impression that he treated them as colleagues. As I already indicated above, this had considerable disadvantages for the camp.

His cancer research (…) and the – as far as I know – few surgical interventions in this area were not damaging. Yet the insights from this research are of far-reaching importance to the whole medical world. They were unique to my knowledge.

After the 'evacuation' of Auschwitz, Wirths first went to Dora-Mittelbau, then Bergen-Belsen and finally to Neuengamme. His heart condition had worsened so much due to his work at Auschwitz that he was almost unfit for duty, additionally his hearing was fading rapidly. He lived in a happy marriage with four children.

W. was very comradely and was also very popular with his comrades. He helped the SS families a lot as a doctor; all had trust in him.

On 20 September 1945 Wirths committed suicide in American custody in Staumühle near Paderborn.

The 'Non-Medical Activities'

It is illuminating what Höß wrote during his time in Cracow prison on the 'non-medical activities of the SS doctors in Auschwitz'.[88] Here no emotions are recognisable either, as soberly and factually he expounds the share of the SS doctors in the Holocaust. Besides the usual tasks, the following arose:

1. For the arriving transports with Jews they had to select the male and female Jews fit for work according to the guidelines given by the RP SS.

2. During the extermination procedure at the gas chambers they had to be present in order to supervise the prescribed application of the poisonous gas Zyklon B by the medical orderlies responsible for disinfection. Furthermore, they had to make sure after the opening of the gas chambers that the extermination was complete.

3. The dentists had to satisfy themselves constantly with spot checks that the prisoner dentists of the special details pulled the gold teeth of all people gassed and placed them into the provided containers. Furthermore, they had to monitor the melting down of the dental gold and its secure storage until delivery.

4. The SS doctors had to constantly sort out in Auschwitz, Birkenau as well as the labour camps, the Jews having become unfit to work who could not likely be restored to fitness again within four weeks, and direct them towards extermination. In addition, Jews suspected of being infected were to be exterminated. The bedridden were to be killed by injections, the others in the

crematoria or bunkers by gas. For the injections phenol, evipan and hydrogen cyanide acid were used.

5. They had to carry out the so-called concealed executions. These were performed on Polish prisoners whose execution had been ordered by the RSHA or the Chief of the Security Police in the General Government. As the executions were not to become known for political or security reasons, a cause of death common within the camp was to be certified.

6. The healthy prisoners thus sentenced to death were brought by the political department to the detention block 11 and there killed by an SS doctor through injection. Sick persons were equally killed inconspicuously by injection in the infirmary. The doctor responsible then had to give a rapidly fatal illness on the death certificate.

7. The SS doctors had to be present during executions of those sentenced to death by summary courts and to confirm their deaths. Likewise, during executions ordered by the RL SS or the RSHA or the Chief of the Security Police in the General Government.

8. In the case of requests of corporeal punishment they had to examine the prisoners concerned for impediments and to be present while the punishment was carried out.

9. They had to perform abortions on foreign women – until the 5th month of their pregnancy.

10. Trials were performed by:

   a) Dr Wirths: cancer research examinations and surgical interventions on Jewesses with cancer or suspected thereof

   b) Dr Mengele: twin research, examinations on identical Jewish twins

   By non-SS doctors:

   c) Prof. Blauberg: sterilisation research. Injections to prevent reproduction by gluing the ovaries together performed on Jewish women.

   d) Dr Schumann: sterilisation attempts by x-rays in order to destroy the reproductive organs of Jewish women.

Regarding the phenol injections, it has to be remarked that an estimated 30,000 people were murdered in this manner. In many cases the camp commander informed the surviving relatives but cynically concealed the cause of death. For example, he wrote to a certain Richard Thederjahn in Forst on 25 November 1942 that his wife had reported sick on 17 November 1942 and as a result had been admitted to the hospital for medical treatment. He wrote:

> She received the best medical and custodial treatment possible. In spite of all efforts applied she could not overcome her illness. I wish to express my condolence for this loss to you. Your wife did not express any dying wishes. I have instructed the prisoner property administration of my camp to send her estate to your address. The death certificate will be sent to you in the next days. Signed Höß, SS Senior Storm Command Leader and Commander.[89]

While Höß deliberately did not give a cause of death, a few days later, on 6 December 1942, SS Under Storm Leader Maximilian Grabner wrote that the woman had died as the result of 'influenza in combination with a heart condition in the hospital here'.[90] The corpse was cremated, and if so desired the husband could have the urn with the ashes of the deceased delivered to him.

Adolf Eichmann, SS Senior Storm Command Leader, head of the Judenreferat [Jewish Department] IV B 4 in the RSHA[91]

Höß noted during his Cracow imprisonment:

> I only met Eichmann when he – after he had received the order to exterminate the Jews by the RL SS – came to me at Auschwitz in order to discuss with me the further details of the extermination operation. Eichmann was a lively, always busy man in his thirties full of energy. He always had new plans and always looked for innovations and improvements. He knew no rest. He was obsessed with the Jewish question and with the 'final solution' ordered! Eichmann had to constantly make immediate and oral reports to the RL SS regarding the preparations and execution of the operations initiated. And only Eichmann was capable of providing accurate information on numbers. He had memorised almost everything. His files were memos with signs incomprehensible to others, which he always carried with him. Even his permanent deputy in Berlin, Günther, could not always provide exhaustive information. Eichmann was constantly on official trips, only rarely one could find him in Berlin in his office.

Höß recounted that Eichmann led in preparing, executing and monitoring the 'Jewish operation', and then continued:

> On Pohl's orders I went to Budapest three times in order to give an estimate on the numbers to be expected of those fit to work. On these occasions I had the opportunity to observe Eichmann in his negotiations with the Hungarian government departments and

the Hungarian army. He behaved in a very assertive and correct manner, but also amiable and courteous and was popular and well received everywhere.

(...) Eichmann was fully immersed in his task and convinced that this extermination operation was necessary.

Höß wrote that he often clashed with Eichmann with regard to delaying transports – most of the time to no avail. Eichmann viewed the final solution as his life's work. 'Considerations of difficulties were unknown to him, he had learned that from the RL SS.'

In this context the opinions that Eichmann voiced about Höß and how the former commander of Auschwitz assessed Eichmann are of interest, for the latter was the one organising the transports to the death camps, especially to Auschwitz, and so had to co-ordinate these closely with him. In the book *Auschwitz. Zeugnisse und Berichte*, co-edited by Hermann Langbein, Eichmann is quoted with the following remarks:

> Höß impressed me because he contrasted pleasantly – at least in my eyes – with the appearance of many an SS drawing room officer. He went about in a casual field shirt. When I visited him, we climbed into his car, drove to any area of his camp or outside, he showed me his new buildings, his administration, his difficulties. Within his administration he had employed prisoners of virtually all nations, even at Höß' house. (...) Höß himself was stocky, short, muscular, extremely quiet and reticent. He was one of those people whom I would count among the Northern Germans – you often had to pull the words from Höß' mouth. He showed no passions, he hardly drank, mainly out of courtesy, he was more or less a social smoker.[92]

Hermann Langbein, a prisoner at Auschwitz, reminds us that Eichmann spoke about Höß in Argentina, when he dictated his biography on tape:

> That Höß as a person suffered from his work, which included the task of physically destroying opponents, I heard from his own mouth, for – as if it was to his own consolation – he once said to me, when we were at his residence (the furniture SS natural timber style, clean, simple, but cosy and nice), that a few days ago the RL had visited the camp, also the physical extermination of our opponents, from the gassing to the cremation. The RL had said in Höß' presence to these SS men: 'These are battles which our future generations will no longer have to fight.' He, Eichmann, gathered that Höß was not representing a bulldog-like, uncomplicated, brutal type of concentration camp commander, but that Höß was a man who was accustomed to sit in judgement on himself and to give account to himself on what he was doing.[93]

This statement stands in stark contrast to the assessment by the Minister for Armament, Albert Speer. He pointed out in his book *Der Slavenstaat* that improvements were made in the Auschwitz labour camp when its commander, Höß, was relieved by SS Senior Storm Command Leader Arthur Liebehenschel: 'So depending on the personal attitude of the individual, much could be turned to good or bad account. When Höß took his place again, the catastrophic conditions were soon restored.'[94] This is confirmed by Hermann Langbein, who spoke of two currents within the SS: 'The one wanted to eliminate all Jews if possible at once, the others wanted to exploit their labour as long as possible. It was a noticeable relief for the camp when in November 1943 the commander Höß was relieved by Liebehenschel. Höß had campaigned fanatically for the death machinery functioning as well as possible. Liebehenschel eased the camp terror, stopped the worst punitive measures.'[95] This also corresponds with the description by SS Senior Company Leader Hans Schillhorn: 'Höß went rigorously against the prisoners and also the SS men.'[96]

Eichmann's statements are important sources, providing information on Höß, but at the same time they serve Eichmann's aim of lessening his own guilt. Hannah Arendt said, for example, that the authorities of the Nazi regime all had the same ambition: to kill as many Jews as possible. After the war everybody wanted to 'keep out' his department at the expense of all others: 'So at least Eichmann explains to himself the fact that the commander of Auschwitz, Rudolf Höß, accused him in his notes of certain things he claims he never committed, if only because he had not been in a position to commit them. Without hesitation he admitted that Höß certainly did not want to put the blame on him for personal reasons, their relations had been of a friendly nature; he merely claimed – yet in vain – that Höß had wanted to exonerate his own office, the Central Economic-Administrative Office, and therefore to foist off all blame on the RSHA.'[97] The collaboration between the SS and the companies was excellent: Höß reported in his statements of the best societal relations with the representatives of the I.G. Farben works.[98]

During interrogation Eichmann said that Höß had been amused by his discomfort in the face of a 'selection' of a transport that had arrived shortly before, i.e. the 'separation of Jews deemed fit to work from those viewed as unsuitable and thus had been condemned to instant death'.[99]

'Eichmann and Höß had discussed the execution of the extermination. (...) In Israel he [Eichmann] declared in a note to his defence counsel that he had to prove to the inveterate liar Höß (...) "that I had nothing to do at all with him and his gas chambers."[100] On the other hand, Höß stated 'that even Eichmann, who was "certainly of robust constitution", had no inclination to switch positions with me'.[101] Furthermore, Höß had attempted in his memoirs written during his Polish imprisonment to paint a disturbing picture of Eichmann in the years 1942/43 and to find out Eichmann's 'innermost, true conviction regarding this "final solution".'[102]

Höß possibly painted Eichmann's picture darker than it was in reality in order to let his own scruples appear more convincing.[103]

On 13 November 1944 the special commissioner in Hungary, SS General Edmund von Veesemayer, informed the Foreign Office that the evacuation of the Jews was taking its scheduled course. 'On the same day Veesemayer's telegram was sent, a group of high SS officers on their journey from Vienna to Budapest encountered one of the marching columns. The officers, among them Rudolf Höß, who in the meantime had transferred to the WVHA, and SS Senior Group Leader Hans Jüttner, chief of staff of the SS Central Leadership Office, were horrified. Having arrived at Budapest, they protested forcefully with Winkelmann against the marches and demanded their termination. Höß, of all people, pointed out that Himmler had announced a "different orientation" no longer intending the slaughter of Jews.'[104]

'Hence, Eichmann was asked by Gideon Hausner, the Israeli chief prosecutor in the trial, whether he viewed anybody involved in the murder of Jews as criminal, for example Höß. Eichmann answered: "He was an unhappy man." He tried under all circumstances to avoid denouncing Höß as a criminal, as he knew exactly that this would fall back onto him sooner or later.'[105]

In contrast, Höß stated that the gassing of Russian prisoners of war had had an extremely calming effect on him, 'as in the foreseeable future the mass extermination of the Jews had to begin and still neither Eichmann nor I had a clear idea of the manner of killing these masses which we had to expect'.[106] And in a later passage he wrote:

> Even Mildner[107] and Eichmann, both certainly of 'robust constitution', had no inclination at all to switch positions with me. Nobody envied me my task. With Eichmann I spoke often and exhaustively about all that was connected to the final solution of the Jewish question, albeit without ever revealing my internal agonies. I tried to find out from Eichmann his innermost, truest conviction regarding this 'final solution', by all means. Yet even under the most advanced influence of alcohol – just among ourselves – he advocated with virtual obsession the total extermination of all Jews within reach. Without mercy, cold as ice, we had to carry out the extermination as quickly as possible. Any consideration, even the slightest, would

come back to roost later. In view of this hard persistence I had to bury my human inhibitions most deeply.[108]

Such human feelings seemed to him like treason against the Führer.

The Eichmann Protocols

Eichmann explained to the Israeli captain Avner Less, interrogating him in Jerusalem, that he inspected the extermination camps on 'Gestapo-Müller's orders for the first time in Auschwitz in 1941 and also met Höß there for the first time.[109] He did not convey any orders to Höß on that occasion. Outside the camp they did not meet, and he had not had a personal relationship to Höß. He had read that Höß had written of 4 million Jews murdered in Auschwitz, but considered this number too high. He never spoke about numbers with Höß. Höß had once merely spoken of 'his installations' in which he could kill 10,000 Jews per day. Another time he had met Höß in Katowice. He had been with SS Standard Leader Mildner, the chief of the Gestapo in Katowice. Höß had joined them and they visited an 'embarrassing restaurant' with whose owner Mildner was acquainted. In Auschwitz the people always kept a three-feet distance from him, Eichmann, as did Höß at the beginning, because they did not wish to reveal their hand.

Referring to Höß' statements before the Nuremberg Military Tribunal, Eichmann said that he could not have known the number given there of 2 million murdered, only Höß, 'for he was the man receiving the transports, not I'. If Höß had stated that he, Eichmann, had conveyed an order according to which gold teeth had to be pried from the corpses and the hair of the women had to be cut, then this was unbelievable. And he swore that this was not true. Höß had made something up.

The allegation by Avner Less that, according to Höß, he had been looking for a gas that was easy to supply and did not require specific installations, Eichmann refuted determinedly:

> This matter is simply invented in the largest part of the statements. I see now that he was solely concerned to leave out his own central office, the SS Central Economic-Administrative Office, from all these matters; especially with regards to the technical details, with which the Gestapo Office had had nothing to do. He wants to exonerate the technical departments responsible in the SS Central Economic-Administrative Office and spare them for reasons unknown to me, but generally known in themselves. I have never discussed this matter – and I swear any oath on this, Captain Sir – in any way with Höß.[110]

On 6 June 1960 Less confronted Eichmann with the following:

> In the English edition of camp commander Rudolf Höß' book much
> is written about you that is missing from the German edition. I have
> translated it for you and will read from it to you: 'I met Eichmann,
> after I had received from the Reich Leader SS the orders for the
> extermination of the Jews, when the former visited me at Auschwitz
> in order to discuss the further details of the extermination process
> with me. Eichmann was a lively, active man in his thirties and
> always full of energy. He always made new plans and was constantly
> looking for innovations and improvements. He could never rest. He
> was obsessed with the Jewish question and with the order given for
> the final solution. He had to constantly make immediate and oral
> reports to the RL SS regarding the preparations and execution of the
> individual operations. Eichmann was completely convinced that if
> he managed to destroy the biological foundation of the Jews in the
> East, then Judaism as a whole would never recover from this blow.'[111]

The fate of the Councillor of Commerce Storfer of the Vienna Central
Office for Immigration seemed to concern Eichmann in a special manner.
He probably wanted to demonstrate that he actually had nothing against
Jews. At least the former served him to prove his 'innocence' and his
'good' relationship to this Jewish prisoner. Eichmann said he received
a telegram from Höß in which Storfer, now a prisoner in Auschwitz,
urgently asked to speak with him. To Höß' information that Storfer had
been assigned to a labour block, he replied: 'Storfer does not need to
work!', which Höß did not accept. Eichmann said he would compose an
official memo, according to which Storfer should maintain the narrow
pebble paths in the garden complex of the commandant's headquarters
with a broom and had the right to sit on one of the benches at any time.
He asked him if this was alright with him, as a result of which Storfer
and he had shaken hands. 'Then he received the broom and sat on the
bench. This was a great inner joy for me. When I returned once more
from Hungary, I heard that Storfer had been shot.'[112]

In Israeli imprisonment Eichmann wrote his 1,200-page memoirs
with the title *Götzen [Idols]*, which were made accessible in 2006 by the
Israeli government. Fundamentally new insights into the extermination
policy of the National Socialists could not be found, instead Eichmann
played down his own role. Therefore only those passages that concern
the relationship of the two mass murderers Eichmann and Höß will be
mentioned here:

> In spring 1940 I received from my immediate superior, the lieutenant
> general of the police Müller, the order to travel to Auschwitz and

to report to him on the actions against the Jews by the commander of the Auschwitz concentration camp. Höß, the commander, said to me that he was killing with hydrogen cyanide acid. Circles of pressed felt were drenched with this poison and thrown inside the rooms where the Jews were gathered. This poison had an instantaneous fatal effect. The corpses were burnt on an iron grate outside. He led me to a shallow pit wherein a large number of corpses were currently burning. It was a horrifying image to my eyes. Only softened by the smoke and the enormous flames. He used some kind of oil for the burning. (...)

The untruths that Höß stated about me after 1945 are pathetic. Yet they can be easily recognised as such, partly through his own statements, as he gave a different report elsewhere, if one makes the effort to study his statements, supplementing this with the literature and documents for comparison.

Höß said, for example, that I had visited him in June 1941, shortly after Himmler's visit to Auschwitz, and that he learned all the details with regards to the alternatives for killing from me. He says that I spoke with him about gassing by exhaust fumes. Yet that such a possibility existed, or rather filled the heads of some SS and police generals, I myself only learned in late autumn 1941, when I was with the then major general of the police Globocnigg [sic] who was immediately subordinate to the General of the Police and of the Waffen-SS Krüger. If Höß further says that I had told him details about the plans for deportation, then this could have been around 20th March 1942 at the earliest, for around that time the secretary of state in the Foreign Office Weizsäcker permitted deportations from France for the first time. Admittedly, the German ambassador in Paris, Abetz, had previously probed Hitler and Himmler regarding this matter; but this I only learned in late autumn 1941, too. The first deportation order going out from the West, i.e. France, Belgium and the Netherlands, concerning larger numbers, which Himmler issued via the head of department IV, was received by my department only shortly before June 1942.

Höß had already undertaken the first trial gassings in Auschwitz on 23rd September 1941, however, as it emerges from his own statements. When I came to Auschwitz for the first time, the gassings were already in process. Höß burnt the corpses on iron grates. And I had to report to Müller just on what Höß was doing; this was the reason why he gave me the order to travel to Auschwitz.

According to his own statement, Höß had only started burning corpses on iron grates in summer 1942, though. He then further mentions that I had spoken to him about the shootings in the East. Yet I only experienced this for the first time in the winter of 1941/42.

I myself recall seeing blooming flowers in the gardens of Auschwitz. It thus must have been the late spring season. Höß was mistaken by a whole calendar year regarding my first visit, to say the least.

Müller did not give me any orders to be conveyed to him. No other person gave me such or similar instructions, either.

I myself never gave him advice on the technical realisation of the gassing, on the contrary I was jolly glad if I did not have to see or hear anything of such matters. I had nothing further to do with these issues than to execute those wretched orders given by my boss, because he wanted to be informed accurately on all these measures.

Höß was not subordinate to the Reich Security Main Office, either, but – as the documents prove clearly – to the SS Central Economic-Administrative Office. Hence he also received his orders from there.

His immediate superiors were the SS Senior Group Leader and General of the Waffen-SS Pohl and the SS Group Leader and Lieutenant General of the Waffen-SS Glücks.

Besides, it was admitted by witness statements and also by the personal declaration of Dr Sigmund Rascher, head of the medical experiments of the Luftwaffe, to a British captain, Payne-Best, that he[113] had invented the gas chambers, and presented such plans at Auschwitz.

If I had made myself noticeable even in the slightest way in this regard at that time by my quasi collaboration, then it would have been more than certain that I would have been mentioned together with many other persons concerning this during the trials after 1945. It remained reserved for Höß and in part Wisliceny to make use of such untrue claims in this area. Hereby Höß used, for greater plausibility, background material from my private life, or rather explanations of my attitude, character and such.

Generally speaking, he tried here to shift the responsibility for the events from the SS Central Economic-Administrative Office to which he belonged to the departments of the chief of Security Police and Security Service [SD] and made specific use of my person for that purpose.[114]

During the trial against Eichmann, Attorney General Gideon Hausner had, among others, the goal of illuminating the relationship between Eichmann and Höß. Hereby he pointed out lies by Eichmann and the contradiction in the widely differing characterisations:[115]

ATTORNEY GENERAL: You wrote in one passage that you were repeatedly in Auschwitz, isn't it so?

EICHMANN: Yes indeed, I have also admitted this, I was there roughly five or six times, I do not know exactly.

ATTORNEY GENERAL: And Höß showed you the entire extermination process from A to Z, correct?

EICHMANN: No, that is not correct.

ATTORNEY GENERAL: No? Höß writes this so, that is known to you …

EICHMANN: Possible, but it is not correct …

(A further question, and Eichmann changes his absolutely negative answer and admits to have seen the extermination process at Auschwitz.)

EICHMANN: Showing is not the right word. He told me of it, and in part I have seen it, namely how the corpses were burnt. That I have seen.

CAPTAIN LESS: Did Höß show you the installations?[116]

EICHMANN: Yes indeed.

EICHMANN: They were already working on it, Captain Sir, when I visited, they were already killing.

When Eichmann, under cross-examination, called Höß' description 'inaccurate' or 'untrue', the attorney general reminded him that Eichmann himself had described Höß in another context as 'punctuality and accuracy personified'.[117] Eichmann confirmed once again that this description of Höß' person was correct. Subsequently, Hausner read Höß' words about his 'friend' Adolf Eichmann:

Eichmann was equally a decided opponent of the idea to select Jews fit to work from the Jewish transports. He viewed this as a constant threat to his plan for the final solution, because of the possibility of mass escape or other events potentially arising that might enable the Jews to survive.

ATTORNEY GENERAL: Was someone who was involved in the extermination of the Jews a criminal in your eyes?

EICHMANN: He had been an unhappy man.

ATTORNEY GENERAL: Was he a criminal or not? Yes or no?

EICHMANN: I do not dare to answer this question, for I was never placed in or confronted with such a situation.

ATTORNEY GENERAL: You saw Höß who did this in Auschwitz; did you consider him at that time a criminal, a murderer?

EICHMANN: I told him that I could never do what he had been ordered to do …

ATTORNEY GENERAL: This is not my question, though. My question is whether you saw him as murderer inside?

EICHMANN: In my interior life?

ATTORNEY GENERAL: No, in your heart.

EICHMANN: This is a question that concerns me quite personally, and if I did not speak it aloud at that time, I won't speak it aloud today, for what my emotional life is telling me is a matter that I alone have to bear.

ATTORNEY GENERAL: You will have to answer that now. How did you view Höß, when you saw him murdering Jews, how did you view him, as a criminal or not?

EICHMANN: I felt sympathy and pity for him.[118]

In 1957 Eichmann had said in Argentina: 'Höß was an amiable comrade and friend to me. Höß was his own registrar concerning his fastidious bureaucratic activities. Höß was perhaps too narrow regarding his horizon in order to process the enormous Auschwitz concentration camp complex.'[119]

The Pery Broad Report

The so-called Broad report was composed in British imprisonment, and it served the then East Berlin lawyer Friedrich Karl Kaul and Joachim Noack as a basis for the 'Auschwitz documentation' *Angeklagter Nr. 6 [Defendant No. 6]*. Although due to the political interests of the former celebrity lawyer Kaul, the interpretation of the report does not hold up to academic standards, and furthermore Broad's statements, as far as they concern his emotions, have to be disregarded from any study, a core remains nevertheless that provides information on Höß, too.

Some remarks are required on Pery Broad and the credibility of his representations: after his A-levels the defendant studied at the Technical University Berlin until December 1941. Then he volunteered for the SS and in January 1942 was drafted into the infantry replacement battalion of the SS division 'North' at Wehlau in East Prussia. Since Broad was very short-sighted, he was not deployed to the front. In April 1942 he was transferred to Auschwitz concentration camp, where he initially served in the guard storm command. When scribes and interpreters were wanted for the political department, he applied and was ordered there in June 1942. Later, independent tasks, such as interrogations, were assigned to him, too. When the camp was evacuated, he took six arrested SS men to Groß-Rosen concentration camp near Wroclaw together with other SS members and absconded with a truck laden with files of the Political Department to Mittelbau concentration camp near Nordhausen in the Harz.

While it is documented in Jadwiga Bezwińska's book *Auschwitz in den Augen der SS* [Auschwitz in the eyes of the SS] that he vehemently condemned the conditions in Auschwitz, he denied knowing anything about this during the Frankfurt Auschwitz Trial.

When Broad was in the British camp for prisoners of war at Gorleben, he voluntarily reported to the commander Cornelis van het

Kaar of the British unit stationed at Gorleben. The unit was tasked with interrogating German prisoners of war. He reported that he had been in Auschwitz and could provide information on the conditions in this camp. As a consequence he was fetched from the prisoner of war camp, received a British uniform and found accommodation with the British unit. His report contains seventy-five typed pages. In addition he compiled a list of people employed at Auschwitz. He remained with the British unit, even when it was redeployed to Munsterlager on the Lüneburg Heath.

Broad had written a longer handwritten report on his experiences in Auschwitz during his short British war captivity. The commander of the British unit reported that Broad had called on him voluntarily in order to write the report.[120] Broad had required three days for this, then the report was forwarded to the headquarters of the 2nd British Army in Celle. Van het Kaar gave his opinion before the State Court Frankfurt that the report was a kind of 'confession'. Broad had wanted to relieve himself of the things he had experienced. Broad, himself a perpetrator, helped the British to the best of his abilities in the evaluation of the German prisoners of war, 'in order to potentially point out to us people who seemed suspicious to him'. According to the Frankfurt jury court, Broad's report was written down by an 'intelligent author who had been amidst the events described and did not want to conceal or whitewash anything, as far as it did not concern his person'. One could tell that the report had been composed from personal and immediate experience: 'It is clear, easy to understand and neatly arranged.'

Yet the fact is: Broad had as a member of the Political Department at Auschwitz, where he had been transferred in June 1942, participated in the mass murder of the Jewish people arriving with the transports organised by the RSHA. He was assigned to ramp duty just like the other members of the Political Department. On one occasion, a prisoner of the prisoner detail that had to load the luggage of the arriving people on the trucks secretly warned a woman on one of the arriving RSHA transports. He told her that there was gas inside the Red Cross vehicles and that they were supposed to be killed and subsequently burnt. Broad was on ramp duty at that time. The woman ran to him and explained to him that she was frightened because she was to be poisoned and killed, as a prisoner had told her. Broad let her point out the prisoner who had told her this and calmed down the woman by saying she ought not to believe him. That man was a criminal, she could see this in his protruding ears and bald head. After the woman had been removed, Broad reported the prisoner. The latter was then punished with 150 blows by stick for the 'dissemination of horror stories', to be carried out by his fellow prisoners on the orders of the SS. He died of the consequences.

Broad knew that innocent Jews were killed based solely on their descent and religion. He further knew that the extermination operations were carried out with the utmost secrecy and by deceiving the victims regarding their impending fate. Furthermore, he knew that the victims were murdered in the gas chambers in the manner described above. Finally, it was obvious to him that he himself promoted the extermination operations with his own activities – monitoring the prisoner details, monitoring the SS members, and monitoring the people selected as unfit to work.

Broad was also ordered by the head of the Political Department Grabner to the so-called emptying of the bunker and for this purpose entered the detention bunker with the other SS members. In at least two cases he was also present during shootings in the yard. His presence during these procedures together with that of other SS members was supposed to show the victims that resistance was futile from the outset. He was further supposed to cut down any potential sudden insurrection by the victims together with the other SS members. All of this Broad clearly knew.

Pery Broad was sentenced to four years in prison for joint abetting of joint murder. He was by no means as innocent as he pretended to be toward the Frankfurt judges. Helene Cougno from Greece, who was a prisoner at Auschwitz, reported that Broad carried out beatings during most of his interrogations. The prisoners expressed among themselves **their surprise that Broad, who 'was extremely intelligent and extremely educated', stooped to interrogate people in this manner.**[121]

Chapter 6

Höß as Head of Department D I

On 10 November 1943 Höß took over the tasks of head of department at D I in the SS Central Economic-Administrative Office and became formal head of this department on 1 May 1944. Under the leadership of Oswald Pohl, the WVHA consisted of five office groups, each containing several departments. The department D I – Central Office – within the office group D Concentration Camps was at first managed by Arthur Liebehenschel and was responsible for:

- D I/1: Prisoner matters
- D I/2: Communications, camp security and guard dogs
- D I/3: Motor vehicles
- D I/4: Weapons and tools
- D I/5: Training of the troop

Pohl had allegedly given Höß the choice to become either commander of Sachsenhausen or head of department at D I. Since Höß, according to his own statements, did not want to manage another camp by any means, he decided upon the executive position in the office D I of the WVHA. Here he controlled, among other things, the operation of gas trucks. Ernst Philipp Schultz, head of the motor vehicle department in DI, stated in his interrogation on 9 April 1947 that his immediate superior had been Senior Storm Command Leader Höß. Schultz was responsible for a motor vehicle pool of 800 vehicles, to which also belonged the notorious gas trucks. Requests for these particularly perfidious murder instruments could be authorised by inspector Glücks or Höß.

Schultz put – as he called it – 'his foot in it' on one occasion, when in August/September 1944 a request for 200 litres of benzine came in for the 'House Elbe' signed by Glücks or Höß. Upon enquiry it was said that he should not meddle in matters that were not his concern.

171

House Elbe was a house near Meißen where special prisoners were kept – French officers who should receive special treatment, according to a Führer's order. Schultz was mistaken in so far that in the outpost camp Meißen-Neuhirschstein, a sub-camp of the concentration camp Flossenbürg with the code name 'House Elbe', 150 prisoners were actually incarcerated from October 1943 onward, predominantly Italians from Dachau and after that many smaller groups of prisoners, among them others from the outpost Dresden SS Pioneers Barracks. In December 1943 220 prisoners were at Neuhirschstein, half of them construction specialists. The most high-profile 'prisoner of honour' was the Belgian king Leopold III with his family, who were kept there in greatest secrecy.

Höß had a certain freedom in shaping his activities and was often on official trips. Together with SS Standard Leader Maurer he could achieve much, he writes in his *Autobiographical Notes*. In view of the desolate situation in the overcrowded concentration camps he said:

> If the prisoners in Auschwitz had been immediately brought into the gas chambers, they would have been spared much suffering. (…) If according to my view expressed repeatedly in Auschwitz only the healthiest and strongest Jews had been selected, fewer persons fit to work could have been reported, but then we would have had some truly fit ones for a long time. So we had high numbers on paper, in reality however, high percentages had to be subtracted in most of the cases. They were only a burden to the camps, took space and food of those fit to work, accomplished nothing, indeed their presence rendered many of those fit to work unfit.[1]

Pity looks different.

It was part of Höß' tasks as 'D I' to inspect camps, among others also Bergen-Belsen. The commander there, SS Senior Storm Command Leader Haas, Höß called a 'sinister, devious man' who acted as he pleased. In the character studies written down in his Cracow prison, Höß stayed true to his judgement of his fellow perpetrators: Haas had no great notion of concentration camps. When towards the end of the war during the evacuation of Auschwitz a large part of the prisoners was transferred to Bergen-Belsen, conditions arose that even he, Höß, who 'was used to quite a lot from Auschwitz had to call gruesome'.[2]

From the period when Höß was head of department in the Central Economic-Administrative Office in Oranienburg dates a letter by Pohl to Himmler, in which the layout and occupancy of the concentration camp Auschwitz is listed in great detail. The reason for this was an overview of the security measures that had been undertaken after the division of Auschwitz into three independent camps and for the case of a mass escape or insurrection, which Himmler seemed to seriously fear:

> *Camp I* contained the enormous men's camp and had at that time an occupancy of about 16,000 prisoners. It was surrounded by a fence and wire obstacles charged with high voltage. In addition there were guard towers equipped with machine guns.
> Circa three kilometres away was *Camp II* with 15,000 male and 21,000 female prisoners. Of them, 15,000 were unfit to work. *Camp III* consisted of all outposts existing as far as Upper Silesia near the industrial works, which were in part very far away from each other. At the time of the report there were 14 outposts with altogether 15,000 male prisoners. The largest outpost was that of I.G. Farben Industries with 7,000 prisoners.
> (…) Of the total number of 67,000 prisoners, those at the outposts (15,000) and those hospitalised (18,000) have to be dropped if the question of risk by a potential insurrection or escape is to be contemplated for Upper Silesia. Then 34,000 prisoners remain who might be considered for an insurrection and would pose a risk, if the security measures were inadequate.[3]

Pohl then detailed in his letter that for Camps I and II, including the members of the command's headquarters, 2,300 SS members could be assigned, for the outpost camps 650 guard details. In addition a police company with 130 men was supposed to be deployed. Besides guard towers and electric wire fencing, a line of bunkers manned by SS members had been created as an internal ring. In the 'case of insurrection' another external ring was to be formed by Wehrmacht units. In this 'external' ring labour camp of I.G. Farben was included, at which around 15,000 civilians were employed apart from the prisoners.

In the event of mass escapes, large-scale manhunts were to be initiated under the direction of the criminal police headquarters in Katowice; finally Luftwaffe units stationed at Auschwitz with a strength of 1,000 men were additionally available, if a mass escape did not coincide with an aerial attack.

The cause for Himmler's fears that the concentration camp might be insufficiently secure was, among others, the fact that due to a dearth of material the 'wire obstacle' around the entire area of the Auschwitz camp demanded by the Reich Leader SS could not be erected. The Central Construction Management had informed Höß of this in October 1943.[4]

Höß wrote about the heads and functions of the individual departments within the office group D of the Central Economic-Administrative Office in detail in the character studies, namely the head of the office group and the individual heads of department – Eicke, Glücks, Liebehenschel, Maurer and Kammler.

Chapter 7

The I.G. Farben Works at Auschwitz

The importance concentration camps held for the German war economy in general has already been briefly described. This was none more true than for Auschwitz, for here the I.G. Farbenindustrie [Dye Industry Syndicate] established Buna [a brand of synthetic rubber] and fuel works for whose construction and operation tens of thousands of prisoners were required. Höß was hence one of the most important partners for the I.G. Farben representatives, as he had to create essential foundations for the establishment of the work, for example to provide a sufficient number of prisoners for the workforce.

It should be pointed out that other German enterprises carried out production at the Auschwitz camp and thereby exploited prisoners. Among them was, as is less known, primarily the Krupp AG from Essen. Some sources say that Krupp maintained a factory for detonators at Auschwitz, but that is incorrect. Rather, members of the Krupp AG, the Central Economic-Administrative Office, and experts discussed with Höß on 16 February 1942 the construction of a manufacturing plant for automatic light anti-aircraft weapons.[1] The first major meeting then took place on 28 August 1942 and included Höß, SS Head Storm Leader Schmincke, Captain Rudolf Gogarten (a chartered engineer) of the High Command of the Army, 'the gentlemen Lang and Gütling' of the Krupp AG and Senior Storm Leader Pfeil of the Central Economic-Administrative Office, in order to inspect the area for the intended anti-aircraft weapons factory.[2]

It can be surmised from an overview of orders that the Krupp works rapidly took shape. On 7 March 1943 Höß received the news from the Central Construction Management (ZLB) that the head of office group C of the WHVA had ordered the construction of three residential

174

barracks for circa 200 core workers of the Krupp AG. The following week, on 14 March 1943, the ZLB requested from Höß prisoners that were supposed to work on Sundays in order to be assigned to the 'building project Krupp'. Several meetings regarding armament constructions for Krupp followed in which Höß always took part. At the end of March 1943 Höß agreed to the construction of accommodation for Krupp employees, and finally in April 1943 he arranged the accommodation of 300 female Krupp employees in the House of the Waffen-SS at Auschwitz. According to the information in the Krupp Archive in Essen provided to the author in July 2014, the production of anti-aircraft cannon at Auschwitz did not commence after all, though.

The work of the I.G. Farbenindustrie in Auschwitz was on a larger scale. First and foremost Reich Marshall Hermann Göring, plenipotentiary for the four-year plan, had advocated the construction of this works for the production of synthetic rubber and fuel. He was aided by Heinrich Himmler, with all his possibilities as Reich Leader SS. During the Second World War the Nazi economy and war machinery could only be maintained with the aid of synthetic benzine, and this came 100 per cent from I.G. Farben factories, which also provided the vast majority of the explosives for the Wehrmacht.

At the end February 1941 the chairman of the I.G. Farben, Otto Ambros, received from the plenipotentiary for special issues in chemical production, Carl Krauch, who was at the same time 'commissioner for the four-year plan', a letter in which the latter informed him that the Auschwitz works had the highest priority in the new arrangement of priority levels issued by General Field Marshal Wilhelm Keitel. He expected of Ambros that he would do his utmost 'to commence production as quickly as possible without regard to costs of any kind'. In addition to the production of Buna[3] a fuel production complex was to be built with a capacity of 755,000 tons a year. Besides the high-performance fuel, raw materials for the manufacture of special ammunition and plastic compounds for the war economy were to be produced at Auschwitz. It was decided to establish this works, Auschwitz-Monowitz, about 9 kilometres east of Auschwitz and 56 kilometres west of Cracow. Gleiwitz, 60 kilometres away, was the nearest large German settlement.

How important the Auschwitz I.G. Farben works was for the war industry can be recognised from the fact that on 24 March 1941 during a construction meeting at Ludwigshafen the agenda was decisively set. Project manager Walter Dürrfeld reported on an encounter with SS Senior Storm Leader Martin Wolf from the Central Office Reich Leadership SS. The latter had promised 'that 700 men from the prisoners in the concentration camp Auschwitz can be allocated to the construction site':

> There is a commitment that the Central Office Reich Leadership SS will avail itself to effect an exchange within the concentration camps of the SS in such a way that specialist workers from the Reich will be transferred to Auschwitz.
>
> All free forces in Auschwitz have to be registered without exception.
>
> The camp command (Höß) takes responsibility for the guarding of the construction site.
>
> If possible, the establishment of workshops within the camp is intended.
>
> The administration of the concentration camp will be instructed to address the question of how far it is possible to take on the food provisioning of the construction site as well.[4]

As a witness during the 1st Frankfurt Auschwitz Trial, the board member of I.G. Farben, Otto Ambros, could supposedly barely remember the events around the establishment of the Auschwitz I.G. Farben works. Documents prove, however, that he was constantly involved in the plans and in the setting up of the works, or was at least informed on all goings on. Indeed, he confirmed that he had chosen the site for the I.G. Buna works. For him – so he said – purely technical considerations had been crucial. It had demanded that the Buna works had to be built in the farthest possible site in the east so that it was safe from aerial attacks. Furthermore, much water was needed for the work, which could be drawn from the Vistula. Finally, there was coal and lime in the region. When Ambros argued in favour of the location of Monowitz, he claimed that he did not know of the existence of the Auschwitz concentration camp yet. The responsible labour bureau Bielitz had, according to him, given their assurance that sufficient 'free' labour forces existed. There had never been talk of the possibility of drafting prisoners. These statements are rather implausible, especially since Ambros was in the loop during each phase of construction, even regarding the tiniest details. Toward the Allies he had admitted that a collaboration with the concentration camp had become necessary for the deliveries of gravel, equipment and similar. Later, Ambros no longer wanted to recall any of this. The responsible chief engineer, Maximilian Faust, had advised him in April 1941 to visit the camp commander. Höß had given him a tour through the camp, which at that time had still been very small. He saw the barracks block, the kitchen, the workshops, the tailor shop and the carpentry shop:

> In passing I was shown the crematorium not in use at that time. I saw the barbed wire charged with electricity, the prisoners in

the striped prisoner garments with their shorn heads, but did not have such a terrible impression of the camp, as I had expected after what was generally heard about the concentration camp at Dachau. The prisoners wore triangles of different colours on their clothing. When I asked Höß about their meaning, he explained to me that these badges showed the reason for which the respective prisoner was in the concentration camp. As far as I recall, I saw during this first visit to Auschwitz professional criminals and homosexuals. Afterwards Höß invited me to a simple dinner.[5]

During this first encounter with Höß a partition of the joint interests was determined, namely that west of the Sola River should be the area of interest of the concentration camp and east of the Sola that of I.G. Farben. With regards to the labour deployment of prisoners, Höß informed him that the I.G. Works Auschwitz did not qualify for this at a larger scale for now, since the concentration camp needed the prisoners itself for its agricultural expansion and so on.

During the 1st Frankfurt Auschwitz Trial, Ambros stated that he met with Höß three times, for example at the inaugural meeting in which roughly twenty departments took part. There he became acquainted with the commander:

The concentration camp had workshops. These workshops were supposed to help in part by taking on metalwork, and in part by carpentry and joinery. The concentration camp operated a large gravel pit. The camp further had a 'Woodworking Workshops GmbH'. The suggestion during this meeting was that I should visit those workshops, which happened a few days later. Through the tour by Höß I got to know the workshops and agreed with him that these should provide carpentry and joinery work, gravel deliveries from the gravel pit and furthermore a medical vehicle in the case of accidents.

Around that time I still had the impression that the whole assistance of the concentration camp was supposed to consist of providing services by these workshops in favour of the works just starting up. It was an almost impossible task to set up a works in the East during the second year of war.

At another encounter we discussed that the concentration camp would possibly be relocated. The Reich Railways wanted to have the premises for a large shunting yard, the town for its expansion.[6]

To the question of what agreements had been made with him regarding the allocation of prisoners, Ambros replied that he recalled that talks had been held regarding their transportation, the additional food and their accommodation, but not with him. Apart from that, prisoners were always assigned by the responsible labour bureau. In contrast, Walter Dürrfeld, Deputy Economic Manager at Auschwitz, had declared that there had been two channels of acquiring prisoners: one via the office of the labour bureau at the Auschwitz camp and the second was the direct route to Höß, which had been created on the orders of the Reich Office for Economic Expansion.

On Ambros' instigation, a staff member of Maximilian Faust made contact with the concentration camp administration, which promised the allocation of up to 600 prisoners. They were required for the erection of a barracks complex that was meant to serve as accommodation for the future I.G. Farben workforce. At first, however, I.G. Farben employed up to 150 men, at this early stage still 'free' labourers. When this did not suffice, the labour bureau explained to the chief project manager Gustav Murr: 'Then only prisoners remain potentially for employment until we fetch further free workers.'[7] Thereupon Murr negotiated with Höß and his adjutant, SS Head Storm Leader Erich Frommhagen, in order to arrange the transportation and the guarding of these prisoners. Murr additionally received lockers and beds for the workers' barracks. He showed himself to disagree with the forced resettlement of the Auschwitz population at Sosnowitz. He protested against this with the mayor, as he could have made use of them as a workforce.

If the crucial prerequisites for the construction of the I.G. Farben works were discussed, Höß took part in the meetings, for example in a detailed meeting at the Auschwitz camp on Friday, 28 March 1941. In the minutes the following people were listed:[8]

> Storm Command Leader Höß, Storm Command Leader Krause, Head Storm Leader Burböck, adjutant of the inspector of the concentration camps Senior Leader Glücks
>
> Storm Leader Schwarz (general work detail leader) and several gentlemen of the staff
>
> From the German Equipment Works GmbH: Senior Storm Command Leader Maurer
>
> From the I.G. Farbenindustrie corporation: chief engineer Faust and chartered engineer Flöter

At this meeting it was clarified in which manner the workshops of the concentration camp could be utilised by I.G. Farben. They were incorporated in the German Equipment Works and could primarily provide the following:

> Barracks and barracks furniture, windows and doors for any type of building, plumbing parts (roof gutters and gutter pipes),

installation of heating systems and sanitary facilities, furniture for apartments and offices in all design, concrete goods (posts and slabs for enclosures), mattresses, palliasses, head rests and so on.

In view of the immense demand by the future I.G. Farben works it was deemed necessary to expand the concentration camp workshops. Furthermore, the delivery of gravel by the concentration camp was agreed:

> The concentration camp already had three mechanical excavators. A crushing and stone plant was to be erected on the banks of the Sola. Thereto a light railway with 15 to 20 km of tracks should be built. On this railway all prisoners employed at the building site were supposed to be transported, too.
>
> Bricks were to be delivered by the East German Construction Materials Works Bielitz O/S.
>
> A telephone line was to be installed over a distance of 5 km to the concentration camp.

The previous evening an intense talk between Höß and the I.G. project manager Walter Dürrfeld had already taken place. They spoke of the 'spirit of an excellent comradeship and the will (...) to support each other to a great extent and to carry out the given tasks in all circumstances and promptly and on schedule'.

Early on, Dürrfeld had sat down with Höß to determine the details of the support. In a construction meeting at Ludwigshafen he informed the company management on the results. According to this, Höß had [shown] himself 'very willing to support the project management to the best of his abilities. For the year 1941 Faust requires approximately 1,000 unskilled labourers who can be provided by the camp.' As the upper limit, Höß named 1,500 during this year:

> In the moment it is not yet possible to accommodate more prisoners. In the year 1942, however, this number can be increased to 3,000 to 4,000. Höß asks that the project management supports him in the erection of barracks by allotting timber shares. This support Höß shall receive, as well as building metal. The deployment of prisoners initially takes place in groups supervised by kapos. Each kapo supervises roughly 20 men.[9]

They also agreed that the concentration camp, operating three mechanical diggers at the Sola River, should initially deliver 400 cubic metres of gravel per day. It was considered expedient to build a light railway for the transportation to the I.G. Farben construction site. For one cubic metre of gravel the concentration camp should receive

3.30 Reichsmark, a price that Dürrfeld called 'manageable'. In order to protect an area of 30,000 acres controlled by the SS between Vistula and Sola from flooding, Höß promised the construction of a dam. Furthermore, it should be possible to call upon the existing workshops inside the concentration camp for the completion of orders by the local I.G. construction management.[10]

During the inaugural meeting of the Auschwitz works on 7 April 1941 in Katowice attended by high-ranking representatives of I.G. Farben, for example Otto Ambros, as well as ministry staff and members of the High Command of the Wehrmacht, it was determined to first complete a Buna factory 'at the highest speed'. The basis for this was provided by the Upper Silesian hard coal as fuel or as raw material for various syntheses. The workforce during the construction period was to comprise 8,000 construction workers and 4,000 metal workers at peak times and later 5,000 to 15,000 men. Words of praise were heaped upon camp commander Höß. It was put about that for the construction period they could count on extensive support by the Auschwitz camp based on an order of the Reich Leader SS. And further: 'The camp commander, Storm Command Leader Höß, had already made preparations for the deployment of his forces. The concentration camp provides prisoners for the construction work, craftsmen for locksmith work and carpentry, supports the work in the provisioning of food for the construction workforce and will carry out the delivery of the construction site with gravel and other construction materials.'

For the work deployment it was determined:

> In principle the complete resettlement of the Polish population from the area in question is intended. The aim of the Reich Leader is to establish here a model for the Eastern settlement, whereby the main focus will be the settlement of specially qualified Germans. In order to avoid a denudation of the eastern territories the resettlement of the Poles will only take place step by step.[11]

Shortly after the inaugural meeting, Ambros recorded that he felt reassured about the project. To the directors Fritz ter Meer and Strauß he wrote on 12 April 1941:

> A certain resistance by lowly desk jockeys could be eliminated quickly. Dr Eckell[12] acquitted himself very well in this matter and furthermore our new friendship with the SS proves to be very beneficial. On the occasion of a dinner given by the command of the concentration camp we further determined all the measures concerning the involvement of the truly excellent management of the concentration camp in favour of the Buna works.

Höß had to support the project in many ways. Time and again he was included in the plans of I.G. Farben. For example, at a site consultation meeting on 6 May 1941 at Ludwigshafen, the I.G. Farben management was concerned with site development for the construction of a settlement with 1,000 apartments: 'It seems advantageous to also call upon the camp commander Höß for support regarding the approval of our settlement plans,' the minutes recorded.[13]

On 26 May 1941 a meeting took place of, among others Ambros, Dürrfeld and Höß, having travelled all the way to Leuna. The focus was the 'provision of prisoners':

It was recorded:

> The commander stressed the order he had received from Reich Leader SS to provide us under all circumstances with prisoners up to the number of 4,500 men. He will perform this task until the requested deadline of mid-June in any case, even if their own operations have to take a back seat. All his dispositions regarding the female Jewish prisoners were aimed at that. We would thus like to request these forces according to demand. In a detailed conversation on the quality of the prisoners I developed the following conditions:
>
> > Firstly, strong prisoners fit to work; secondly, daily the same prisoners for the same workplace; thirdly, greater liberty in assigning the prisoners; fourth, incentivising the prisoners to better performance.
> >
> > Regarding the first point, the commander promised to take care of a good selection. He would have to be actually informed on any complaints. Yet he had to admit that his staff of junior leaders was inadequate and partly bad. For the second item he promised likewise to instruct his staff to pay attention during deployment that no greater shifts occurred in the allocation of prisoners in cases of sickness notification, which often were extremely numerous in bad weather.
> >
> > Regarding the third: our suggestions to man the entire fence with a cordon and to let the prisoners work freely inside the fence he considered only manageable if sharp controls are carried out at the gates. In particular each person passing a gate would need to remove any head coverings (shorn hair).
> >
> > Regarding the fourth point we suggested a primitive piecework system (jokingly called FFF system)[14] was suggested to the commander and we asked for his support in its realisation. The commander considered the system definitely doable. We agreed to address all these open questions in the week after Pentecost and to speak with the adjutant and the work deployment leader. The realisation was to be put into action immediately.

Höß fulfilled the demand for 'strong' and fit prisoners as far as possible. I.G. Farben representative chief engineer Max Faust wrote in his weekly report 90/91 for the period from 8 to 21 February 1943:

> Visit of Senior Storm [sic] Leader Maurer. We discussed the numerous enforcements of Camp IV. Senior Storm Command Leader Maurer promised to increase the number of prisoners to 4,000 shortly, perhaps even to 4,500. The deployment of these numbers can only take place if they are employed behind the work's fence and if the area is cordoned off, considering the low number of guard posts. It was hence decided to fence in the entire section for synthesis. Further the Senior Storm Command Leader Mauer promised that all weak prisoners can be removed so that an almost equal performance to that of a German unskilled labourer can be guaranteed.[15]

For the prisoners concerned, removal by I.G. Farben usually meant death.

On the other hand, Faust complained several times to Höß that in total twelve prisoners had been shot because of petty reasons, for example the accidental stepping over the cordon. Equally, Faust supported the cause of two master craftsmen who had been arrested 'for the abetting of prisoners'. In this case Faust made several phone calls to Höß in order to finally free the two men.

It should be added that Gerhard Maurer, most recently SS Standard Leader, was primarily responsible for the labour assignment of concentration camp prisoners, whereby the talk here was always just about 'protective custody prisoners'. SS Group Leader Oswald Pohl, who as head of the SS Central Economic-Administrative Office had a particular interest in the construction of the work, stated on 28 August 1947 in an affidavit that he had had on average once a week a staff meeting with Maurer, during which he was presented with compilations of numbers and deployment locations.[16] After Himmler had ordered the expansion of the labour deployment to the private industry, Maurer also had to visit these firms and to maintain contact with them, just like with the I.G. Farben Works at Auschwitz.

Although some aspects spoke for the location of Auschwitz, the I.G. Farben experts were rather dissatisfied on the whole.[17] The work was more difficult than in other parts of the Reich, they complained, as the start of construction had fallen into a period when the economy was strained as never before. The location was considered especially favourable in economic and technical terms with respect to safety from aerial attacks as well as 'for reasons of strengthening Germanness in the east', but enormous distances had to be bridged, which in particular with the beginning of the eastern campaign and the resulting strained traffic situation led time and again to unexpected delays. Further they complained:

> The works is built on formerly Galician ground with a very low level of civilisation and culture compared to Reich territory. No water supply, no organised removal of faecal waste, no inns, no educational establishment, no German cinema in the 'town' of Auschwitz. There is a lack of suitable accommodation for the workforce participating in the construction, no shopping facilities etc. Although the regional leader and the district president, the commander of the concentration camp and the head of the district authority support us in a vigorous manner to a great extent, the particular difficulties in this newly incorporated region make it awkward, if not impossible, to meet the demands of the construction site.

Nevertheless, they succeeded in fulfilling the workload to a large extent. For Spring 1942 it was deemed necessary to increase 'the workforce from currently [October 1941] 2,700 men (thereof 10 per cent Germans, 50 per cent concentration camp prisoners) to 10,000 men during the months of March to May 1942 (thereof at least 3,000 Germans and 4,000 voluntary civilian foreigners, preferably Poles and Slovaks)'. Furthermore, the required barracks camps with all the fixtures (kitchen, beds, blankets, linen etc.) for a capacity of 15,000 beds were to be provided. For the accommodation of the office staff and qualified construction and assembly workforce of the construction companies and the I.G. parent plants (foremen, technicians, typists) a residential complex with rooms for single and multiple occupancy for roughly 1,500 people was to be erected.

In summer 1941 – after the erection of the main camp Auschwitz I – the camp administration started to deploy prisoners daily to Monowitz following an agreement with I.G. Farben. These had to march on foot to their worksite at first, but were later brought in cattle wagons with 100 men each to the premises in the morning and back in the evening. On the insistence of I.G. Farben, a prisoner camp was established directly on the works site in 1942.

The close collaboration described between SS and industry was by no means an exception, but I.G. Farben received numerous freedoms. For the armament industry, or rather the conduct of the war, the works planned at Auschwitz were of essential importance. SS Senior Group

Leader Pohl, mighty head of the WVHA, submitted the following affidavit regarding this:

> In deviation from the generally valid rules in individual cases, arrangements were made which took the special circumstances of the operations into consideration. This was, for instance, the case with the Monowitz camp situated in the immediate vicinity of the Buna works in Auschwitz. This was built in 1942 at the expense of the I.G. Farbenindustrie to accommodate the prisoners assigned to the construction of the work by the Auschwitz concentration camp on Göring's order. The construction of this accommodation became necessary, after the initial daily transportation of prisoners from and to the Auschwitz concentration camp could no longer be carried out for traffic reasons. Besides the erection of the appropriate camp, including accommodation for the required guard details, I.G. Farben also took care of the food supply.[18]

This statement is instructive of Pohl's mindset: he took the view that the prisoners were not cheap, but to the contrary expensive workers. He stated as a reason for this that the companies had to pay the same wages as to the civilian workers. According to a survey in 1943, only 10 per cent of the prisoners achieved full performance in 70 per cent of all eligible enterprises, all others only 20 to 80 per cent of the performance of a civilian worker.

Something else rankled with those responsible at I.G. Farben. There was a constant lack of guard details so as to increase the deployment of prisoners. A ratio of one guard to forty prisoners was desirable, but that was never reached. Most of all, however, progress at the I.G. Farben works was time and again delayed by epidemics, too. 'In order to completely avoid the introduction of epidemics, the SS is informed with immediate effect that the I.G. will take on the provisioning of the prisoners in Camp IV themselves. This is to prevent epidemics being introduced with the fetching of food from the concentration camp.'[19] In September 1942 a sense of alarm spread through the I.G. project management, for: 'The deployment of prisoners and Jews by the concentration camp is currently impossible due to hygienic reasons. In order to be able to assign newly arrived, uninfected Jews and prisoners, a camp is to be completed at the construction site, which can accommodate them.'[20]

Likewise, there was as a rule an extremely high absence rate through sickness. Yet I.G. Farben undertook little to change this. On the contrary, despite the difficulties Dürrfeld gave the instruction that jumpers, protective vests, fur-lined vests etc. had to be handed in under all circumstances.[21] Whoever did not comply with this ought not to receive any protective winter clothing the following winter.

Nobody of those responsible at I.G. Farben wanted to know anything of the appalling conditions in Auschwitz and in particular of the mass gassings. Especially telling is here an affidavit that Höß submitted a few months prior to his execution regarding Dürrfeld, the I.G. Farben director and project manager of the I.G. works at Auschwitz-Monowitz:

> He was the acting director of the Buna work in Auschwitz until the completion of the building project. All matters with regards to administration, construction and machinery were under his control. He also visited the Auschwitz camp itself. He knew of the gassings of people in Birkenau and was anxious of how to explain these terrible things to his staff and subordinates. Dr Dürrfeld, just like the other managing directors, was responsible for the bad treatment of the inmates in the same way as I had been responsible as commander of the concentration camp for the excesses of the least junior officer.[22]

The responsibility for the selection and deployment of the SS members to Auschwitz-Monowitz lay with Höß. Only a few examples shall be listed here:

SS Head Storm Leader Heinrich Schwarz was from November 1943 commander of the Auschwitz-Monowitz camp and had learned his 'craft' under Höß. In Spring 1943 he had carried out a selection, after which several hundred prisoners were taken to Birkenau to be gassed. On 5 March 1943 he reported to the SS Central Economic-Administrative Office and gave an account of a selection of a transport having arrived at Auschwitz shortly before from Berlin: 'If the transports from Berlin continue to roll in with so many women and children along with old Jews, I do not expect much in terms of deployment. Buna needs most of all younger or stronger bodies.'[23] Most noticeably Schwarz was in evidence during executions, the last time during the evacuation march in Gleiwitz, where he furnished some of the criminal prisoners with weapons and others were badly mistreated by his own hand.

The camp leader was SS Senior Storm Leader Vinzenz Schöttl, a 'quiet' civil servant who barely surfaced during mistreatments, but was present during executions on several occasions. He was a heavy alcoholic who loved his comfort and avoided any excitement as much as possible. Schöttl was known to many prisoners from Dachau as a notorious thug. He tried to establish a 'jovial' relationship with the prisoners, especially to those whom he already knew from Dachau.

The same was true for SS Head Company Leader Josef Remmele, member of the SS guard detail, a feared thug who preferred criminal prisoners and participated in the robbing of new arrivals. After the war he was sentenced to death by a US court and executed.

SS Senior Company Leader Bernhard Rakers had been transferred for disciplinary reasons – as head chef he had embezzled groceries – from Sachsenhausen to Auschwitz, initially did his detention in the command bunker of Auschwitz I and then went to Monowitz as detail leader for the I.G. Farben premises. He commanded the entire Buna detail. In the morning he accompanied the slave labourers of the I.G. Farbenindustrie to the works' premises, together with SS guard detail under his command. In the evening he escorted the prisoners back to the camp. At the I.G. construction site, Rakers, the SS guard details, the kapos and the I.G. foremen controlled the work details of the subcontractors commissioned by I.G. Farben. Complaints about Rakers because of his cruelty and brutality against prisoners led to his release. He was not transferred to his disadvantage, however. Instead, he ascended to report leader in the Buna/Monowitz concentration camp. In this function he had to perform, among other things, the roll calls and to determine the camp numbers. In December 1944 Rakers was once again transferred for disciplinary reasons from Buna/Monowitz to the outpost Gleiwitz II (German Carbon Black Works with its base in Dortmund).

The deployment leader for the entire period was SS Senior Company Leader Wilhelm Stolten. On the evacuation transport from Gleiwitz to Buchenwald he shot a number of prisoners who had left the wagons for a toilet trip and were no longer able to climb back on board for lack of strength. According to reports by surviving prisoners, after the liberation of the camp Stolten was recognised by prisoners in Mecklenburg, apprehended and battered to death.

The following account of a survivor reflects the cruelties to which the prisoners were subjected at Auschwitz-Monowitz. It serves to present the later protestations of innocence by the I.G. Farben chief manager given at Nuremberg in the proper light:

> The principal punishment of the camp was beatings, which like in other camps were executed on a support. This punishment was officially ordered and consisted of 20–25 blows by stick. (...) Another punishment handed out by the Political Department was the standing inside the sleeve. The sleeve was the space that surrounded the entire camp between the electrically charged wire and the other wire and had a width of roughly 60–80 cm. Into this sleeve those prisoners were placed who were ordered by the Political

Department for penal investigations, or those who had been caught in so-called punishable acts. This coercive measure was also used against civilians by the Political Department, if those were caught inside the work in any kind of relationship to prisoners. (…)

At irregular intervals selections were carried out in the Monowitz camp. This happened directly on SS orders, but indirectly on the instruction of the I.G. works' management who did not want any sick prisoners in the camp. There was an agreement with the works' management that no prisoner was allowed to spend more than 15 days in the infirmary. The long-term sick were to be replaced by healthy persons, which in most cases meant death for the prisoners concerned lying in the infirmary, as in such cases they were transported to Birkenau.[24]

During the Nuremberg I.G. Farben trial in 1947 Dürrfeld declared in contrast:

Concentration camp and I.G. work are two totally separate areas, two different intellectual worlds, linked on the outside by the same name, but between them an abyss:
There the concentration camp – here an I.G. work!
There extermination – here development by the I.G.!
There a mad order – here the will for creative achievement!
There despair – here keenest hope!
There humiliation and degradation – here care for the people!
There death – here life!

Against this histrionic exclamation contemptuous of human life shall be held the following factual statements: at the end of October 1942 the SS transferred the first group of prisoner functionaries from the main camp at Auschwitz to the newly opened concentration camp at Buna/Monowitz. In the following weeks the number of camp inmates grew rapidly. On 27 October 1942 a deportation train from the concentration camp at Westerbrok in the Netherlands arrived with 841 Jewish prisoners, of whom merely 224 men were selected as 'fit for work' and committed to Monowitz. The remaining deportees were gassed at Birkenau. Two days later followed a transport with prisoners from Dachau, who were supposed to work at the construction of the Buna works of I.G. Farben. On 30 October 1942 in the main camp roughly 800 male Jewish prisoners from the German Reich were selected as 'fit to work' by the SS and transferred to Monowitz. At the end of October 1942 2,100 prisoners were in the Buna/Monowitz camp. In September 1943 5,400 of the 6,500 inmates were assigned as labourers to I.G. Auschwitz. In summer 1944 the camp numbers reached their peak with more than 11,000 prisoners as a consequence of the deportation of hundreds of thousands, Jews from Hungary to Auschwitz. Some of the deportees selected as 'fit to work' at the ramp in Birkenau were committed to Buna/Monowitz and there accommodated in tents. On New Year's Day 1945, 10,350 prisoners were in Buna/Monowitz.[25]

There are widely differing estimates on the number of those who died at I.G. Farbenindustrie Auschwitz. A fundamental reason for this is the systematic destruction of files carried out shortly before the end of the war both by the SS and the staff of I.G. Farbenindustrie. Besides the incompletely preserved prisoner register and death registers of the concentration camp Buna/Monowitz, statements regarding the number of prisoners murdered there are mostly based on the estimates of former inmates. These range from at least 23,000 to 40,000 at most. In historical research the statements differ from 10,000 dead by the Polish historian Piotr Setkiewicz and 'in total 30,000 prisoners who died directly from the work for I.G. Farben', which Bernd C. Wagner assumes.

Chapter 8

After the Collapse

The Flight

Shortly before the end of the National Socialist regime, SS Senior Group Leader Oswald Pohl, SS Standard Leader Enno Lolling and Rudolf Höß undertook a last inspection trip to several concentration camps in March 1945. To the British military police officer Hanns Alexander, who had tracked him down in the north of Schleswig-Holstein, Höß recounted among other things that the group had visited the camps at Neuengamme, Bergen-Belsen, Buchenwald, Dachau and Flossenbürg.[1] Furthermore, they had been to Leitmeritz (Litoměřice)[2] near Aussig (Ústi nad Labem) and had inspected another large camp at the Elbe. Pohl had received the order to make this trip by Reich Leader SS Heinrich Himmler. Likewise, Himmler had instructed the camp commanders not to kill any more Jews and to do everything in their power to reduce the rate of mortality among the prisoners. Equally the commanders had to prepare the evacuation of certain camps. Bergen-Belsen in particular had been in a 'terrible' state, Höß criticised. Tens of thousands of dead were lying about. All the latrines were full and overflowing. There was no opportunity to obtain groceries, since the State Food Agency refused to deliver anything to Bergen-Belsen. He, Höß, had then instructed the camp commander to have fire wood gathered in the forests nearby and to burn the corpses of the thousands of dead. Evidently the state of the camp upset the 'sense of tidiness' of Höß, who in Auschwitz had organised the inconceivable factory-style murder of millions of people.

At the end of April 1945 SS Senior Group Leader Richard Glücks gave the order to transfer the Oranienburg office group to the nearby Ravensbrück concentration camp. There they remained for about six days and then continued on to Barth in Pomerania.

Pohl describes the last weeks of freedom thus:

> Around mid-April 1945 Group Leader Lörner conveyed to me Himmler's order to leave Berlin with the Central Economic-Administrative Office and to relocate at my own discretion. I left one group under Senior Leader Dr Salpeter, who wanted to remain in Berlin. The office groups A, B and C went to Southern Germany, namely A and B at first to Dachau and Bayrischzell, C to several locations, mostly to where there were building projects. I myself repaired with my staff to Dachau, and when Dachau was threatened in the command vehicle to Brüningsau near Halfing, from where on 13th May I marched on foot to Northern Germany. The office group D still remained in Oranienburg at Group Leader Glück's request and was supposed to evade the approaching front towards the north (Mecklenburg, Schleswig-Holstein). Fixed plans had not been made.[3]

Höß writes in his *Autobiographical Notes* that he had heard of Hitler's death when he was fleeing with his family. The same thought crossed his and his wife's mind:

> Now we have to go, too! With the Leader our world had also perished. Did it still make sense to us to continue living? We would be pursued and looked for everywhere. We wanted to take poison. I had obtained this for my wife so that she and the children would not fall into the hands of the Russians while alive during an unexpected advance. Yet for the sake of our children we did not do it. (…) We should have done it nevertheless. I later regretted it time and again. (…) We were linked and chained to *that* world – we ought to have perished with it.[4]

The cohesion of the individual groups loosened rapidly after the departure from Berlin. Office Group D maintained communication from Oranienburg to Dachau the longest, as they had their own radio link. After the evacuation from Oranienburg news from this group ceased, too.

Pohl continued: 'From there [Ravensbrück] we received the order to redeploy to Rendsburg in Holstein.' Even the families were evacuated to Rendsburg, for which Höß organised the transports according to his own statement. Here, at the North Sea–Baltic Sea Canal, appeared, according to Höß, 'Glücks with his wife and his driver, Mrs Ricke with her daughter and the latter's two children, Lolling with wife and son, Sommer with his wife and children and Mrs Salpeter'. Salpeter himself, the assistant of Senior Group Leader Pohl and head of the legal department in the SS Central Economic-Administrative Office, had remained in Berlin. Among the group were Höß with his wife and children, [Wilhelm] Burger with Mrs Kleinheisterkamp, the wife of a commander of a division of the Waffen-SS.[5] 'She was Swedish, went to the Swedish consulate and we never saw her again.' To these were added Senior Storm Command Leader Werner Siemann of Office II at the Office Group D and finally the deputy head of Office Group D, SS Storm Command Leader Gerhard Maurer, with his driver.

Two trucks with luggage and communications material had been lost near Rostock, since anti-tank ditches across the roads could not be passed. Because Höß could not find accommodation for the group in Rendsburg, they stayed overnight in a stable near Klein Benecke, 20 kilometres north of Rendsburg. The following day they succeeded in finding shelter for the women and children in a school building of the Colonial School at the North Sea–Baltic Sea Canal.

After a discussion between Glücks and SS Senior Group Leader Hans Adolf Prützmann, head of the SS partisan fighter units, Flensburg was the next destination of the SS refugees on 1 May 1945. Höß, however, found lodgings for his family in St Michaelisdonn. His contact was Mrs Thomsen, who had previously been a teacher at Auschwitz and was the sister of Höß' wife Hedwig and thus his sister-in-law. Her husband, a former member of the Artaman League and SS Senior Storm Leader, had held a leading position in the agricultural department at Auschwitz until its dissolution.

Höß brought the salvaged luggage to St Michaelisdonn, then travelled to Rendsburg and farther to Flensburg, where the chief of police, SS Senior Group Leader Hinz, was still in office. The latter advised Höß and the other SS refugees to hide for now in a forest along the road to Apenrade. In the evening Höß and his people visited Hinz again in the hope of receiving through him a decision by Himmler on their next steps. On Hinz' advice they repaired to the navy school at Mürwik, where they met Himmler on 3 May 1945. Gerhard Paul went on the record about this: 'In the evening Rudolf Höß and the head of the inspection of the concentration camps, Richard Glücks, are meeting with Himmler. Höß describes the head of the SS as "fresh as a daisy and in the best of moods". Himmler gives the two of them the order to cross the unfenced part of the border to Denmark disguised as non-commissioned officers of the army and to go into hiding there. Legally speaking this is desertion on official orders.'[6]

Holger Piening gives in his book *Westküste 1945* [Western Coast 1945] the following account: 'He radiant and in the best of moods – and meanwhile the world had perished, our world. If he had said: Well, gentlemen, this is the end. You know what you have to do.

191

Then I would have understood it – that would have corresponded with that which he had preached for years to the SS: self-sacrifice for the idea. Yet now he gave us as his last order: Go into hiding among the Wehrmacht!'[7]

This version is confirmed by Glücks. Himmler was no longer able to issue orders and had advised him and Höß to cross the border to Denmark as members of the Wehrmacht. The remaining members were supposed to try somehow to pass as refugees. SS Group Leader Karl Gebhardt, chief clinician with the Reich Physician SS and head of the SS hospital Hohenlychen, was to house women and children.

Höß himself described the meeting such:

> On 3rd May I met Himmler for the last time. As ordered the rest of the concentration camp inspection had followed Himmler until Flensburg. There Glücks, Maurer and I report to him. He is just coming from a meeting with the remainder of the Reich government. He is fresh as a daisy and in the best of moods. He welcomes us and orders immediately that Glücks and Höß should pass under different names as non-commissioned officers of the army as stragglers across the unfenced section of the border to Denmark and go into hiding there.[8]

The next day Hinz explained to the refugees that the best way to go into hiding was to impersonate members of the navy and to disguise themselves. Navy Captain Wolfgang Lüth, most recently flotilla commander, furnished the Nazi criminals with pay books under false names with the express approval of Grand Admiral Karl Dönitz, who as Hitler's successor was the last 'head of state' of the Third Reich. Höß took on the name Franz Lang and received the appropriate kit for a marine.

SS Storm Command Leader Heinrich Bünger had papers issued with the name Wolff, Glücks called himself Sonnemann and Lolling Dr Gerlach. The other members of the office group did not need to take on false names, in Höß' opinion, because they were not in immediate danger.

The path now led Höß – furnished with ordinary marching orders – to the navy communications school at Rantum on the island of Sylt. He described this episode during his interrogation by Captain Alexander as follows:

> I myself intended to interrupt the journey for a visit with the Tober family (Mrs Tober was a daughter-in-law of Mrs Thomsen[9] of St Michaelisdonn) in Bredstedt. I separated from Maurer and Burger at the crossroads to Walsbüll where my road to Bredstedt turned

off and arranged to meet them again the next day in Niebüll. When I arrived there the following day, I found nobody present. From Niebüll I went to Rantum, where I reported to the navy communications school.

Höß was incredibly lucky: because the British intended to take SS criminals into custody at the navy communications school, the marines, now including Höß, were taken from Rantum to Brunsbüttel on the mainland, to the so-called detention area G. There he could make repeated contact with his family:

> During my stay in Brunsbüttel I was visited two or three times a week by my son Klaus-Bernd. On one occasion my wife visited me. Three days after my arrival at Brunsbüttel I paid my first visit to Mrs Thomsen in St Michaelisdonn and asked her to inform my wife of my presence. This visit took place on the 1st or 2nd June, and on that occasion I stayed overnight with Mrs Thomsen. The next day I returned.

Shortly after, Rudolf and Hedwig Höß met in a sandy field near the sugar factory of St Michaelisdonn. In the evening Höß met his wife again – this time at the house of his sister-in-law. Towards the end of June a second visit at St Michaelisdonn took place, where Höß met his wife again alone in the same field.

After he had been quartered for four weeks with a farmer, he had an early release on 5 June 1945 during Operation Barleycorn, since he had claimed to be a farmer. His next stop was a farmer called Hansen in Gottrupel near Handewitt – an address he had been given by the navy lieutenant Lietz. He then stayed overnight in Flensburg with Lietz' wife and her parents. The next morning the labour bureau assigned him to the farmer Peter Hansen in Gottrupel. Höß seemed to feel confident, for he even made himself useful as recording clerk at the local council. Sönke Dwenger wrote about this on 20 January 2007 in the *Dithmarscher Landzeitung* [Dithmarschen Regional Newspaper]:

> The people in the village 'all liked him', the farmer later recounted; to the farmer's wife he seemed 'polite and modest – and hard-working. He was always working! And he often sat over books at night.' His notorious black leather coat and his briefcase remained in Gottrupel; the coat was very useful for painting jobs, the children used the briefcase of the mass murderer as a satchel.[10]

On 4 May 1945 Höß had met his brother-in-law, Fritz Hensel, in the building of the garrison administration in Flensburg, then shortly before Christmas 1945 once more on a street in Flensburg. A few days later Hensel came to Höß at Gottrupel and told him that he would visit the latter's wife shortly, and handed him two letters that Hedwig Höß had written to him. Now Höß was informed of his family's situation for the time being.

Since he had separated from the members of the office group, he had allegedly heard nothing more of them. His son mentioned that SS Under Company Leader Pfersich and the scribe Eberle of the Auschwitz personnel office had supposedly been seen in or near St Michaelisdonn. SS Standard Leader Maurer had told Höß of his intention to go to Halle, where besides his mother he had further relatives and acquaintances and thus the opportunity to go into hiding and build up a new existence. Burger wanted to go to his relatives in Lower Bavaria, where his wife might be. His brother-in-law owned a brewery, and he had a chance to find employment there.

Höß' oldest son, Klaus-Bernd, was particularly suspected by the British of still being in contact with his father. Yet the former asserted that he last saw Höß on 3 May 1945 in Flensburg. A letter and the SS death head ring had been the last messages for his mother.

The British knew that Hedwig stayed at St Michaelisdonn at the sugar factory, and they assumed that Höß would try to make contact with his wife.[11] The captain of the 92nd Squadron FSS (Force Support Squadron) gave the strict order to avoid any contact with Hedwig in an attempt to lull her into a false sense of security. However, her house was kept under constant observation by disguised civilian informers. Captain Cross suggested extending the observation for another four weeks. If nothing happened in the meantime, they could arrest her and 'grill' her for a week in order to break her. Several times the British surrounded the area of the sugar factory and even searched the sewers, the contemporary witness Hans Peter Jansen recalls.

Contact was also made with the unit in Marne, but they could not contribute anything significant. There were several suspects, a man threw a bicycle in the direction of a guard and fled, another fit the description of Höß but was not the wanted man.

Inconsistencies and the Creation of Legends

Hedwig Höß was extraordinarily reticent on the subject of Auschwitz after the war. His daughter Ingebritt also showed little interest in speaking about the subject. To the British journalist Thomas Harding, Ingebritt said that it would be best not to recall all these events. On the capture of her father, she said that she was around thirteen years old at that time. She was sitting with her siblings at the table, when British soldiers shouted again and again: 'Where is your father?' She got a severe headache, went outside and cried under a tree. She calmed down then, but would suffer from migraines for years. This started up again after she had received a letter from Harding after several decades.

Her older brother and her mother were led away by the British, her brother was abused. Her mother heard his cries of pain in the next room. Like any other mother, she wanted to protect her son and finally gave up her father's location. The British Nazi hunter Captain Hanns Alexander now gathered a team and set off to the barn in Gottrupel where Höß was hiding. Höß woke up and denied he was the wanted concentration camp commander. Alexander wanted to see his wedding ring. Höß replied that he was unable to get it off his finger. Alexander allegedly threatened to cut off the finger. Höß then took off the ring, and inside was found the engraving 'Rudolf and Hedwig'.

Alexander describes the search for Höß differently.[12] According to him, Hedwig Höß had been arrested on Thursday, 7 March 1946. At first Sergeant Koolish of the 92nd FFS Lunden Detachment tried to interrogate her at the prison in Lunden, but she refused to provide any useful information. She behaved rather dramatically, Alexander noted, 'but we began a war of nerves and hoped to be successful within a couple of days'. It was decided to arrest the oldest son and use him as leverage. Klaus-Bernd was arrested on Friday afternoon by members of the 92nd FFS. He gave a frightened impression, and Alexander decided to question him at short intervals: 'Höß junior explained that he had not seen his father since 3 May 1945 in Flensburg. The last news of his father was a letter to his mother and the death head ring of his father.' The following day mother and son refused to eat, but on Monday, 11 March 1946, Hedwig started to talk and revealed the address of her husband and his alias – not voluntarily, but because Alexander had threatened to hand her son to the Russians and let him be deported to Siberia.

According to Ingebritt, Hedwig and the children barely scraped by in the period that followed. They stole coal from trains for their heating, had no shoes and wrapped rags around their feet. As former prominent National Socialists they were allegedly shunned by the local population. In around 1960 Hedwig finally moved to a small house in Ludwigsburg near Stuttgart, where she lived with one of her daughters.

Ingebritt's statements are, however, partly imprecise or even incorrect. Hedwig and her children did not need to steal coal from trains, for they were living in a room at the manager's apartment of the sugar factory of St Michaelis, and this was the only building there with functioning heating. Later they were housed in a barrack in the village centre, which had originally been erected for the Reich Labour Service. Contemporary witness Hans Peter Janssen told the author of this book that the Höß children went to school together with the village youth and were by no means shunned. They settled quickly at St Michaelisdonn, took part in the annual bird shooting and made friends.[13]

Also, the date given for Hedwig's move to Ludwigsburg – 'around 1960' – is demonstrably incorrect. According to the information by the town archive of Ludwigsburg provided to the author of this book on 13 January 2014, Hedwig moved on 19 August 1954 close to Stuttgart, namely to Hirschbergstraße 47 in the Ludwigsburg district of Eglosheim.[14] Of the children, daughter Heidetraut is already missing from the records of the registration office at that time; apparently she did not take part in the move. Son Hans-Jürgen was registered from 1957 in Besigheim in the administrative district of Ludwigsburg, and for daughter Ingebritt the last entry reads 'married since 1961 at Gibraltar to Alan D. Peck'. Hedwig remained in Ludwigsburg until 15 March 1965 and then moved to Stuttgart-Botnang with daughter Annegret.

In contrast to soldier widows, Hedwig evidently did not receive a pension. The German Pension Insurance refuses any information on this for inconceivable reasons. It has to be suspected, but cannot be proved, that she was supported by National Socialists, who found shelter in Schleswig-Holstein in great numbers. She who had played an important role at Auschwitz was subject to no restrictions of any kind regarding travel. When she was in Washington in her later years, she minded her grandchildren while her daughter was working.

Hedwig's final visit to the USA dates to September 1989. She was now eighty-one years old and frail. She was supposed to fly back to Germany, but she told her daughter that it was too cold there and that she wanted to stay longer. On 15 September 1989 she declared after dinner that she was tired and wanted to go to bed. The next day Ingebritt knocked on the door and found that her mother had died in her sleep. The daughter found a local crematorium, where Hedwig was incinerated – under a false name. Ingebritt postponed the memorial service in order to allow time for relatives from Germany to take part. On 3 March 1990 at 11am there was a short service in an inter-confessional cemetery. Hedwig Höß found her final resting place among the graves of Jews, Christians and Muslims.

The End on the Gallows

Rudolf Höß was arrested on 11 March 1946 at 11pm in Gottrupel in Flensburg district at the house of the farmer Hansen by Captain Cross, 92nd FFS. The apprehension that he might commit suicide turned out to be baseless, since shortly before the vial with the poison had broken. Höß himself described in his *Autobiographical Notes* his arrest in the following manner:

> Since I assumed when first roused from sleep that this was one of the robberies frequently occurring there, the arrest succeeded. I was badly badgered by the field security police. I was dragged to Heide, to those barracks of all places from where I had been released by the British eight months before. My first interrogation came about with 'striking' proof. What is written in the minutes I do not know, although I signed it. Yet alcohol and whip were *too much*[15] even for me. The whip was my own, which by chance had found its way into my wife's luggage. My horse had hardly ever felt its sting, even less prisoners. Yet the interrogator was apparently of the opinion that I had incessantly thrashed prisoners with it.[16]

The latter comment is basically typical of Höß: he who had countless people tortured and murdered in the most brutish manner complained about having been walloped with a whip!

After he had been arrested, he at first preferred to be called Franz Lang, before he had to admit to being Rudolf Höß after all. Photos for comparison did not leave any doubt. On the way from the site of his arrest to the prison cell, while he was sitting in the cargo area of a truck under guard by three sergeants, he spoke a lot and admitted outright and without showing discernible emotions to being responsible for the deaths of ten thousands of people.

It is further to be learned from the record of the interrogation that Captain Alexander called a Major Bramwell of Operation Haystack on 12 March 1946 around 12pm. It was agreed that he would send a car and an escort as quickly as possible in order to bring Höß to Heide. Höß was first put into a cell of the guard detail of the 5th Royal Horse Artillery (RHA), and one guard observed him day and night.

After a few days he was transferred to Minden in Westphalia, repeatedly interrogated and after three weeks transferred to Nuremberg 'with a prisoner of war fetched from London, the defence witness for Fritzsche', the head of the press and information office in Goebbels' Ministry for Propaganda. 'I had come to Nuremberg, because Kaltenbrunner's [head of the Reich Security Main Office] defence counsel had requested me as a witness', as Höß states in his *Autobiographical Notes*.[17]

On 25 May 1946 Höß was driven to the airport together with Curt von Burgsdorff, governor of Cracow district, Josef Bühler, deputy of the general governor in Cracow, and Amon Göth, commander of the

Jewish camp Plaszow near Cracow, and handed over to Polish officers. On 30 July 1946 he was transferred to Cracow. Poland had, meanwhile, established a Supreme National Tribunal (Naczelny Trybunal Narodowy, NTN), which was to hold trials of the main National Socialist perpetrators. Among them were also forty staff members of Auschwitz, including Höß.

On the suggestion of Jahn Sehn, the chief prosecutor of the Polish tribunal, Höß wrote his letters and memoirs between October 1946 and April 1947, also as a memory aid for the court proceedings.

The trial against the forty-seven-year-old Höß began on 11 March 1947 in a hall of the Związek Nauczycielstwa Polskiego (ZNP), the union of Polish teachers in Warsaw, which could seat 500 people.[18] A simultaneous translation into several languages was possible. The audience consisted mainly of former prisoners of the camp. During the trial Höß was calm and controlled. He had no illusions about what he could expect. He insisted until the end that not 5 or 6 million people had perished in Auschwitz, but at most 1.5 million. At the end of the trial he asked for permission by the court to have his wedding ring sent to his wife. On 2 April the court pronounced the sentence: death by hanging. The day after the sentence former camp prisoners wrote a petition to the authorities for Höß to be executed on the camp's grounds.

On 11 April 1947 Höß wrote his last letters to his wife and his children, of which copies are kept at the Institute for Contemporary History in Munich, with the Federal Commissioner for Stasi documents (BstU) and with the International Tracing Service in Bad Arolsen (ITS).[19]

> My dearest Mutz!
> My life journey had now come to an end.
> A truly sad lot was attributed to me by fate. How happy the comrades who were allowed to die an honourable soldier's death.
> Calm and collected I am facing the end.
> From the outset it was entirely clear to me that I too had to perish with the[20] world to which I had dedicated myself body and soul, when it was shattered and destroyed. I had unwittingly become a cog in the monstrous German extermination machine and was working in an exposed position. As commander of the extermination camp Auschwitz I was entirely responsible for all that was happening there, whether I knew of it or not. Most of all the terrible and horrific occurrences there I only learned during the investigation and during the trial itself. It is indescribable how I was deceived, how my instructions were bent and what has been

carried out supposedly on my orders. The guilty will not, so I hope, escape their judgement.

How tragic: I who by nature was soft, good-hearted and always obliging became the greatest annihilator of humans who carried out every extermination order coldly and to the last consequence. Through the long-lasting iron training in the SS with the aim of turning every SS man into a mindless tool for the execution of all plans by the RL SS, I myself had become an automaton blindly obeying every order.

My fanatical patriotism and my most exaggerated sense of duty were excellent preconditions for this training.

It is hard to admit to oneself in the end that one has trodden the wrong path and thus has brought this end upon oneself.

Yet what use is all this pondering of wrong or right. In my view the life journeys of us all are predetermined by fate, by sage divination, and unalterable.

Painfully bitter and difficult for me is the farewell from you all, you my dearest, best Mutz, and you my darling children. That I have to leave you my poor unfortunates behind in hardship and misery. Fate has burdened you, my unhappy wife, with the hardest share in our doom. To the endless pain of our being torn apart is added the deep worry about your future life, the worry about our children. But, dearest darling, take comfort, do not despair!

Time also heals the deepest, most aching wounds which in the first pain one believes one will not survive.

Millions of families were torn apart by this disastrous war or wholly destroyed.

Yet life goes on. The children grow older. May you, dearest, best Mutz, only be blessed with strength and health so that you can care for them until they can stand on their own feet.

My misguided life places upon you, dearest, the sacred duty to raise our children to true humanity coming deeply from the heart. Our dear children are all good-natured. Encourage all these good stirrings of the heart in every way, make them sensitive to any human suffering.

What humanity is I have learned only here in the Polish prisons. I who as commander of Auschwitz visited so much harm and suffering on the Polish people – though not personally and not on my own initiative – was met with a human understanding that has often and deeply shamed me. Not only by the higher officials, but also by the simplest guards. Many among them were former prisoners of Auschwitz or other camps. Just now during my last days I experience a humanity which I would have never expected. In spite of all what has happened – they still see in me a human being.

My dearest Mutz, I beg you, do not harden under the harsh blows of fate, preserve your good heart. Do not be deterred by adverse circumstances, by the hardship and misery which you have to suffer. Never lose faith in humanity.

Try as soon as possible to leave the bleak environs there.

Apply for a change of name. Take on your maiden name again. This should no longer be met with difficulties. My name is simply scorned throughout the world, and you my poor darlings will only have unnecessary difficulties under my name, especially the children in their future progress. Klaus, for example, would certainly have had an apprenticeship long ago if he had not been called Höß.

It is best if my name vanishes with me, too.

With this letter it was permitted to me to have my wedding ring sent to you.

Wistfully I remember the time of our spring in life, when we put these rings on each other. Who suspected *this* end to our life together?

Eighteen years ago in just this season we once found each other. A difficult path was before us. But brave and cheerful we began our life together.

We were not granted many 'sunny days', more hard efforts, much, much suffering and worry. Only step by step we advanced.

How happy were we in our children whom you, dearest Mutz, gave to us gladly and happily time and again. In our children we saw our life's work. To create a home for them as a firm support and to raise them to useful people was our constant concern. Often and often I have now traced back our common path during my imprisonment; all incidents and events remembered again and again.

What happy hours we were allowed to experience – but through how much hardship, illness, sorrow and grief we had to pass, too.

I thank you, my dear good comrade who has shared bravely and faithfully joy and sorrow with me through all the years, I thank you from the depth of my heart for all the good and beautiful which you have brought into my life, for all your constant love and care. Forgive me, my dear, if I have ever offended or hurt you.

How deeply and painfully do I regret today every hour which I did not spend with you, dearest Mutz, and the children, because I believed that work would not permit it or other obligations which I deemed important.

A kind fate allowed me to hear from you, my dears, once more. I received all eleven letters dated from 31st December to 16th February. How glad was I, especially during the days of the trial, to read your lines. Your concern and love for me, the dear chatter of the children, gave me new courage and the strength to withstand everything.

I am particularly grateful to you, dearest, for the last letter you wrote during the early hours of Sunday morning. As if you poor dear had known that these were the last words to reach me. How bravely and clearly you write about everything. Yet what bitter sorrow, what deep pain between the lines. I know how deeply our two lives are linked. How difficult it is to part from each other.

I wrote to you, my dear Mutz, on Christmas, on 26th January, and on 3rd and 16th March. And hope that you have received those letters. Yet how little can be said in writing and under those circumstances. How much has to remain unspoken what cannot be put into writing. However, we have to resign ourselves to it.

I am so grateful that I was allowed to hear the little about you and that I could tell you, my darling, that which was on my mind at least in essentials.

All my life I was a withdrawn fellow, never liked to let anybody see the innermost of my heart, squared everything with my own conscience. How often have you, dearest, regretted this and felt painfully that you yourself who was closest to me could take part so little in my inner life.

So I have carried around for years all my doubts and gloom concerning the righteousness of my work and the necessity of the orders given to me. I could not and was not allowed to talk to anybody about it. It will now become understandable to you, dearest Mutz, why I became more and more withdrawn, more and more remote. And you, dearest Mutz, all you my loved ones, had to suffer from it unintentionally, and could not explain to yourselves my dissatisfaction, my absent-mindedness, my often being morose. Yet that was the case, I regret it bitterly.

During my long, lonely imprisonment I had enough time and peace to ponder my whole life deeply. I have revised my whole conduct.

Due to my recent realisations I see today for myself clearly, harshly and bitterly enough that the entire ideology, the whole world in which I believed so firmly and steadfast was based on false premises and inevitably had to collapse one day.

So my actions in the service of this ideology were completely wrong, though I had faith in the righteousness of the idea. Now it was entirely logical that strong doubts arose inside me that if my renunciation of God was not also subject to wholly false premises.

It was a hard struggle. However, I have regained my faith in our Lord.

More I cannot write to you, dearest, about these matters, it would lead too far.

Should you, my dear Mutz, in your misery find strength and comfort in the Christian faith, follow the compulsion of your heart. Do not be deterred from it by anything. You should not simply follow me, either. You should decide for yourself herein.

The children will in any case take a different path through their school than the one which we have been following so far. Klaus may later, when he will have become more mature, decide for himself and find orientation for himself.

So of our world only wreckage remains, from which those left behind have to build a new and better world.

My time is running out.

Now it is time to say farewell for good to you, my dears, whom I loved most in the world.

How difficult and painful is parting.

I thank you, dearest Mutz, once again for all your love and care and all that which you brought to my life. In our children I will remain always with you and around you, my poor unfortunate wife.

I go in the optimistic hope that after all the sadness and difficulty you, my dears, will still find a place in the sun, that you will find a modest opportunity in life and that you, dearest Mutz and dearest children, will be blessed with a quiet and content happiness.

All my dearest and heartfelt wishes accompany you all, my dears, on your future path in life.

I am most grateful to all dear, good people who stand by your side in your hardship and who help you and send them my best regards.

Final kind regards also to our parents, to Fritz and all the other dear old friends.

For the last time, I send you my best regards with a heavy heart, my dears, all my dear children, my Annemäusl, my Burling, my Puppi, my Kindi and my Klaus, and my best, dearest Mutz, my poor unfortunate wife. Remember me fondly.

Until the last breath remains with you, all my loved ones,

Your *Vati*

Last letter by Rudolf Höß to his children, 11 April 1947:[21]

My dearest children!

Your daddy has to leave you now. Only your dear mummy remains – may she stay with you for a long, long time. You do not understand yet what dear mummy means to you, what a treasure she is for you. A mother's love and a mother's care is the most beautiful and valuable thing on earth. I recognised this only when it was too late and have regretted it for the rest of my life.

To you, my dearest children, I am therefore addressing my final urgent plea: never forget your darling mummy! With what selfless love has she always nurtured and cared for you. Her life was dedicated just to you. How many beautiful things in life has she denied herself for your sakes. How worried was she, when you were sick, how patient and untiring was she in her care for you then. She was never at rest, if you were not all around her. Only for your sakes is she bearing now all this bitter hardship and suffering. Do not forget this ever in your lives!

Help her to bear her painful lot. Be nice and good to her. Help her to the best of your abilities. In this manner give her a part of the gratitude she deserves for her love and care of you day and night.

Klaus, my dearest boy!
You are the oldest. You are about to go out into the world. You now have to find your own path in life. Out of your own strength you will have to make a life for yourself. You have good abilities, use them. Hold on to your good heart. Become a person who is primarily led by a warm, feeling humanity. Learn to think and judge for yourself. Do not accept everything brought to you without criticism and as axiomatic. Learn from my life. My greatest mistake in life was that I trusted blindly everything which came from 'above' and did not dare to doubt the truth of the given facts in the slightest.

Go through life with open eyes. Do not become one-sided, weigh the pro and contra in all matters.

For everything you undertake do not let only the intellect speak, but listen first and foremost to your heart's voice. Much will not be understandable to you yet, my dear boy. Yet always remember this, my final advice.

I wish you, my dear Klaus, much happiness in your life. Become a useful, upright fellow with your heart in the right place.

Kindi and Puppi, my dear big girls!
You are still too young to perceive the full impact of the harsh fate allotted to us. Especially you, my dearest girls, are now duty-bound to stand at your poor, unfortunate mummy's side in a helpful and loving way. To surround her with all your heartfelt child's love in order to show her how much you love her and want to help her in her hardship. I can only ask you, my dearest girls, most urgently to listen to your dear mummy!

She will show you the right path with her selfless love and care for you and will furnish you with the lessons you will need for life to become good, useful persons. As different as you two are in your characters, so you both – you, my dear imp, and you, my dear little housewife – have soft, sensitive hearts. Keep them for your later life.

This is the most important matter. Later you will understand this and remember my last words.

My Burling, you dear little lad!
Keep your loving, happy child's attitude. The harsh reality of life will tear you, my dear boy, early enough from your child's land. I am happy to hear from mummy that you make good progress in school.

Your dear daddy cannot tell you anything any more soon. You poor little lad have only your dearest mummy left caring for you. Follow her obediently and thus remain 'Daddy's dear Burling'.

My dear little Annemäusl!
How little was I allowed to experience of you, dear little creature. Mummy dearest shall take you, my Mäusl, firmly in her arms on my behalf and tell you of your dear daddy and how much he loved you.

May you remain for a long time Mummy's little sunshine and continue to give her much joy. May you, dear sunny creature, help poor, dear Mummy over all the dark hours.

Once more I ask you all, my dearest children, to take my final words to heart. Remember them always and forever.

Stay fond of
your *Vati*

The execution was scheduled for 14 April, but was brought forward due to the worry that the inhabitants of Auschwitz might try to lynch him on the way to the camp.

The platform of the gallows was erected at dawn by German prisoners. It cannot be excluded that they were also the executioners. The camp could only be entered with a special ID. Uniformed guards with rifles were standing everywhere. Höß was brought there at 8am. Inside the camp he was led to the building of the former commandant's headquarters. There he asked for a cup of coffee. After he had finished his drink, he was brought into one of the cells of the bunker in Block 11 called the Block of Death. Exactly on time at 10am, he was led outside. He was calm. With a steady, almost ceremonious step he strode across the main road of the camp. As his hands were tied behind his back, the hangmen helped him onto the stool above the trap door. The gallows were approached by a priest, for whose presence the condemned had asked. It was a Salesian[22] of the Auschwitz parish, Reverend Tadeusz Zaremba. The prosecutor read the sentence aloud, the executioner threw the noose around Höß' neck, the condemned corrected its fit with his head. When the executioner removed the stool from under the feet of the former commander, his body fell through the opening trap door. The priest began to speak the prayers for the dying. It was 10.08am. The death was determined by a doctor at 10.21am. Höß' corpse was burnt.

The execution of Höß was the last public execution in Poland. The Polish press reported only briefly on it. Newspapers were apparently not allowed to write about this event. It emerges from Höß' file that the state authorities had decided at the beginning of 1947 to no longer admit the public to executions of German war criminals, after the execution of Arthur Greiser, the regional leader of the so-called Reichsgau [Reich region] Wartheland, on the slopes of Poznan Citadel in summer 1946 had attracted masses of people and degenerated in such a manner that there were children among the onlookers, ice cream, drinks and sweets were sold and that after the hanging of the condemned people fought over pieces of the hangman's rope. Therefore the Polish Ministry of Justice had decided that the execution of the commander of Auschwitz-Birkenau should occur in a 'small circle' – it was witnessed by former prisoners as well as high-profile personalities from the Ministry of Justice, the prosecutor's office and the Urząd Bezpieczeństwa (UB), the Office for Security – still more than a hundred people.

Under the heading 'Rudolf Hoess komendant Auschwitz *na szubienicy*' the Polish journalist Andrzej Gass published on 6 February 2008 an article that also discussed the ban on photography during Höß' execution:

> Dąbrowiecki told me that only he and one other man unknown to him had taken photographs. All others had their cameras taken away. They were standing only a few feet from the gallows. The second photographer was in Dąbrowiecki's opinion probably from the Office of Security. After the execution this man disappeared and the photographer was approached by two functionaries of the Ministry for Public Security. They took the camera out of his hands, removed the roll of film and said that it was confiscated on the order of the Ministry of Justice. Dąbrowiecki informed his superiors. The bosses of 'Polish Film' wanted to publish the photos via their foreign service, they believed that they would become a worldwide sensation. On 21 April 1947 the agency approached the Minister of Justice Henryk Świątkowski in an official letter regarding the return of the confiscated negatives. On 6 June the minister refused approval for the distribution of photos from the execution, he determined that these should remain in the archive forever.[23]

Measured against the suffering he had caused hundred thousands of others, Höß' end was unspectacular. The Poles who now belonged to the victors had dealt with him in an extraordinarily humane manner.

None of the other Nazi perpetrators has committed as much to paper as Höß during the period between arrest and the execution of the death sentence. He did not consider himself guilty in any way, and thus had no cause to be repentant.

Höß demonstrates in an alarming manner where absolute obedience can lead a person. He was in no way a sadist who enjoyed killing. At most he gained pleasure from carrying out his 'work' neatly. It is unlikely that Höß would have risen within the party hierarchy or within the SS in case of a continuation of the war. He was the born recipient of orders and possessed no leadership qualities. He managed the mass murder and set aside personal sensitivities – as far as they existed at all. Such people existed in the Third Reich in great numbers. Höß could organise and perfect the murder – not more. He was no ideologue and no orator. Therefore no legends have grown around him, he thus represents no symbolic figure for the neo-Nazis of the twentieth and twenty-first century. At least this he has spared human kind.

Perhaps it was after all the fear of death that caused Höß to return into the fold of the church. Contemplation and repentance were certainly not the reasons. A last service was provided to the people by Höß, though involuntarily: his corpse was burnt, the ashes thrown into the Sola River and not, like he would have done, ground and spread across the fields as fertiliser.

Acknowledgements

Without the support of the staff of numerous archives this book could have not been written. Here I would like to highlight as an example the commitment with which Karen Strobel, M.A., of the City Archive Mannheim searched for the 'bride' of Höß with whom he corresponded during his Brandenburg jail time. I would also like to thank Regina Witzmann of the City Archive Ludwigsburg who spontaneously offered support to me. As with previous books, Manuela Gehrke of the 'Stasi Documents Office' was of great assistance to me; this is also and very much true for Dr Sabine Dumschat of the Federal Archive Berlin-Lihcterfelde who searched above and beyond for documents on Höß and struck it rich. Further thanks is due – once again – to Michael Klein, Regina Grüner und Cesrin Schmidt of the Federal Archive reading room, also in Berlin-Lichterfelde, furthermore to Dr Susanne Urban, ITS Bad Arolsen, Stefanie Shala of the registry office of the state capital

Stuttgart, Erika Bartecki of the Gransee office and Jörg Rau of the Local Heritage Society Buberow.

I could relinquish the manuscript with confidence to my editor Dr Annalisa Viviani, who attended to it with dedication, toil and a high level of expertise.

APPENDICES

Abbreviations

	German	English	
A.L.	Arbeitslager	Labour camp	
Arb.Eins. Fü	Arbeitseinsatzführer	Labour of work assignment leader	
Arb.Min.	Arbeitsminister	Minister for Employment	
BArch	Bundesarchiv, Berlin-Lichterfelde	Federal Archive, Berlin-Lichterfelde	
BfdV	Beauftrager für den Vierjahresplan (Göring)	Commissioner for the four-year-plan (Göring)	
BdS	Befehlshaber der Sicherheitsolizei und des SD	Commander of the security police and the SD [Security Service]	
Btl., Batl.	Bataillon	Battalion	
BstU	Bundesbeauftrager für die Unterlagen der Staatssicherheit der ehemaligen DDR	Federal Commissioner for the Records of the State Security Service of the former German Democratic Republic	
BV	Berufsverbrecher, eigentlich; befristete Vorbeugehäftlinge	Professional criminals, actually; temporary prisoners in preventative detention	
DAW	Deutsche Ausrüstungswerke	German Equipment Works	
DEST	Deutsche Erd- und Steinwerke	German Earth and Stone Works Company	

208

DNVP	Deutschnationale Volkspartei	German National People's Party	
DWB	Deutsche Wirtschaftsbetriebe (WVHA)	German Economic Enterprises (WVHA)	
E.B.B.Br.	Eisenbahnbau-Birgaden	Railway construction brigades	
FKL	Frauenkonzentra-tionslager	Women's concentration camp	
FSS		Field Security Section	
Geb. Kom	Gebietskommissar	Regional commissioner	
Ge.Insp.	Generalinspekteur	General inspector	
Gen. Kdo	Generalkommando	General command	
Gen. Kom.	Generalkommissar	General commissioner	
Gestapa	Geheimes Staatspolizeiamt	Office of the Secret State Police	
Gestapo	Geheime Staatspolizei	Secret State Police	
GG	Generalgouvernement	General Government	
GGr.	Generalgouverneur	General Governor	
Gruf.	Gruppenführer	Group Leader	
HStuf	Hauptsturmführer	Head Storm Leader	
IBV	Internationaler Bibelforschungsverein	International Bible Students Association [Jehovah's Witnesses]	
IfZ	Institut für Zeitgeschichte, München	Institute for Contemporary History, Munich	
I.K.L.	Inspektion der Konzentrationslager, auch Inspekteur	Inspection of concentration camps, also inspector	
IMG	Internationaler Militärgerichtshof	International Military Court	
IMT	Internationales Militärtribunal (Nürnberg)	International Military Tribunal (Nuremberg)	

Insp.KL		Same as I.K.L.	
Kapo		Prisoner with a position similar to a foreman	
Kdo	Kommando	Commando, detail	
Kdt.	Kommandant	Commander, commandant	
Kdtr.	Kommandantur	Commandant's/ command's headquarters	
Kgf.	Kriegsgefangene	Prisoners of war	
KL	Konzentrationslager	Concentration camp	
Kp.	Kompanie	Company	
KZ	Konzentrationslager	Concentration camp	
MdR	Mitglied des Reichstags	Member of the Reichstag	
NTN	Naczelny Trybunal Narodowy	Supreme National Tribunal	
NSDAP	Nationalsozialistische Deutsche Arbeiterpartei	National Socialist German Workers' Party	
NSV	Nationalsozialistische Volkswohlfahrt	National Socialist People's Welfare	
Nürnb. Dok.	Nürnberger Dokumente	Nuremberg documents	
Oberf.	Oberführer	Senior leader	
OGruf	Obergruppenführer	Senior Group Leader	
OKH	Oberkommando des Heers	High Command of the Army	
Ostubaf	Obersturmbannführer	Senior Storm Command Leader	
OStuf	Obersturmführer	Senior Storm Leader	
Pol. Abtlg.	Politische Abteilung	Political Department	
Pol.Fü	Polizeiführer	Police leaders or chiefs	
PVH	Polizeivorbeugehaft	Police preventative custody	

RASS	Reichsarzt SS	Reich Physician SS	RP SS
RFSS	Reichsführer SS	Reich Leader SS	RL SS
RGBl	Reichsgesetzblatt	Imperial Law Gazette	
R.H.A.		Royal Horse Artillery	
RSHA	Reichssicherheits-hauptamt	Reich Security Main Office	
SA	Sturmabteilung der NSDAP	Storm Troopers [paramilitary branch] of the NSDAP	
SAG	Sanitätsgefreiter	Medical orderly	MO
Sanka	Sanitätskraftwagen	Medical vehicle	MV
SD	Sicherheitsdienst	Security Service	
Sipo	Sicherheitspolizei	Security police	
Sh. (also Shn.)	Sachsenhausen		
SS	Schutzstaffel der NSDAP	Protection Squadron [paramilitary and security organisation] of the NSDAP	
Stapo	Staatspolizei, auch Geheime Staatspolizei	State Police, also Secret State Police	
VGH	Volksgerichtshof	People's Court	
WVHA	Wirtschafts-Verwaltungshauptamt der SS	SS Central Economic-Administrative Office	
ZAL	Zwangsarbeiter	Forced labourer	

Chronology[1]

1940

March/April:

Höß explores in Auschwitz the possibilities for setting up a concentration camp.

Reich Leader SS Himmler gives Richard Glücks, SS Senior Group Leader and Inspector of the Concentration Camps, the order to set up a concentration camp at the artillery barracks of Auschwitz.

Glücks appoints Höß commander of the future concentration camp Auschwitz.

Höß arrives at Auschwitz with five SS members.

May:

Höß is provided by the mayor of Auschwitz with 300 Jews for clearance work.

Höß is officially appointed commander.

Thirty criminal German prisoners from Sachsenhausen selected by Höß arrive in Auschwitz under the leadership by report leader Gerhard Palitzsch and are appointed as prisoner functionaries.

June:

The first 728 Polish prisoners are committed from Tarnów prison.

July:

Escape by the prisoner Tadeusz Wiejowski from the concentration camp Auschwitz; the prisoners have to line up and stand on the muster ground from 6pm until 2pm the next day.

Höß files an application with Reich Leader SS Himmler to shoot sixteen Polish prisoners who had assisted Wiejowski in his escape.

August:

The camp administration sets up a punishment detail.

Activation of the crematorium with an incinerator, which operates until July 1943.

1941

January:
Setting up of a camp orchestra, which has to play during the exit and entry march of the prisoners and to perform concerts for the camp commander.

I.G. Farben board member Otto Ambros travels through Silesia looking for the site of a fourth Buna work.

February:
Reich Marshall Göring, in his function as commissioner for the four-year plan, instructs Himmler to provide concentration camp prisoners for the construction of the Buna works, and orders the resettlement of all Poles from the town of Auschwitz. Into their apartments move Germans, who are supposed to build the Buna works for I.G. Farben.

Completion of a second incinerator.

March:
Himmler inspects Auschwitz concentration camp. He is accompanied by: SS Group Leader Karl Wolff, head of Himmler's personal staff, SS Storm Command Leader Heinrich Vogel, senior head of department at the Central Economic-Administrative Office, SS Under Storm Leader Edmund von Thermann, regional leader and governor of Silesia, SS Brigade Leader Fritz Bracht, SS Senior Group Leader and Higher SS and Police Leader in Wroclaw Heinrich Schmauser, SS Senior Group Leader Richard Glücks. Himmler orders the expansion of Auschwitz to 30,000 prisoners, the erection of a camp for 100,000 prisoners of war as well as a camp for I.G. Farben with 10,000 prisoners.

Meeting of representatives of the SS and I.G. Farben regarding their collaboration at Auschwitz.

April:
Höß selects ten prisoners as retaliation for the escape of one of them and sentences them to death by starvation. By 26 May all of them have died.

June:
The first prisoner transports from Czechoslovakia arrive.

Höß sentences another ten prisoners to death by starvation. They die by 27 June.

Another ten prisoners die by 30 June inside the 'bunker'.

July:

Soviet prisoners of war are brought to the camp and murdered in the gravel pit.

A special commission selects on Himmler's orders 575 prisoners, who are brought to the 'Asylum Sonnenstein' and are gassed there.

In Berlin, Himmler discusses with Höß the technical aspects of the 'final solution'. Höß receives the order for the mass extermination of Jews in Auschwitz and is supposed to present the necessary construction plans within four weeks.

August:

Beginning of the killing of sick prisoners by phenol injections.

Eichmann visits Auschwitz concentration camp in order to discuss with Höß the details of the extermination operation. They agree on the fact that the killing will only be possible with the aid of gas. At the same time the murder of sick prisoners and those unfit to work by poison injections is begun.

September:

First mass murder with Zyklon B of c.600 Russian prisoners of war and roughly 300 other prisoners.

Arrival of the first prisoner transport from Yugoslavia.

October:

Commencement of construction of the Birkenau camp. SS Senior Group Leader Hans Kammler declares, according to Höß, that a camp for 200,000 and not just for 100,000 prisoners of war will be built.

November:

First executions with small calibre weapons by a shot in the neck. Initially killed are 151 mostly Polish prisoners.

Almost 5,000 prisoners of war and other inmates die during this month. In Birkenau mass graves are dug.

1942

January:

Birkenau is determined as the site of the mass extermination of the Jews; the first gassings are carried out in a remodelled farmhouse.

March:

Arrival of the first women's transport with almost 1,000 prisoners from Ravensbrück.

Arrival of the first RSHA transport organised by Eichmann with 999 Slovakian Jewesses.

Arrival of the first RSHA transport with 1,112 Jews from Paris.
The Russian prisoners of war camp is dissolved. Of more than 10,000
prisoners, just 945 are still alive. They are brought to the newly
established Birkenau camp.

April:
Further RSHA transports with Slovakian Jewesses.

May:
First selection at Birkenau.
Commencement of construction of Crematorium II at Birkenau.

July:
Himmler inspects Auschwitz concentration camp; he has a thorough
demonstration of the gassing and the burial of the corpses, and
in addition he observes the corporal punishment of women.
He promotes Höß to SS Senior Storm Command Leader.

August:
First RSHA transport from Belgium.
First RSHA transport from Yugoslavia.
Relocation of the women's camp from the main camp to Birkenau.
Eruption of a spotted fever epidemic; the 'Buna detail' has to cease its
work because of it.

September:
In Chelmo, Höß views the installations for the burning of corpses in
order to destroy the bodies from the mass graves at Birkenau.
In Birkenau 2,000 corpses are stacked, doused with petroleum and
burnt.
Order by the WVHA to hand over all possessions of the Jews deported
to Auschwitz to the Reich Bank or the Main Welfare Office of Ethnic
Germans.

October:
First RSHA transport from Terezin [Theresienstadt].

November:
In the women's camp SS doctor Horst Schumann establishes a trial
station.
Commencement of construction of the Crematoria IV and V at Birkenau.

30 November:
The burning of 107,000 corpses dug up from the mass graves is
completed. Bone remnants are ground and spread as fertiliser over
the fields.

December:
Beginning of the sterilisation experiments in the women's camp; sterilisation of 200 prisoners by X-rays.

1943

February:
Arrival of the first gypsy transport from Germany.
General roll call in the women's camp; 1,000 Jewesses are selected and murdered in the gas chambers.
Operation Factory in Berlin; Jewish armament workers and their families are deported to Auschwitz.

March:
Arrival of the first RSHA transport from Greece.
Registered are 162,000 prisoners.
Activation of the Crematoria II and IV.

April:
Höß and the head of the crematoria, SS Head Company Leader Moll, receive the War Merit Cross First Class with Swords.
Activation of Crematorium V.

June:
Activation of Crematorium III at Birkenau.

July:
Höß and I.G. Farben factory manager Dürrfeld visit the coal mines at Fürstengrube and Janinagrube; Höß promises the allocation of prisoners.

September:
Transport with 5,000 Jews from Terezin [Theresienstadt].

October:
First RSHA transports from Italy.

November:
Höß is transferred to the WVHA at Oranienburg; his successor is SS Senior Storm Command Leader Arthur Liebehenschel.

1944

May to September:
Extermination of the Hungarian Jews during Operation Reinhardt.

May:
Höß takes on the function of garrison commander at Auschwitz. He orders the installation of five pits for burning corpses.
Completion of the 'ramp' of Birkenau.
Arrival of ninety RSHA transports with 250,000 Jews.
SS Storm Command Leader Richard Baer becomes commander of the camp Auschwitz I and relieves Liebehenschel.

June:
Arrival of about sixty RSHA transports with 150,000 Jews.

July:
Allied aerial reconnaissance takes pictures of the complex.

August:
155,000 people are imprisoned.
Liquidation of the gypsy camp and of the Lodz ghetto.
Survivors of the Warsaw uprising are brought to Auschwitz.
Arrival of about thirty-five RSHA transports with c.100,000 Jews.

September:
Aerial attacks on the I.G. Farben works.

October:
Setting up of a new women's camp.
Uprising of the special detail; Jewish prisoners set Crematorium IV on fire.

November:
The gassings at Auschwitz are terminated.
Himmler orders the destruction of the gas chambers and crematoria.

December:
Demolition of the crematoria.
Further aerial attacks on the I.G. Farben works.

1945

17 January:
Commencement of the evacuation of the camp.

27 January:
Liberation of the camp by Soviet troops; they find 5,000 prisoners unable to march left behind.

SS Ranks, their Translation and their Equivalents in the British Armed Forces

SS-Mann or Schütze	SS Private	Private
SS-Oberschütze	SS Head Private	-
SS-Sturmmann	SS Storm Man	Lance Corporal
SS-Rottenführer	SS Band Leader	Corporal
SS-Standartenjunker	SS Standard Officer Cadet	-
SS-Unterscharführer	SS Under Company Leader	Sergeant
SS-Scharführer	SS Company Leader	Platoon Sergeant Major
SS-Standartenoberjunker	SS Standard Senior Officer Cadet	-
SS-Oberscharführer	SS Senior Company Leader	Company Sergeant Major
SS-Hauptscharführer	SS Head Company Leader	Battalion Sergeant Major
SS-Stabsscharführer	SS Staff Company Leader	Similar to Company Sergeant Major
SS-Sturmscharführer	SS Storm Company Leader	Regimental Sergeant Major
SS-Untersturmführer	SS Under Storm Leader	Second Lieutenant
SS-Obersturmführer	SS Senior Storm Leader	Lieutenant

SS-Hauptsturmführer	SS Head Storm Leader	Captain
SS-Sturmbannführer	SS Storm Command Leader	Major
SS-Obersturmbannführer	SS Senior Storm Command Leader	Lieutenant Colonel
SS-Standartenführer	SS Standard Leader	Colonel
SS-Brigadeführer und Generalmajor der Waffen-SS	SS Brigade Leader and Major General of the Waffen-SS	Brigadier
SS-Gruppenführer und Generalleutnant der Waffen-SS	SS Group Leader and Lieutenant General of the Waffen-SS	Major General
SS-Obergruppenführer und General der Waffen-SS	SS Senior Group Leader and General of the Waffen-SS	Lieutenant General
SS-Oberstgruppenführer und Generaloberst der Waffen-SS	SS Supreme Group Leader and Colonel General of the Waffen-SS	General

Facts about Auschwitz Concentration Camp[1*]

The complex encompassed an area of 40 square kilometres and also contained an extensive restricted zone. In the years 1940 to 1941 the inhabitants of the municipal district of Auschwitz where the concentration camp was to be erected, as well as those of eight neighbouring villages, were relocated. In the town and its vicinity 1,200 buildings were demolished in order to create space for the concentration camp as well as for SS barracks and residences for the German workforce.

Under the first camp commander, Rudolf Höß, the construction of the camp began in May 1940, later called Auschwitz I or main camp. The first stage of construction was planned for 7,000 prisoners and consisted of twenty-eight two-storey brick buildings as well as wooden auxiliary buildings. The average occupancy was 18,000 prisoners. The entire area was surrounded by a double fence of barbed wire under high voltage. Above the entrance gate to the camp was written the cynical motto ARBEIT MACHT FREI [Work brings freedom].

On Heinrich Himmler's orders, the construction of the camp Auschwitz II or Birkenau was begun in October 1941. This – significantly larger than the main camp – encompassed 250 wooden and stone barracks. The highest occupancy of Birkenau was c.100,000 prisoners in 1943. In contrast to the main camp, Birkenau was planned from the beginning as an extermination camp. Here was also found the 'ramp' on which the selection of new arrivals was carried out. Birkenau was divided into the following protective custody camps:

- men's camp
- women's camp (from 26 March 1942)
- quarantine camp
- family camp Terezin [Theresienstadt] (from autumn 1943)

- camp for the Hungarian Jews (from May 1944)
- gypsy camp (from spring 1943)
- prisoner infirmary
- camp 'Mexico'
- storage camp 'Canada'

In Birkenau stood the crematoria II to V (completed from 22 March to 25 June 1943), which were furnished with one gas chamber each and according to SS information could burn 4,756 corpses per day. During an uprising on 7 October 1944 prisoners blew up the gas chamber of Crematorium IV. In November 1944 the SS dismantled the extermination installations and blew up the crematoria.

In the vicinity of Auschwitz concentration camp industrial works were located that 'rented' prisoners as labourers from the SS. The I.G. Farben works in the suburb of Monowitz, for example, produced synthetic rubber (Buna). For the prisoners working there the SS set up the outpost Auschwitz-Monowitz on 31 May 1942, which from December 1943 became the centre of the Auschwitz III concentration camp. In addition, the SS operated its own economic enterprises and mines. In total there were fifty such outposts.

Auschwitz concentration camp was evacuated from 17 to 19 January 1945 by the SS. Until then 405,000 prisoner numbers were assigned, of which c.132,000 were to women. Those who were sent to the gas chambers immediately did not receive a number. Their figure is estimated at 1.2 million people. Due to the advance of the Soviet front the SS began to evacuate the camp and sent all prisoners able to walk on 'death marches' to other camps. On 27 January the Red Army liberated the camp and discovered roughly 5,000 sick and dying prisoners left behind.

Prisoner Categories

Jews: From 1942 onward the largest group. 200,000 were registered.

Political prisoners: 160,000, mostly Poles who were arrested during different repressive operations or due to their activities in the resistance.

'Antisocials': Among this category were primarily 21,000 registered Roma.

Soviet prisoners of war: c.15,000, of which 12,000 were registered.

Prisoners to be educated: People who were committed to the concentration camp for factual or alleged violation of workplace discipline; their number is estimated at c.11,000.

Police prisoners: Exclusively Poles who came to the camp due to the overcrowding in the Gestapo prisons at Katowice and Myslowice and there waited for their summary justice sentences. Their number is estimated at several thousands.

Criminals: Several hundreds, mostly of German origin. From this group the camp administration frequently chose the so-called prisoner functionaries (kapos).

Jehovah's Witnesses: Registered were at least 138 prisoners, who came mainly from Germany.

Homosexuals: At least several dozen mainly of German origin.

Number of dead (estimates):

- Jews: 1 million
- Poles: 70,000 to 75,000
- Roma: 21,000
- Soviet prisoners of war: 14,000
- Others: 10,000 to 15,000
- in total: c.1.1 million

Affidavit by Höß during the Nuremberg Main Trial of War Crimes

During the Nuremberg Main Trial of War Crimes Höß was examined as a witness for the defence of Ernst Kaltenbrunner, Chief of the Security Police and the SD as well as head of the Reich Security Main Office, on 1 and 2 April 1946. The statements made by Höß during the examination were summarised in an affidavit in English. This affidavit was signed by Höß on 5 April 1946. The document number of the Nuremberg trial is 3868-PS and US-819.

I, Rudolf Franz Ferdinand Höß, testify after prior lawful swearing-in and declare the following:

1. I am forty-six years old and member of the NSDAP since 1922; member of the SS since 1934; member of the Waffen-SS since 1933. From 1st December 1934 I was a member of the SS guard unit, the so-called Death Head Unit.

2. Since 1934 I was working continually in the administration of concentration camps and served in Dachau until 1938; then as adjutant in Sachsenhausen from 1938 until 1st May 1940, at which time I was appointed commander of Auschwitz. I commanded Auschwitz until 1st December 1943 and estimate that at least 2,500,000 victims have been executed and exterminated there by gassing and subsequent cremation; at least half a million died by starvation and illness, which amounts to a total number of 3 million dead. This figure represents approximately 70 or 80 per cent of all persons sent as prisoners to Auschwitz; the remaining were selected and used for slave labour in the industries of the concentration camp. Among the executed and cremated persons were approximately 20,000 Russian prisoners of war (who were previously selected by the Gestapo from the

223

prisoner of war camps); these were committed at Auschwitz to the Wehrmacht transports commanded by regular officers and forces of the Wehrmacht. The remainder of the total number of victims entails approximately 100,000 German Jews and large number of inhabitants, mostly Jews, from the Netherlands, France, Belgium, Poland, Hungary, Czechoslovakia, Greece and other countries. Approximately 400,000 Hungarian Jews were executed by us in Auschwitz alone during summer 1944.

3. WVHA (Central Economic-Administrative Office) led by Senior Group Leader Oswald Pohl was responsible for all administrative matters in the concentration camps such as accommodation, food provisioning and medical care. Before the establishment of the RSHA the Office of the Secret State Police (Gestapo) and the Reich Office of the Criminal Police were responsible for the arrests, commitments to concentration camps, for punishments and execution there. After the formation of the RSHA all these functions were carried out as before, but according to the orders signed by Heydrich as head of the RSHA. While Kaltenbrunner was head of the RSHA, the orders regarding protective custody, commitments, punishments and special executions were signed by Kaltenbrunner or Müller, the Gestapo chief, as Kaltenbrunner's deputy.

4. Mass executions by gassing commenced in the course of summer 1941 and lasted until autumn 1944. I personally supervised the executions in Auschwitz until 1st December 1943 and know due to my current service in monitoring the concentration camps for the WVHA that these mass executions proceeded as mentioned previously. All mass executions by gassing occurred under the direct orders and under the supervision and responsibility of the RSHA. I received all orders immediately from the RSHA to carry out these mass executions.

5. On 1st December 1943 I became head of Office I in Office Group D of the WVHA, and in this office I was responsible for the compilation of all issues arising between the RSHA and the concentration camps under management by the WVHA. I held this position until the end of the war. Pohl as head of the WVHA and Kaltenbrunner as head of the RSHA often conferred in person regarding the concentration camps and communicated frequently verbally and in writing.

On 5th October 1944 I presented a detailed report to Kaltenbrunner in his office at the RSHA, Berlin, regarding the concentration camp

Mauthausen. Kaltenbrunner asked me for a brief oral extract from this report and said he would reserve every decision until he would have the opportunity to peruse it in all details. This report dealt with the assignment to labour of several hundred prisoners sentenced to death, so-called 'nameless prisoners'.

6.　The 'final solution' of the Jewish question meant the complete eradication of all Jews in Europe. I had the order to create extermination facilities in Auschwitz in June 1942. At that time three further extermination camps already existed in the General Government: Belzec, Treblinka and Wolzek. These camps were under the operational command of the Security Police and the SD. I visited Treblinka to see how the exterminations were carried out. The camp commander of Treblinka told me that he had liquidated 80,000 in the course of half a year. He was mainly involved in the liquidation of all Jews from the Warsaw ghetto. He used monoxide gas, and in his opinion his methods were not very effective. When I constructed the extermination buildings in Auschwitz, I therefore used Zyklon B, crystallised hydrogen cyanide acid which we threw into the death chamber through a small opening. It took 3 to 15 minutes, depending on the weather conditions, to kill the people inside the death chamber. We knew when the people were dead because their screaming stopped. We usually waited half an hour before opening the doors and removing the corpses. After the corpses had been removed, our special details took off their rings and pried the gold from the teeth of the bodies.

7.　Another improvement towards Treblinka was that we built gas chambers which could hold 2,000 people at once, while the 10 gas chambers at Treblinka held only 200 people each. The manner of how we selected our victims was the following: two SS doctors served at Auschwitz in order to examine the arriving prisoner transports. The prisoners had to walk past one of the doctors who gave their decisions by sign at their passing. Those fit to work were sent to the camp. Others were sent immediately to the extermination complex. Young children were exterminated without distinction, as they were unable to work due to their young age.

Another improvement we made towards Treblinka was the fact that in Treblinka the victims almost always knew that they were supposed to be exterminated, while in Auschwitz we made the effort to fool the victims by letting them believe that they had to undertake a delousing process. Of course they frequently realised our true intentions, too, and we had sometimes unrest and difficulties because of it. Very frequently women wanted to hide their children under their clothes, but if we found them, the children were of course sent to their extermination. We were supposed to carry out the exterminations in secret, but the foul, nauseating smell originating from the incessant burning of bodies permeated the whole region, and all people living in the surrounding localities knew that exterminations were taking place at Auschwitz.

8. From time to time special prisoners came from the local Gestapo office. The SS doctors killed such prisoners by benzine injections. The doctors had the instruction to issue common death certificates and could choose causes of death according to their whim.

9. From time to time we performed medical experiments on female prisoners among which were experiments on sterilisation and cancer. Most of these people dying during the experiments had already been sentenced to death by the Gestapo.

10. Rudolf Mildner was during the period from about March 1941 until September 1943 chief of the Gestapo in Katowice, and as such head of the Political Department at Auschwitz which carried out the third degree interrogations. In this function he often sent prisoners to Auschwitz for incarceration or execution. He visited Auschwitz on several occasions. The Gestapo court, the SS summary court, interrogating persons accused of various crimes, such as escaped prisoners of war etc., often gathered at Auschwitz, and Mildner was frequently present during the interrogation of such persons who usually were executed at Auschwitz according to their sentence. I showed Mildner the extermination complex in Auschwitz in its entirety, and he was very interested, as he had to send Jews from his region to their execution at Auschwitz.

I understand English, as it is written above.

The statements above are true; I made this declaration voluntarily and without coercion. After reading the statements I signed and administered the same in Nuremberg, Germany, on the fifth day of April 1946.

Rudolf Franz Ferdinand Höß

Archives

APMO, Archiwum Państwowe Muzeum Auschwitz-Birkenau
Amtsarchiv [District Office Archive] Gransee
Botschaft der Republik Polen [Embassy of the Republic of Poland]
Brandenburgisches Landeshauptarchiv [Brandenburg Central State Archive]
Bundesarchiv [Federal Archive] Berlin-Lichterfelde
Bundesarchiv, Außenstelle [Branch] Ludwigsburg
Bibliothek des Deutschen Bundestags [Library of the German Parliament]
BstU – Bundesbeauftragter für die Unterlagen der Staatssicherheit der ehemaligen DDR [Federal Commissioner for the Records of the State Security Service of the former German Democratic Republic]
Die Beauftragte der Bundesregierung für Kultur und Medien [Commissioner of the Federal Government for Culture and Media]
Domstiftsarchiv Brandenburg [Archive of the Cathedral Chapter Brandenburg]
Gemeindeverwaltung, Standesamt/Gewerbeamt, Neukirch/Lausitz [Municipal Administration, Registry and Trade Office Neukirch/Lusatia
Gemeinde [Municipality] St Michaelisdonn
Heimatverein [Local Heritage Society] Buberow
Historisches Archiv [Historical Archive] Krupp
Institut für Zeitgeschichte [Institute for Contemporary History] Munich-Upper (IfZ)
International Tracing Service Bad Arolsen (ITS)
Landesarchiv [State Archive] Berlin
Landesarchiv [State Archive] Schleswig-Holstein
Landgericht [State Court] Schwerin
Politisches Archiv Auswärtiges Amt [Political Archive Foreign Office]
Staatsbibliothek [State Library] Berlin
Stadtarchiv [Town Archive] Baden-Baden
Stadtarchiv [Town Archive] Dachau; Registry Office Dachau

Stadtarchiv [Town Archive] Flensburg
Stadtarchiv [Town Archive] Ludwigsburg
Stadtarchiv [Town Archive] Mannheim
Stadtarchiv [Town Archive] Schwerin
Stadtarchiv [Town Archive] Stuttgart
Stuttgart, Amt für öffentliche Ordnung (Abt. Altkartei) [Office for Public Order, Department for Old Files]
Zentrum für Historsiche Forschung Berlin der Polnischen Akademie der Wissenschaften [Centre for Historical Research Berlin of the Polish Academy of Sciences]

Selected Bibliography

Adler, H.G./Langbein, H./Lingens-Reiner, Ella (eds), *Auschwitz. Zeugnisse und Berichte*. 3rd revised edition Cologne 1984.

Arendt, Hannah, *Eichmann in Jerusalem. A Report on the Banality of Evil*. London 2006.

Bezwińska, Jadwiga, *Auschwitz in den Augen der SS*. Warsaw 1992, State Museum Auschwitz-Birkenau 1997.

Black, Peter, *Ernst Kaltenbrunner: Ideological Soldier of the Third Reich*. Princeton 1984.

Brandt, Rolf, *Albert Leo Schlageter. Leben und Sterben eines deustchen Helden*. Hamburg 1937.

Bronnen, Arnolt, *Roßbach*. Berlin 1931.

Cesarani, David, *Eichmann: His Life and Crimes*. New York 2005.

Czech, Danuta: *Auschwitz Chronicle, 1939–1945*. New York 1997.

Demant, Ebbo (ed), *Auschwitz 'direkt von der Rampe weg'*. Reinbek 1979.

Deselaers, Manfred, *And Your Conscience Never Haunted You: The Life of Rudolf Hess, Commander of Auschwitz*. Auschwitz-Birkenau State Museum 2013.

Eichmann, Adolf, *False Gods: The Jerusalem Memoirs*. London 2015.

Forschungsstelle für Zeitgeschichte Hamburg (ed), *Der Dienstkalender Heinrich Himmlers 1941/42*. Hamburg 1999.

Fraenkel, Heinrich/Manvell, Roger, *Heinrich Himmler: The Sinister Life of the Head of the SS and Gestapo*. Barnsley 2017.

Französisches Büro des Informationsdienstes über Kriegsverbrechen (ed.), *Konzentrationslager, Dokument F 321*. 18th edition Frankfurt/M. 2005.

Friedman, Towiah (ed), *We Shall Never Forget: An Album of Photographs, Articles and Documents: The Trial of the Nazi Murderer Adolf Eichman[n] in Jerusalem*. Haifa 1991.

Fröhlich, Elke (ed), *Die Tagebücher von Joseph Goebbels 1924–1945*, Munich 1987–2008.

Gilbert, Gustave M., *Nuremberg Diary*. New York 1947.

Harding, Thomas, *Hanns and Rudolf: The German Jew and the Hunt for the Kommandant of Auschwitz*. London 2014

Harris, Whitney R., *Tyranny on Trial*. New York 1995.

Heydecker, Joe/Leeb, Johannes (eds), *The Nuremberg Trials*. London 1962.

Höß, Rainer, *Das Erbe des Kommandanten: Rudolf Höß war der Henker von Auschwitz: er war mein Großvater. Geschichte einer schrecklichen Familie.* Munich 2013.

Höß, Rudolf, *Commandant of Auschwitz*. Introduced by Primo Levi. London 2000.

Hoffman, Michael, *Die Shoah vor Gericht in Polen. Verfolgung und Verurteilung von nationalsozialistischen Verbrechern auf dem Gebiet des Volksrepublik Polen.* Munich 2011.

Hohmann, Joachim S./Wieland, Günther (ed.), *Konzentrationslager Sachsenhausen bei Oranienburg. 1939– 1945.* Frankfurt/M. 1997.

International Military Court Nuremberg (ed), *The trial of German major war criminals: proceedings of the International Military Tribunal sitting at Nuremberg, Germany.* London 1946.

Institut für Zeitgeschichte/Norbert Frei (ed.), *Standort- und Kommandanturbefehle des Konzentrationslagers Auschwitz 1940–1945.* Munich 2000.

Institute of Documentation for the Investigation of Nazi War Crimes in Israel/Friedman, Towiah (ed),
Rudolf Höß. Commandant in Auschwitz. Haifa 1997

Janssen, Hans Peter, *Von Rehedyk nach St. Michaelisdonn. 400 Jahre Kirchen- und Dorfgeschichte. 1611– 2011.* Husum 2011.

Kaul, Friedrich Karl/Noack, Joachim (eds), *Angeklagter Nr. 6. Eine Auschwitz-Dokumentation.* Berlin 1966.

Kempner, Robert M.W., *SS im Kreuzverhör: Die Elite, die Europa in Scherben schlug.* Nördlingen 1987.

Kielar, Wieslaw, *Anus Mundi: 1,500 Days in Auschwitz/Birkenau*. New York 1980.

Klee, Ernst, *Das Personenlexikon zum Dritten Reich. Wer war was vor und nach 1945.* 4th edition Frankfurt/M. 2013.

Kogon, Eugen, *The Theory and Practice of Hell: The German Concentration Camps and the System Behind Them.* New York 2006.

Komitee der Antifaschistischen Widerstandskämpfer in der DDR (ed), *SS im Einsatz. Eine Dokumentation* über die Verbrechen der SS. Berlin 1957.

Kompisch, Kathrin, *Täterinnen. Frauen im Nationalsozialismus.* Cologne/Weimar/Vienna 2008.

Lang, Jochen von (ed), *Das Eichmann-Protokoll. Tonbandaufzeichnungen der israelischen Verhöre.* Berlin 1982.

Langbein, Hermann, *People in Auschwitz*. Chapel Hill 2016.

Langbein, Hermann (ed), *Der Auschwitz-Prozess. Eine Dokumentation.* Vol. 1, 2nd print of the 1965 edition, Frankfurt/M. 1995.

Lasik, Aleksander (ed), *Auschwitz 1940–1945. Studien zur Geschichte des Konzentrations- und Vernichtungslagers Auschwitz.* Auschwitz-Birkenau 1999.

Longerich, Peter, *Heinrich Himmler*. Oxford 2012.

Morsch, Günter/Ley, Astrid (ed), *Das Konzentrationslager Sachsenhausen 1936– 1945. Ereignisse und Entwicklungen.* Berlin 2008.

230

Naujoks, Harry, *Mein Leben im KZ Sachsenhausen 1936–1942. Erinnerungen des ehemaligen Lagerältesten.* Berlin 1989.

Oertzen, F.W. von, *Die deutschen Freikorps 1918–1923.* 6th edition Munich 1939.

Overy, Richard: *Interrogations: Inside the Minds of the Nazi Elite.* London 2002.

Paul, Gerhard, *Der Untergang 1945 in Flensburg,* published by the State Agency for Civic Education Schleswig-Holstein, Kiel 2012.

Piening, Holger, *Westküste 1945. Nordfriesland und Dithmarschen am Ende des Zweiten Weltkriegs.* Heide 2000.

Pohl, Oswald, *Credo. Mein Weg zu Gott.* Landshut 1950.

Poliakov, Leon/Wilf, Josef (eds): *Das Dritte Reich und die Juden. Dokumente und Aufsätze.* Berlin 1955.

Pozner, Vladimir, *Abstieg in die Hölle.* Berlin 1982.

Pressac, Jean-Claude, *Auschwitz: Technique and operation of the gas chambers.* New York 1989.

Riedel, Dirk, *Ordnungshüter und Massenmörder im Dienst der 'Volksgemeinschaft'.* Berlin 2010.

Schmorak, Dov. B., *Der Prozess Eichmann. Dargestellt an Hand der in Nürnberg und Jerusalem vorgelegten Dokumente sowie der Gerichtsprotokolle.* Vienna/Stuttgart/Basel 1964.

Schulte, Jan Erik: *Zwangsarbeit und Vernichtung: Das Wirtschaftsimperium der SS: Oswald Pohl und das SS- Wirtschafts- Verwaltungshauptamt 1933–1945.* Paderborn 2001.

Segev, Tom, *Soldiers of Evil: Commandants of the Nazi Concentration Camps.* Faringdon 1990.

Sobolewicz, Tadeusz, *But I survived.* Auschwitz-Birkenau State Museum 1998.

Speer, Albert, *Infiltration: How Heinrich Himmler Schemed to Build an SS Industrial Empire.* London 1981.

Thalhofer, Elisabeth, *Entgrenzung der Gewalt: Gestapo-Lager in der Endphase des Dritten Reiches.* Paderborn 2010.

Tuchel, Johannes, *Die 'Inspektion der Konzentrationslager' 1934–1938: Vorgeschichte, Struktur und Funktion einer Organisation im nationalsozialistischen Herrschaftsapparat.* Berlin 1989.

Picture Credits

Amtsverwaltung Gransee und Gemeinden [Administration Gransee and municipalities]: fig. 10

Brandenburgisches Landeshauptarchiv: figs. 3, 4, 5, 6

Bundesbeauftragte für die Unterlagen der Staatssicherheit der ehemaligen DDR, MfS, HA iX/11, ZM67: fig. 14

IfZ/Rainer Höß: fig. 13

Polish Press Agency: fig. 15

Private archive of the author: fig. 9, 11

Town Archive Baden-Baden: fig. 1

Town Archive Dachau: fig. 8

Town Archive Mannheim: fig. 2, 7

Yad Vashem, Jerusalem: fig. 12Fig. 1: Birth certificate

Fig. 2: Entry in the Mannheim register

Fig. 3: Facsimile of a letter by Rudolf Höß to the Brandenburg penitentiary

Fig. 4: Facsimile of letter by Rudolf Höß from the Brandenburg jail

Fig. 5: Letter by Senior Lieutenant Gerhard Roßbach (retired) to the administration of the penitentiary Brandenburg on the Havel

Fig. 6: Envelope of the letter by Höß to his 'bride'

Fig. 7: Official registration card of Helene Huber

Fig. 8: Official registration card regarding the move of Mr and Mrs Höß to Dachau

Fig. 9: Title page of Oswald Pohl's book *Credo. Mein Weg zu Gott* published 1950.

Fig. 10: Marriage certificate of Rudolf Höß and Hedwig Hensel

Fig. 11: Landscape by Fritz Hensel

Fig. 12: Heinrich Himmler and Rudolf Höß during a visit at Auschwitz

Fig. 13: The Höß family in their Auschwitz villa in autumn 1943. From left to right: Ingebritt, Hedwig Höß with the newborn Annegret, Hans-Jürgen, Heidetraut, Rudolf Höß and Klaus-Bernd

Fig. 14: A page from Höß' farewell letter to his wife and his children

Fig. 15: Höß was sentenced as a war criminal to death by hanging and executed on the site of the former main camp Auschwitz I on 16 April 1947.

Notes

Introduction

1 Rudolf Höß: *Kommandant in Auschwitz. Autobiographische Aufzeichnungen*, edited by Martin Broszat, Munich 2013, 24th edition, p.231.
2 Archive Sachsenhausen, P 3 Matejka, Vladimir.
3 Rudolf Höß: *Kommandant in Auschwitz. Autobiographische Aufzeichnungen*, p.231.
4 *Op. cit.*, p.235.
5 BstU, MfS HA IX/11. ZM 67, Annotation Höß. Undated.
6 Archive of the Fritz Bauer Institute, 1st Frankfurt Auschwitz Trial, Case against Mulka, Witness Interrogation Heinrich Dürmayer, 58th day of trial, 22 June 1964.
7 Letter to Caesar, reproduced in: Leon Poliakov/Josef Wulf (eds): *Das Dritte Reich und die Juden*, Berlin 1955, p.139.
8 Jadwiga Bezwińska: *Auschwitz in den Augen der SS.* Statement by Stanislaw Dubiel, Warsaw 1992, p.290.
9 Hermann Langbein (ed): *Der Auschwitz-Prozess. Eine Dokumentation.* Frankfurt/ M. 1995, vol. 1, p.88.
10 Robert M.W. Kempner: *SS im Kreuzverhör: Die Elite, die Europa in Scherben schlug.* Nördlingen 1987, p.79f.
11 Hermann Langbein (ed.): *Der Auschwitz-Prozess.*
12 Jadwiga Bezwińska: *Auschwitz in den Augen der SS.* Statement by Stanislaw Dubiel, p.291f.

1. The Life Lies of Rudolf Höß

1 BArch, R 3003, Assassination Trial, statement by Höß before the Reich Court Leipzig, 22 August 1923.
2 Wilhelm Kreuz in collaboration with Sara Kettner: Die Klasse Höß. Ein Projekt von Schülern der Klassenstufe 12 im Schuljahr 2005/2006, in: 200 Jahre Vereinigtes Großherzogliches Lyceum – Karl-Friedrich-Gymnasium Mannheim, pp.165–174.
3 Rudolf Höß: *Kommandant in Auschwitz. Autobiographische Aufzeichnungen,* p.34.
4 *Op. cit.*, p.34.
5 Gustave M. Gilbert: *Nürnberger Tagebuch. Gespräche der Angeklagten mit dem Gerichtspsychologen.* 14th edition, Hamburg 2012, p.259ff.
6 *Op. cit.*
7 Rudolf Höß: *Kommandant in Auschwitz. Autobiographische Aufzeichnungen,* p.34f.
8 *Op. cit.*, p.35.
9 *Op. cit.*, p.40f.
10 The Free Corps Roßbach was formed on the order of the governorate of Graudenz fortress in West Prussia by the then twenty-five-year-old lieutenant Gerhard Roßbach (1893–1967) from the remains of a machine gun training commando.

233

Until the turn of the year 1918/19 the Roßbach troop was deployed south of the Strasburg district in West Prussia as border protection. On 19 October 1919 the Free Corps set off for the Baltic states. It supported the beleaguered troops of the Voluntary Russian Western Army [Freiwillige Russische Westarmee] and the Iron Division and was deployed along the front of Daugava River. Returned to the Reich, Roßbach received the order to dissolve his free corps in Ratzeburg in Mecklenburg. Large parts, however, remained in East Prussia and found work there in cover enterprises that were supposed to ensure the illegal retention of the troop. After the renewed dissolution on 20 May 1920 many of the men were placed in agricultural jobs in Mecklenburg and Pomerania.

11 Joseph Goebbels: *Die Tagebücher*, Part I, Notes 1924–1941, Munich 1999. Entry dated 13 May 1926, p.80.
12 E.W. von Oertzen: *Die deutschen Freikorps 1918–1923*, 6th edition, Munich 1939, p.104f.
13 Rudolf Höß: *Kommandant in Auschwitz. Autobiographische Aufzeichnungen*, p.49f.
14 BArch R 3003, Reich Court Leipzig, Trial Höß and others.
15 BArch R 3003, results of the preliminary investigation. The Reich chief prosecutor, Leipzig, 19 February 1924.
16 Ibid.
17 Ibid.
18 Ibid.
19 Central State Archive Schwerin. 10.9-H/8 Nachlass Hildebrandt, Friedrich Karl, Nr. 104 (Schutzverfilmung S138)
20 Ibid.
21 Jean-Claude Pressac: *Die Krematorien von Auschwitz: Die Technik des Massenmordes*. Munich 1994, p.12.
22 Rudolf Höß: *Kommandant in Auschwitz. Autobiographische Aufzeichnungen*, p.52.
23 BArch R 3003, Letter from Höß to Mrs Härtel, Brandenburg, 25 March 1928.
24 Rudolf Höß: *Kommandant in Auschwitz. Autobiographische Aufzeichnungen*, p.56.
25 Ibid., p.65 (emphasis in the original).
26 Ibid., p.67 (emphasis in the original). All italics in the text were taken from the original.
27 Ibid., p.71.
28 Central State Archive Brandenburg, Rep 29 Brdbg. Nr. 6691, letter by the Reich chief prosecutor to the directorship of the Brandenburg penitentiary, Leipzig, 1 April 1924.
29 Central State Archive Brandenburg, Rep 29 Brdbg. Nr. 6691, personal statement Höß, Brandenburg, 22 April 1924.
30 Central State Archive Brandenburg, Rep 29 Brdbg. Nr. 6691, note of the penitentiary director, Brandenburg, 4 June 1924.
31 Central State Archive Brandenburg, Rep 29 Brdbg. Nr. 6691, letter by Schnütgen to the board of the penitentiary, Neuhof, 11 June 1924.
32 Central State Archive Brandenburg, Rep 29 Brdbg. Nr. 6691, letter by the Reich chief prosecutor to the penitentiary, Leipzig, 13 February 1925.
33 Central State Archive Brandenburg, Rep 29 Brdbg. Nr. 6691, letter by Beckmann to the penitentiary board, Kalsow, 25 October 1924.
34 Central State Archive Brandenburg, Rep 29 Brdbg. Nr. 6691, letter by the penitentiary direction to Beckmann, Brandenburg, 1 November 1924.
35 Central State Archive Brandenburg, Rep 29 Brdbg. Nr. 6691, letter by Roßbach to the penitentiary board, Munich, 3 March 1926.
36 Central State Archive Brandenburg, Rep 29 Brdbg. Nr. 6691, letter by the penitentiary board to Roßbach, Brandenburg, 10 March 1926.

37 Central State Archive Brandenburg, Rep 29 Brdbg. Nr. 6691, letter by Roßbach to the penitentiary board, Munich, 1 April 1926.
38 Central State Archive Brandenburg, Rep 29 Brdbg. Nr. 6691, letter by the penitentiary board to E. Heins, Munich, Munich, Brandenburg, 19 June 1926.
39 Roßbach had founded a 'sports band Ekkehard', possibly the 'Sports School Ekkehard' is identical with that institution.
40 Rudolf Höß: *Kommandant in Auschwitz. Autobiographische Aufzeichnungen*, p.66.
41 Central State Archive Brandenburg, Rep 29 Brdbg. Nr. 6691, letter by Höß to Helene Huber, Mannheim, Brandenburg, 19 June 1924.
42 Rudolf Höß: *Kommandant in Auschwitz. Autobiographische Aufzeichnungen*, p.66.
43 Central State Archive Brandenburg, Rep 29 Brdbg. Nr. 6691, attestation of employment, non-employment, detention, sickness etc.
44 Rudolf Höß: *Kommandant in Auschwitz. Autobiographische Aufzeichnungen*, p.72.
45 Central State Archive Brandenburg, Rep 29 Brdbg. Nr. 6691, statement by Höß, Brandenburg, 28 November 1927.
46 Central State Archive Brandenburg, Rep 29 Brdbg. Nr. 6691, letter by Mrs Kadow to the penitentiary board, Wismar, 1 October 1926.
47 Central State Archive Brandenburg, Rep 29 Brdbg. Nr. 6691, letter by the penitentiary board to Mrs Kadow, Brandenburg, 6 October 1926.
48 Rudolf Höß: *Kommandant in Auschwitz. Autobiographische Aufzeichnungen*, p.74.
49 BArch, R 3003, petition for pardon of Höß dated 5 September 1927.
50 BArch, R 3003, letter by Lehmann to the Minister of Justice Hergt, Munich, 18 April 1928.
51 Bavarian State Library, Munich Centre for Digitalisation, meetings of the Reichstag, vol. 423.1928, minutes of 13 June 1928, p.15ff.
52 Ibid.
53 Ibid.
54 Ibid.
55 Central State Archive Brandenburg, Rep 29 Brdbg. Nr. 6691, and Rudolf Höß: *Kommandant in Auschwitz. Autobiographische Aufzeichnungen*, p.75.
56 Fröhlich, Elke (ed.), *Die Tagebücher von Joseph Goebbels. Sämtliche Fragmente. Teil I, Aufzeichnungen 1924–1941, Band I, 27.6.1924–31.12.1930*, entry dated 19 July 1928.
57 Rudolf Höß: *Kommandant in Auschwitz. Autobiographische Aufzeichnungen*, p.76 (emphases in the original). See also: Manfred Deselaers: 'Perspektive der Täter. Das Beispiel des Kommandanten Rudolf Höß', in: *Dialog an der Schwelle von Auschwitz*. Cracow 2003.
58 Rudolf Höß: *Kommandant in Auschwitz. Autobiographische Aufzeichnungen*, p.77.
59 Town archive Dachau, official registration cards.
60 Certified document of the registry office Dachau, Dachau, 20 February 2014.

2. The Personality

1 BArch, VBS 1/1040057735, recommendation minutes of the leadership corps of the commandant's headquarters of the concentration camp Dachau.
2 BArch, VBS 1/1040057735, evaluation of Höß, May 1943.
3 BArch, VBS 1/1040057735, letter of the administration of the concentration camp Dachau to the regional leadership Munich-Upper Bavaria, Dachau, 14 May 1936.
4 BArch, VBS 1/1040057735, letter of the Reich leadership of the NSDAP to the regional group Death Head Unit Upper Bavaria, Munich, 25 November 1936.
5 Andrea Riedle: *Die Angehörigen des Kommandanturstabs im KZ Sachsenhausen*. Berlin 2011, p.79.

6 BArch, VBS 1/1040057735, Letter by Bormann to Rreich treasurer, regarding SS Head Storm Leader Rudolf Höß, membership number 5 357 166, Sachsenhausen (northern railway), Friedlandstr. 11.

7 BstU, MfS, HA IX, no. 23036, notes by Höß, Cracow.

8 Rudolf Höß: *Kommandant in Auschwitz. Autobiographische Aufzeichnungen*, p.103.

9 This is the code name for the systematic murder of all Jews and Roma of the so-called General Government. Between July 1942 and October 1943 more than 2 million Jews as well as around 50,000 Roma were murdered in the extermination camps.

10 Pery Broad: 'Erinnerungen', in: Jadwiga Bezwińska: *Auschwitz in den Augen der SS*, p.182f.

11 Rudolf Höß: *Kommandant in Auschwitz. Autobiographische Aufzeichnungen*, p.233.

12 Ibid. p.235.

13 IfZ Arch, ZS 2455, AZ 825/4/92, statement by Isaak Egon Ochshorn, September 1945.

14 Oswald Pohl: *Credo. Mein Weg zu Gott*, Landshut 1950, p.39.

15 *Ibid.*

16 Archiv des Fritz Bauer Instituts, 1. Frankfurter Auschwitz-Prozess, Strafsache gegen Mulka u.a., Landgericht Frankfurt a.M., 88. Verhandlungstag, Einlassung des Angeklagten Boger, 145. Verhandlungstag, 25 March 1965.

17 Archiv des Fritz Bauer Instituts, 1. Frankfurter Auschwitz-Prozess, Strafsache gegen Mulka u.a., Landgericht Frankfurt a.M., 88. Verhandlungstag, Einlassung des Zeugen Horst Huley, 88. Verhandlungstag, 11 September 1964.

18 Archiv des Fritz Bauer Instituts, 1. Frankfurter Auschwitz-Prozess, Strafsache gegen Mulka u.a., Landgericht Frankfurt a.M., 88. Verhandlungstag, Einlassung des Zeugen Leopold Heger, 88. Verhandlungstag, 11 September 1964.

19 Richard Overy: *Verhöre. Die NS-Elite in den Händen der Allierten 1945*, Munich 2002, Document 16: conflict of competence, p.392ff.

20 Ibid., p.393.

21 Ibid., p.395.

22 Ibid., p.397.

23 Ibid., p.398.

24 Ibid., p.398f.

25 Ibid., p.403.

26 Ibid., p.404.

27 BstU, MfS, HA XX, No. 3560, concentration camp Auschwitz, fact file.

28 Gustave M. Gilbert, Nürnberger Tagebuch. Gespräche der Angeklagten mit dem *Gerichtspsychologen*, p.242ff.

29 This number has turned out to be too high; the number of 1.1 million murdered probably corresponds with reality to great extent.

30 Gustave M. Gilbert, *Nürnberger Tagebuch. Gespräche der Angeklagten mit dem Gerichtspsychologen*, p.242ff.

31 Gustave M. Gilbert, *Nürnberger Tagebuch. Gespräche der Angeklagten mit dem Gerichtspsychologen*, p.251ff.

32 *Der Nürnberger Prozess gegen die Hauptkriegsverbrecher vom 14. November 1945–1. Oktober 1946*. Munich/Zurich 1984, volume XI, 108th day, Monday, 15 April 1946.

33 Gustave M. Gilbert, *Nürnberger Tagebuch. Gespräche der Angeklagten mit dem Gerichtspsychologen*

34 Ibid.

35 Ibid.

36 Gustave M. Gilbert, *Nürnberger Tagebuch. Gespräche der Angeklagten mit dem Gerichtspsychologe*, p.259ff.

37 Gustave M. Gilbert, *Nürnberger Tagebuch. Gespräche der Angeklagten mit dem Gerichtspsychologe*, p.243ff.

38 Archiv der Gedenkstätte Sachsenhausen, SS-Wirtschafts-Verwaltungshauptamt, Befehl Maurers, betr.: Jüdische Häftlinge, Oranienburg, 5 October 1942.

39 Gustave M. Gilbert, *Nürnberger Tagebuch. Gespräche der Angeklagten mit dem Gerichtspsychologe*, p.327.

40 He meant Otto Ohlendorf, SS Group Leader and Lieutenant General of the Police, commander of Deployment Group D and head of department (Security Service [SD] homeland) in the Reich Security Main Office.

41 Karl Dönitz, Grand Admiral, last head of state of the German Reich.

42 Gustave M. Gilbert, *Nürnberger Tagebuch. Gespräche der Angeklagten mit dem Gerichtspsychologe*, p.238.

43 Hans Michael Frank, Hitler's lawyer and supreme legal practitioner during the 'Third Reich'.

3. Höß and the SS

1 Harry Naujoks: *Mein Leben im KZ Sachsenhausen 1936–1942*. Berlin 1989, p.84.

2 Rudolf Höß: *Kommandant in Auschwitz. Autobiographische Aufzeichnungen*, p.104.

3 Elisabeth Thalhofer: *Entgrenzung der Gewalt. Gestapo-Lager in der Endphase des Dritten Reiches*. Paderborn 2010, p.118.

4 BStU, MfS, HA IX, no. 23036, camp regulations, handwritten notes by Höß, Cracow, 1 October 1946.

5 BstU, camp regulations, III. Protective custody camp, Cracow, 1 October 1946.

6 Archiv des Fritz Bauer Instituts, 1. Frankfurter Auschwitz-Prozess, Strafsache gegen Mulka u.a., examination of the witness Gustav Murr, 138th day of trial, 19 February 1965.

7 Aleksander Lasik et al. (eds.): *Auschwitz 1940–1945. Studien zur Geschichte des Konzentrations- und Vernichtungslagers Auschwitz*. Auschwitz-Birkenau, 1999.

8 BArch, R 49/3111, Reich Commissioner for the Strengthening of the German National Character on a meeting with Höß regarding the resettlements on the areal of the concentration camp Auschwitz, Auschwitz, 19 February 1941.

9 BArch, R 49/3111, letter by Höß to the representative of the RKF in Katowice, Senior Storm Command Leader Frommhagen, Auschwitz, 22 March 1941.

10 Archiv des Fritz Bauer Instituts, 1. Frankfurter Auschwitz-Prozess, Strafsache gegen Mulka u.a., examination of the witness Ludwig Damm, 80th day of trial, 21 August 1964.

11 Archiv des Fritz Bauer Instituts, 1. Frankfurter Auschwitz-Prozess, Strafsache gegen Mulka u.a., examination of the witness Jan Pilecki, 45th day of trial, 14 May 1964.

12 Emphasis (capitals) in the original.

13 BstU, MfS, HA IX, no. 23036, notes Höß, Cracow, November 1946.

14 Himmler's official appointment calendar, entry dated 1 March 1941, p.123.

15 Wieslaw Kielar: *Anus Mundi. Fünf Jahre Auschwitz*. Frankfurt/M. 1979, p.77.

16 Public Record Office, W = 309/217, interrogation of Höß by Hanns Alexander, 14 March 1946.

17 Cited in: Vladimir Pozner: *Abstieg in die Hölle*. Berlin 1982, p.151.

18 Thomas Harding: *Hanns and Rudolph. The true story of the German Jew who tracked down and caught the Kommandant of Auschwitz*. New York 2013

19 www.dailymail.co.uk/news/article-2415618/Rudolf-Hoss-daughter-pictured-The-Auschwitz-commandants-Balenciaga-model-daughter-kept-secret-40-years.html, accessed on 23 June 2014.

20 Rudolf Höß: *Kommandant in Auschwitz. Autobiographische Aufzeichnungen*, p.77 (emphasis in the original).
21 In the written record of the interrogation erroneously noted as 'Heuhasen'.
22 Interrogation of Rudolf Franz Ferdinand Höß – alias Franz Lang, 14 March 1946.
23 Communication of the registry office Neukirch/Lusatia to the author, Neukirch, 7 February 2014.
24 Marriage certificate, issued on 29 August 1929, Gutengermendorf.
25 Rainer Höß: *Das Erbe des Kommandanten*. Munich 2013, p.53.
26 Ibid.
27 Birth dates of the other Höß children: Heidetraut, 9 April 1932; Ingebritt (also: Inge-Britt), 18 August 1933 in Sallentin; Hans-Jürgen, 1 May 1937 in Dachau, Annegret, 20 September 1943 in Auschwitz.
28 Thomas Harding: *Hanns and Rudolph. The true story of the German Jew who tracked down and caught the Kommandant of Auschwitz*, p.139.
29 Ibid., footnote p.140.
30 Rainer Höß: *Das Erbe des Kommandanten*, p.146.
31 BArch, NS 4/405, note by Rudolf Höß, re: bonus for the head supervisor of the women's concentration camp Auschwitz, Miss Mandl, Auschwitz, 27 March 1944; Mandl was sentenced to death in Poland and executed on 2 December 1947.
32 Internationaler Militärgerichtshof Nürnberg (ed): *Der Nürnberger Prozess: Das Protokoll des Prozesses gegen die Hauptkriegsverbrecher vom 14. November 1945 bis 1. Oktober 1946*, Interrogation of Höß, 108th day of trial, 15 April 1946, Munich 1984, vol. 12, p.441ff.
33 Gustave M. Gilbert, *Nürnberger Tagebuch. Gespräche der Angeklagten mit dem Gerichtspsychologe*, p.251ff.
34 See also: Anilie Bednarskije (spelling according to Thomas Harding; spelling according to Deselaers: Bednarska), in: Manfred Deselaers: *'Und Sie hatten nie Gewissensbisse?' Die Biografie von Rudolf Höß, Kommandant von Auschwitz, und die Frage seiner Verantwortung vor Gott und den Menschen*, Leipzig 2001.
35 Thomas Harding: *Hanns and Rudolph. The true story of the German Jew who tracked down and caught the Kommandant of Auschwitz*, p.303, footnote to p.142.
36 Manfred Deselaers: *'Und Sie hatten nie Gewissensbisse?' Die Biografie von Rudolf Höß, Kommandant von Auschwitz, und die Frage seiner Verantwortung vor Gott und den Menschen*. He refers to APMO Osw. Bednarska, report 703, dated 29 December 1962, communication by Kazimierz Smolen, APMO, Höß trial 25, 92 (p).
37 Ibid.
38 IfZArch, AZ 1753/55, esp. ZS 599a, statement Eleonore Hodys before Morgen, SS Senior Storm Command Leader Höß, Munich, October 1944.
39 Archiv des Fritz Bauer Instituts, 1. Frankfurter Auschwitz-Prozess, Strafsache gegen Mulka u.a., 4 Ks 2/63, examination of the witness Hedwig Höß on the 113th day of trial, 19 November 1964.
40 Kathrin Kompisch, *Täterinnen. Frauen im Nationalsozialismus*. Cologne/Weimar/Vienna 2008, p.211.
41 Rainer Höß: *Das Erbe des Kommandanten*, p.118.
42 Standort- und Kommandanturbefehle des Konzentrationslager Auschwitz 1940–1945, p.16, commandant's headquarters special order, Auschwitz, 7 February 1941.
43 Ibid.
44 This refers to the storage barrack of the concentration camp Auschwitz.
45 Hermann Langbein: *Menschen in Auschwitz*, Vienna/Munich 1972, p.351f.
46 Ibid., p.457ff.
47 Archiv des Fritz Bauer Instituts, 1. Frankfurter Auschwitz-Prozess, Strafsache gegen Mulka u.a., examination of the witness Friedrich Skrein on 13 July 1964.

48 Hermann Langbein: *Menschen in Auschwitz*, p.516f.
49 Ibid., p.516.
50 Ibid., p.595.
51 Ibid., p.518.
52 Standort- und Kommandanturbefehle des Konzentrationslager Auschwitz 1940–1945, p.183, Garrison Order 27/42, 7 October 1942.
53 Ibid., p.218, circular letter, Auschwitz, 6 February 1943.
54 IBV = Internationale Bibelforschungsvereinigung = Jehovah's Witnesses.
55 Standort- und Kommandanturbefehle des Konzentrationslager Auschwitz 1940–1945, p.287, Garrison Order 22/43, Auschwitz, 3 June 1943.
56 Ibid., p.303, Garrison Order 24/43, Auschwitz, 8 July 1943.
57 Hermann Langbein: *Menschen in Auschwitz*, p.458f.
58 Ibid., p.459f.
59 Canada is the code name for the camp's clothing store.
60 Jerzy Rawic, in: Jadwiga Bezwińska: *Auschwitz in den Augen der SS*, p.20.
61 Ibid.
62 Wilhelm Kmak, committed to the concentration camp on 30 August 1940, worked as a painter there.
63 Report by Janina Szcurek, Oswiecim, 13 January 1963, quoted in: Jadwiga Bezwińska: *Auschwitz in den Augen der SS*, p.293ff.
64 Hermann Langbein: *Menschen in Auschwitz*, p.143ff.
65 BArch, VBS 1 1040051533, letter NSDAP membership office Munich to regional leadership Vienna, Munich 17 August 1939.
66 Ibid.
67 BArch, VBS 1 1040051533, chief prosecutor as head of the prosecuting authority at the special court Hanover, letter to the Nazi financial and party administration Austria regarding membership of national comrade Eleonore Hodys, currently penitentiary Hanover, Leonhardtstraße, Hanover, 15 October 1938.
68 BArch, VBS 1 1040051533, letter of the NSDAP membership office to the chief prosecutor as head of the prosecuting authority at the special court Hanover, Munich, 30 April 1940.
69 Hans Aumeier (1906–1948), SS Storm Command Leader, head of the protective custody camp. In January 1942 he replaced Karl Fritzsch as head of the protective custody camp in the main camp of Auschwitz. He was arrested by the British in spring 1945 and interrogated. Aumeier was extradited to Poland and sentenced to death during the Auschwitz trial in Cracow. He was executed in 1948.
70 Internationaler Militärgerichtshof Nürnberg (ed): *Der Nürnberger Prozess: Das Protokoll des Prozesses gegen die Hauptkriegsverbrecher vom 14. November 1945 bis 1. Oktober 1946*, vol. 20, p.549ff.
71 1st Frankfurt Auschwitz trial.
72 Correct: Clauberg station, named after the gynaecologist Carl Clauberg who performed forced sterilisations on hundreds of female concentration camp prisoners as SS doctor in Auschwitz.
73 IfZArch, AZ 1753/55, esp. ZS 599a, statement by Eleonore Hodys before Morgen, October 1944.
74 Hermann Langbein: *Menschen in Auschwitz*, p.461f.

4. The Cynic
1 Jadwiga Bezwińska: *Auschwitz in den Augen der SS*, p.16.
2 Ibid., p.17.
3 Ibid., p.16.

4 Internationaler Militärgerichtshof Nürnberg (ed): *Der Nürnberger Prozess: Das Protokoll des Prozesses gegen die Hauptkriegsverbrecher vom 14. November 1945 bis 1. Oktober 1946*, vol. 11, p.446.
5 Ibid., p447.
6 So-called antisocials.
7 Harry Naujoks: *Mein Leben im KZ Sachsenhausen 1936–1942*. Berlin 1989, p.141f.
8 Ibid.
9 Ibid., p164.
10 1st Frankfurt Auschwitz Trial, 67th day of trial, statement Kurt Leischow, 17 July 1964.
11 Cf. also Harry Naujoks: *Mein Leben im KZ Sachsenhausen 1936–1942*. Berlin 1989, p.176ff.
12 *Ibid.*, p177f.
13 1. Frankfurter Auschwitz-Prozess, Strafsache gegen Mulka u.a., 84th day of trial, 31 August 1964.
14 IfZArch, AZ 5069/73, eps. ZS/A 15.
15 Standort- und Kommandanturbefehle des Konzentrationslager Auschwitz 1940–1945, p.252, command order 8/44, Auschwitz, 20 April 1943.
16 Jadwiga Bezwińska: *Auschwitz in den Augen der SS*, p.287ff, statement by Stanislaw Dubiel.
17 Standort- und Kommandanturbefehle des Konzentrationslager Auschwitz 1940–1945, p.52f, command order 15/41, Auschwitz, 4 July 1941.
18 Ibid., p.61, command order 21/41, 20 August 1941.
19 Ibid., p.68, command order 25/41, 20 September 1941.
20 Ibid., p.73, command order 28/41, 17 October 1941.
21 Ibid., p.76, command order 30/41, 7 November 1941.
22 Ibid., p.85, command order 33/41, 4 December 1941.
23 Ibid., p.263, command order 11/43, 6 May 1943.
24 Ibid., p.349, garrison order 45/43, 8 October 1943.
25 Ibid., p.394, garrison order 3/44, 19 January 1944.
26 Vladimir Pozner: *Abstieg in die Hölle*, p.151f.
27 www.wider-das-vergessen.org/index.php?option=com_content&view=article&id=62%3Ader-auschwitz-erlass&catid+7&Itemid=36&limitstart=6, accessed 23 June 2014. Rena Jacob: Orchester im Vernichtungslager Auschwitz.
28 Standort- und Kommandanturbefehle des Konzentrationslager Auschwitz 1940–1945, p.218, circular letter, Auschwitz, 6 February 1943.
29 Standort- und Kommandanturbefehle des Konzentrationslager Auschwitz 1940–1945, command order, 10/42, Auschwitz, 6 June 1942.
30 Ibid., command order 21/42, Auschwitz, 24 October 1942.
31 Ibid., command order 8/43, Auschwitz, 16 March 1943.
32 Ibid., garrison order 29/44, 25 November 1944.
33 Ibid., garrison order 51/43, Auschwitz, 16 November 1943.
34 Ibid., command order 2/43, Monowitz, 20 December 1943.
35 BStU, MfS, HA, X/11 ZM 28, garrison order Höß, 1 October 1943.

5. Höß and his Fellow Perpetrators

1 Rudolf Höß: *Kommandant in Auschwitz. Autobiographische Aufzeichnungen*, p.11.
2 BStU, MfS, HA IX, handwritten notes by Höß in Cracow prison, end of 1946.
3 Archiv des Fritz Bauer Instituts, 1. Frankfurter Auschwitz-Prozess, Strafsache gegen Mulka u.a., examination of the witness Kurt Leischow, 67th day of trial, 17 July 1964.
4 Himmler's official diary, entry Friday, 17 July 1942, p.491f.

5   IfZArch, ZS 694-24, interrogation of Caesar, Nuremberg, 13 February 1947.
6   Rudolf Höß: *Kommandant in Auschwitz. Autobiographische Aufzeichnungen*, p.177.
7   *Ibid.*
8   Hermann Langbein (ed.), *Der Auschwitz-Prozess*, vol. 1, p.182.
9   All quotes: BStU, MfS, HA IX, no. 23036, notes Höß, Cracow, November 1946
10 BstU, MfS, HA IX/11, ZS A 15/100, special order 15/43, Auschwitz, 7 July 1943.
11 Musulmen were called those prisoners who were extremely malnourished and barely able to work any longer.
12 Wieslaw Kielar: *Anus Mundi. Fünf Jahre Auschwitz*, p.129f.
13 All quotes: BstU, MfS, HA IX, no. 23036, notes Höß, Cracow, November 1946.
14 Emphasis by Höß.
15 Cf. also deposition Pohl, Nuremberg, 27 August 1947.
16 BstU, MfS, HA IX, no. 23036, notes Höß, Cracow, November 1946.
17 Jadwiga Bezwińska: *Auschwitz in den Augen der SS*, statement by Stanislaw Dubiel.
18 All emphases made by Höß.
19 Jadwiga Bezwińska: *Auschwitz in den Augen der SS*, diary of Kremer, p.217.
20 Emphasis by Höß.
21 IfZArch, ZS 673, 1-13, interrogation of Kaltenbrunner on 13 September 1946.
22 Archive of the Memorial Sachsenhausen, SS Central Economic-Administrative Office, Office Group D, concentration camp, order Glücks re further processing of cut hair, Oranienburg, 6 August 1942.
23 Standort- und Kommandanturbefehle des Konzentrationslager Auschwitz 1940–1945, p.125f, command order 1/42, 15 April 1942.
24 IfZArch, ZS 673, 1-13, interrogation of Kaltenbrunner on 13 September 1946.
25 BstU, MfS, HA IX, no. 23036, notes Höß, Cracow, November 1946.
26 BstU, MfS, HA IX, no. 23036, notes Höß, Cracow, November 1946.
27 BstU, MfS, HA IX, no. 23036, notes Höß, Cracow, January 1947.
28 BstU, MfS, HA IX, no. 23036, notes Höß, Cracow.
29 In the rank of an SS Under Company Leader August Schlachter managed from May 1940 till November 1941 the SS department for new constructions concentration camp Auschwitz/Upper Silesia responsible for the setup of the main camp.
30 Karl Bischoff, SS Storm Command Leader, head of the central construction department.
31 BstU, MfS, HA IX, no. 23036, notes Höß, Cracow, December 1946.
32 BstU, MfS, HA IX/11, ZM 67, letter by Kammler to Höß, I.G. Farben, 11 October 1941.
33 BstU, MfS, HA IX/11, ZM 67, letter by Höß, Auschwitz, 8 February 1941.
34 BstU, MfS, HA IX, no. 23036, notes Höß, Cracow, January 1947.
35 BstU, MfS, HA IX, no. 23036, notes Höß, Cracow.
36 1st Frankfurt Auschwitz Trial, 103rd day of trial, statement by Kurt May, 22 October 1964.
37 BArch NS 3/405, letter to Pohl re allowances for camp commanders, Oranienburg, 25 November 1943.
38 BstU, MfS, HA IX, KZ Auschwitz, case file, list outposts Auschwitz III. Mentione are: location/company, owner, production.
39 1st Frankfurt Auschwitz Trial, 89th day of trial, statement by Ernst Rönisch, 14 September 1964.
40 1st Frankfurt Auschwitz Trial, 103rd day of trial, statement by Elise Heinisch-Utner, 22 October 1964.
41 1st Frankfurt Auschwitz Trial, 103rd day of trial, statement by Erna Mulka, 22 October 1964.
42 Archiv des Fritz Bauer Instituts, 1st Frankfurt Auschwitz Trial, statement by Adolf Trowitz, 103rd day of trial, 22nd October 1964.

43 Archiv des Fritz Bauer Instituts, 1st Frankfurt Auschwitz Trial, Case against Mulka, examination of the witness Hildegard Bischoff, Frankfurt/M., 69th day of trial, 24 July 1964.

44 This is probably a mistake; the author could not find an SS school there.

45 1st Frankfurt Auschwitz Trial, 23rd day of trial, statement by Joachim Caesar, 5 March 1964.

46 Jadwiga Bezwińska: *Auschwitz in den Augen der SS*, statement by Stanislaw Dubiel, p.291f.

47 BstU, MfS, HA IX, no. 23036, notes Höß, Cracow, November 1946.

48 Cf. Tom Segev: *Die Soldaten des Bösen. Zur Geschichte der KZ-Kommandanten*, Reinbek 1992, p.101f.

49 Emphasis in the original.

50 Standort- und Kommandanturbefehle des Konzentrationslager Auschwitz 1940–1945, p.410ff, garrison order, 14 February 1944.

51 Standort- und Kommandanturbefehle des Konzentrationslager Auschwitz 1940–1945, special order for the concentration camp and the women's concentration camp, Auschwitz, 17 April 1942.

52 Standort- und Kommandanturbefehle des Konzentrationslager Auschwitz 1940–1945, p.413f, command order 4/44, Monowitz, 22 February 1944.

53 Robert M.W. Kempner: *SS im Kreuzverhör. Die Elite, die Europa in Scherben schlug*, p.128.

54 IfZArch, ZS 67/2-1, interrogation of Pohl on 25 January 1947.

55 BstU, MfS, HA IX, no. 23036, notes Höß, Cracow.

56 Emphasis in the original.

57 Archiv des Fritz Bauer Instituts, 1st Frankfurt Auschwitz Trial, Case against Mulka, State Court Frankfurt/M., 116th day of trial, 27 November 1964.

58 BstU, MfS, HA IX, no. 23036, notes Höß, Cracow, November 1946.

59 Ibid.

60 Emphasis in the original

61 BstU, MfS, HA IX, no. 23036, notes Höß, Cracow, January 1947.

62 Supreme Hygienist.

63 Tesch and Stabenow.

64 Medical Vehicles.

65 Medical Orderly.

66 BstU, MfS, HA IX, no. 23036, notes Höß, Cracow, November 1946.

67 BstU, MfS, HA IX, no. 23036, notes Höß, Cracow, November 1946.

68 Emphasis in the original.

69 BstU, MfS, HA IX, no. 23036, notes Höß, Cracow, November 1946.

70 Emphasis in the original.

71 BstU, MfS, HA IX, no. 23036, notes Höß, Cracow.

72 Ibid.

73 Emphasis in the original.

74 BstU, MfS, HA IX, no. 23036, notes Höß, Cracow, November 1946.

75 Ibid.

76 Standort- und Kommandanturbefehle des Konzentrationslager Auschwitz 1940–1945, p.359, garrison order 51/43, Auschwitz, 16 November 1943.

77 Bruno Brodniewicz was a German prisoner functionary and prisoner number 1 as well as the first camp senior of Auschwitz.

78 Johann Schwarzhuber, SS Senior Storm Leader and protective custody camp leader of the men's camp in Auschwitz-Birkenau.

79 Emphasis in the original.

80 1st Frankfurt Auschwitz Trial, 55th day of trial, 4 June 1964.

81 Friedrich Karl Kaul/Joachim Noack (eds): *Angeklagter Nr. 6. Eine Auschwitz-Dokumentation*, Berlin 1966, p.53f.

82 Archiv des Fritz Bauer Instituts, 1. Frankfurter Auschwitz-Prozess, Strafsache gegen Mulka u.a., examination of witness Otto Küsel, 73rd day of trial, 3 August 1964.

83 BstU, MfS, HA IX, no. 23036, notes Höß, Cracow.

84 BstU, MfS, HA IX, no. 23036, notes Höß, Cracow, December 1946.

85 This area encompassed more than two dozen barracks in which the robbed property of the prisoners was collected. In order to restrict thefts, the wire barrier around the new effects store in construction section II in Birkenau was charged with high voltage from Thursday, 16 December 1943.

86 BstU, MfS, HA IX, no. 23036, notes Höß, Cracow, December 1946.

87 Emphasis in the original.

88 BstU, camp regulations, the non-medical activities of the SS doctors in the concentration camp Auschwitz, October 1946.

89 Friedrich Karl Kaul/Joachim Noack (eds): *Angeklagter Nr. 6. Eine Auschwitz-Dokumentation*, p.140, letter by Höß, Auschwitz, 25 November 1942.

90 *Ibid.*, p.141, letter by Grabner, Auschwitz, December 1942.

91 BstU, MfS, HA IX, no. 23036, notes Höß, Cracow, November 1946.

92 H.G. Adler/Hermann Langbein? Ella Lingens-Reiner (eds): *Auschwitz. Zeugnisse und Berichte*, Frankfurt/M. 1984, 3rd revised edition, p.204f.

93 Hermann Langbein, *Menschen in Auschwitz*, p.348f.

94 Albert Speer: *Der Slavenstaat: Meine Auseinandersetzung mit der SS*, Stuttgart 1981, p.25.

95 Hermann Langbein: *Der Auschwitz-Prozess*, vol. 1, p.119f.

96 Hermann Langbein, *Menschen in Auschwitz*, p.461.

97 Hannah Arendt: *Eichmann in Jerusalem. Ein Bericht von der Banalität des Bösen*, Munich 1964, p.103.

98 *Ibid.*, p.111.

99 *Ibid.*, p.146.

100 *Ibid.*, p.148.

101 *Ibid.*, p.166.

102 *Ibid.*, p.224.

103 Eichmann, p.224f.

104 Eichmann, p.271f.

105 Eichmann, p.411.

106 Rudolf Höß: *Kommandant in Auschwitz. Autobiographische Aufzeichnungen*, p.189f.

107 SS Standard Leader Rudolf Mildner, chief of the Gestapo headquarters Katowice.

108 Rudolf Höß: *Kommandant in Auschwitz. Autobiographische Aufzeichnungen*, p.199.

109 BstU, MfS, HA IX/11 ZUV, no. 84, vol. 84, protocols of the interrogation of Eichmann, Police d'Israel, Quartier General 6eme Bureau, I, 1-606.

110 Jochen von Lang (ed): *Das Eichmann-Protokoll. Tonbandaufzeichnungen der israelischen Verhöre*, Vienna 1991, p.79.

111 *Ibid.*, p.93.

112 *Ibid.*, p.137f.

113 Emphasis in the original.

114 Adolf Eichmann, *Götzen*, Jerusalem 1961.

115 *Ibid.*, p.233, 99th day of trial, Jerusalem, 17 July 1961.

116 Dov B. Schmorak: *Der Prozess Eichmann*, p.233, police interrogation, tape 9, 6 June 1960.

117 *Ibid.*, p.246f, 95th day of trial, Jerusalem, 13 July 1961.

118 *Ibid.*, p.246f, 95th day of trial, Jerusalem, 13 July 1961.

119 Ibid., p.248, 95th day of trial, Jerusalem, 13 July 1961.
120 Archiv des Fritz Bauer Instituts, 1. Frankfurter Auschwitz-Prozess, Strafsache gegen Mulka u.a., State Court Frankfurt/M., examination of witness Cornelis van het Kaar, 95th day of trial, 1 October 1964.
121 Archiv des Fritz Bauer Instituts, 1. Frankfurter Auschwitz-Prozess, Strafsache gegen Mulka u.a., examination of the witness Helene Cougno, 67th day of trial, 17 June 1964.

6. Höß as Head of Department D I

1 Rudolf Höß: *Kommandant in Auschwitz. Autobiographische Aufzeichnungen*, p.204ff.
2 *Ibid.*, p.210ff.
3 Letter from Pohl to Himmler re security measures in Auschwitz, Berlin, 5 April 1944.
4 BstU, MfS, HA IX/11, ZM 67, note CCM for Höß, Auschwitz, October 1943.

7. The I.G. Farben Works at Auschwitz

1 BstU, MfS, HA IX/11, ZM 67, note on the construction of a Krupp factory, 16 April 1942.
2 BstU, MfS, HA IX/11, ZM 67, note dated 28 August 1942.
3 Buna stands for the polymerisation of butadiene with natrium, a process for the manufacture of synthetic rubber.
4 BstU, B 102/60752, minutes I.G. work Auschwitz, 1st construction meeting on 24 March 1941 at Ludwigshafen on the Rhine, Ludwigshafen, 31 March 1941.
5 Committee of the anti-fascist resistance fighters in the GDR (eds): *SS im Einsatz. Eine Dokumentation über die Verbrechen der SS*, Berlin 1957, p.436ff, statement by Otto Ambros.
6 Archiv des Fritz Bauer Instituts, 1. Frankfurter Auschwitz-Prozess, Strafsache gegen Mulka u.a., statement by Otto Ambros, 149th day of trial, 12 April 1965.
7 Archiv des Fritz Bauer Instituts, 1. Frankfurter Auschwitz-Prozess, Strafsache gegen Mulka u.a., examination of the witness Gustav Murr, 138th day of trial, 19 February 1965.
8 BArch, NS 4 AU/11, minutes of a meeting at the concentration camp Auschwitz on Friday, 28 March 1941.
9 BstU, MfS, HA XX, 3623, I.G. Werk Auschwitz, minutes of the construction meeting on 1 April 1941, Ludwigshafen, 3 April 1941.
10 BstU, MfS, HA XX, 3623, I.G. Werk Auschwitz, minutes of the site consultation meeting on 24 March 1941, Ludwigshafen, 31 March 1941.
11 BstU, B 102/60752, record of the inaugural meeting on 7 April 1941 in Katowice, Ludwigshafen, 16 April 1941.
12 Johannes Eckell, member of staff in the Reich Office for Economic Expansion, head of the chemical department.
13 BstU, MfS, HA XX, 3623, I.G. Werk Auschwitz, minutes of the site consultation meeting of 6 May 1941, Ludwigshafen, 12 May 1941.
14 FFF stands here for 'Freedom, Food, Females'.
15 Archiv des Fritz Bauer Instituts, 1. Frankfurter Auschwitz-Prozess, Strafsache gegen Mulka u.a., examination of the witness Faust, 143rd day of trial, 11 March 1965.
16 IMT, Pohl, affidavit, Nuremberg, 28 August 1947.
17 BstU, B 102/60752, letter by I.G. Farben, Ambros and Dürrfeld, Auschwitz work, to the general plenipotentiary for special issues in chemical production, Prof. Dr Kracuh, Ludwigshafen, 25 October 1941.
18 IfZArch, ZS 567/1-4, affidavit by Oswald Pohl, Nuremberg, 20 October 1947.

19 BstU, MfS, HA XX, 3623, I.G. Werk Auschwitz, minutes of the site consultation meeting of principal group 2, 14 November 1941.
20 BstU, MfS, HA XX, 3623, I.G. Werk Auschwitz, minutes of the site consultation meeting on 8 September 1942, Ludwigshafen, 24 September 1942.
21 BArch R 8128/A 1894, I.G. Werk Auschwitz, report on the TA meeting, 24 May 1944.
22 Archiv des Fritz Bauer Instituts, affidavit, 20 May 1946, Nuremberg follow-up trial Case VI, ADB 72 (d), sheet 130.
23 N. Blumental (ed.): *Dokumenty i materialy*, vol. 1, Obozy, Łódź 1946, p.109.
24 BstU, MfS, HA XX, 3560, concentration camp Auschwitz, factual file.
25 See Wollheim Memorial.

8. After the Collapse

1 Public Record Office, interrogation of Rudolf Franz Ferdinand Höß – alias Franz Lang, 14 March 1946, 230 hrs.
2 The first transport with 500 prisoners from the concentration camp Dachau reached Leitmeritz on 24 March 1944. Since there was no accommodation at first, these first prisoners accommodated 7km away in the Little Fortress, the Gestapo prison in Theresienstadt (Terezin). In summer 1944 prisoners erected a camp in the immediate vicinity of the quarry. In total 18,000 prisoners went through the concentration camp Leitmeritz, most of the transports came from the main camp Flossenbürg as well as the concentration camps Groß-Rosen, Auschwitz-Birkenau and Dachau. Roughly half of them were Poles, further major prisoner groups came from the Soviet Union, Germany, Hungary, France and Yugoslavia. Around 4,000 Jews were deported by the SS to leitmeritz, most of them from Poland, some also from Hungary. From February 1945 also hundreds of women were coerced into forced labour at Leitmeritz. Due to the bad living conditions and many epidemics, mortality within the camp was very high. Armament production also frequently came to a standstill due to the bad state of health among the prisoners. In April 1945 the SS commenced the dissolution of the camp under chaotic conditions. Roughly 1,200 prisoners stayed behind.
3 Archive of the Memorial Sachsenhausen, statement Pohl.
4 Rudolf Höß: *Kommandant in Auschwitz. Autobiographische Aufzeichnungen*, p.222f.
5 Matthias Kleinheisterkamp, General of the Waffen-SS, Commanding General of the 9th SS Army Corps.
6 Gerhard Paul: 'Der Untergang 1945 in Flensburg'. Presentation on 10 January 2012 on the occasion of the exhibition 'Was damals Recht war ...' in Flensburg town hall. State Agency for Civic Education Schleswig-Holstein, Kiel 2012, p.10f.
7 Holger Piening: *Westküste 1945. Nordfriesland und Dithmarschen am Ende des Zweiten Weltkriegs*, Heide 2000, p.104.
8 BstU, MfS, HA IX, notes by Höß in the prison of Cracow.
9 He means Käthe Wede, married Thomsen.
10 Sönke Dwenger: 'Britische Soldaten bewachten den SS-Mann beim Rundgang mit zwei Äxten', in: *Dithmarscher Landzeitung*, 20 January 2007.
11 Archive of the Memorial Sachsenhausen, D1L WO 309/217, Senior Storm Command Leader Höß.
12 Captain Hanns Alexander: Report on interrogations and activities during the search for members of Office Group D in the Flensburg region.
13 Conversation of the author on 21 January 2014 with Hans Peter Janssen.
14 Town archive Ludwigsburg, information to the author, Ludwigsburg, 13 January 2014.
15 Emphasis in the original.

16 Rudolf Höß: *Kommandant in Auschwitz. Autobiographische Aufzeichnungen*, p.225.
17 Ibid.
18 http://historia.focus.pl/wojny/rudolf-hoess-komendant-auschwitz-naszubienicy-214, accessed 23 June 2014
19 Archive of the ITS, notes of the former camp commander Rudolf Höß, No. 82346797#1,(1.1.2.0/0005/0159), letter by Höß to his wife, 11 April 1947.
20 Emphasis in the original.
21 Archive of the ITS, notes of the former camp commander Rudolf Höß, No. 82346797#1,(1.1.2.0/0005/0159), letter by Höß to his wife, 11 April 1947.
22 Societas Sancti Franscisci Salesii.
23 http://historia.focus.pl/wojny/rudolf-hoess-komendant-auschwitz-naszubienicy-214, accessed 23 June 2014.

Appendices
Chronology

1 This is based on the information of the following institutions and publications: Federal Archive Berlin-Lichterfelde, Archive of the Fritz Bauer Institute (Archiv des Fritz Bauer Instituts), Institute for Contemporary History (IfZ) Munich, Danuta Czech: *Kalendarium der Ereignisse im Konzentrationslager Auschwitz-Birkenau 1939–1945*, Reinbek 1989.

Facts About Auschwitz Concentration Camp

1 * Panstwowe Museum Auschwitz-Birkenau; Linz University.

Index

Abetz, German ambassador in Paris, 165
Alexander, Hanns, 189, 192, 195, 197
Allach, porcelain manufacturer, 100
Alps, 104
Altenau, 13
Altona, 121
Anderl, Johann, 66
Annegret, 56, 196
Annemäusl, 202, 204
Arendt, Hannah, 161
Artaman League, 20–1, 25, 28, 52, 93, 191
Aumeier, Hans, 67–9, 73, 90–2, 96, 138–40, 149
Auschwitz documentation *Angeklagter*, 168
Auschwitz in den Augen der SS, Jadwiga Bezwińska's book, 63, 168
Auschwitz. Zeugnisse und Berichte, 160
Autobiographical Notes, 3, 30, 55, 75, 87, 172, 190, 197

Bach-Zelewski, Erich von dem, 47
Bad Arolsen (ITS), 198, 206
Baden-Baden, 1
Baer, Richard, 33, 63, 93, 124, 143–5
Balenciaga, 55
Baranowski, Hermann, 42, 111
Bartecki, Erika, 207
Batawia, Stanislaw, 37, 75–6
battles of Kut-el-Amarna and Baghdad, 4

BdS, Befehlshaber der Sicherheitspolizei, 111
Beckmann from Kalsow, 12
Bednarska, Angela, 64
Bednarskije, Anieli, 57
Beer Hall Putsch, 7, 20
Bergen-Belsen, 157, 172, 189
Berlin-Lihcterfelde, 206
Berlin-Wannsee, 13, 20
Bernhard Jurisch, 8–9
Bezpieczeństwa, Urząd, 205
Bezwińska's, Jadwiga, 63, 76, 168
Bielitz, 69, 176, 179
Bischoff, Karl, 29, 92, 112, 115–16, 122
Bismarckhütte outpost, 150
Black Corps ['Schwarzer Korps'], 28
Blumenreuther, Karl, 134
Böhner, Karl, 57
Bormann, Martin, 6–8, 26–8, 67–8, 94
Bracht, Fritz, 47, 89–90
Brandenburg prison, 9–10, 13, 17, 25, 34, 52, 68, 206
Breiden, Hugo, 74
Brodniewicz, Bruno, 147, 150
Brookhart, Smith. W., 34–5
Broszat, Martin, 87
BstU, Federal Commissioner for Stasi documents, 87, 198
Bückel, Josef, 106
Bühler, Josef, 197
Bünger, Heinrich, 192
Burgsdorff, Curt von, 197

Caesar, Joachim, 60, 89, 92, 120,
    122, 133, 168
Cougno, Helene, 170
Credo, *treatise*, 31
Cyrankiewicz, Polish prime
    minister, 150
Czajkowska, Zofia, 83

Damm, Man Ludwig, 45
Danschke, Wilhelm, 81
Darré, Richard Walter, 21, 28
DAW = German Equipment
    Works, 100
Der Slavenstaat, 161
Deselaers, Manfred, 57
DEST = German Earth and Stone
    Works Company, 100, 120
Dithmarschen Regional
    Newspaper, 193
Dithmarscher Landzeitung
    [Dithmarschen Regional
    Newspaper], 193
Dönitz, Karl, 41, 192
Drexel, 69
Dubiel, Stanislaw, 57, 59–61, 80, 99
Dumschat, Sabine, 206
Dürrfeld, Walter, 175, 178–81,
    184–5, 187

Ebermayer, Ludwig, 8
Ebert, Friedrich, (Reich President), 25
Eichmann, Adolf, 30, 47, 159, 167
Eicke, Theodor, 92–3, 99–100, 106–9,
    111–12, 123, 136, 138–9, 141,
    146, 173
Emil de Martini, 7–8, 149
Engelbrecht, Friedrich, 63
epidemic, 55, 96
Etzenhausen, registry office, 21

Farben Industries, 46–7, 116, 119, 161,
    173–88
Fememord, 2
Fénèlon, Fania, 82
FFF system, 181

FFS, 195–6
Fichtinger, 72, 74
Frank, Hans Michael, 41
Free Corps Roßbach, 2, 4–7, 11–13, 15,
    28, 112
Frick, Wilhelm, 18–19, 94–5
Fricke, Bruno, 12–13
Fridericus, 19
Friedlandstr, 27
Fritzsch, Karl, 92, 136–9,
    146–7, 149
Frommhagen, Erich, 178
FSS (Force Support Squadron), 194
Fürstengrube, 119

Gass, Andrzej, 205
GDR, 87
Gebhardt, Karl, 141, 192
Gender, Theodor, 52, 92–3, 106
Gering, 71–3
Gerlach, 192
German National Freedom Party
    (DVFP), 7
Gestapo, 43, 47, 51, 78, 97, 99, 104–5,
    129, 150, 163
Gilbert, Gustave M., 3, 37–9, 41, 56, 75
Globocnik, Odilo, 92, 117–18, 125
Glücks, Richard, 24, 47, 90–2, 104–6,
    109–11, 123–4, 135–7, 140–2, 144,
    146, 149, 166, 171, 173, 178, 189–92
Goebbels, Joseph, 5, 20, 28, 39–40,
    122, 197
Gogarten, Rudolf, 174
Golden Party Badge, 28, 130
Göring, Marshall Hermann, 20,
    37, 41, 72, 120, 175, 184
Göth, Amon Leopold, 30,
    32, 197
Götzen [Idols], 164
Grabner, Maximilian, 128, 159
Grand Ducal Karl-Friedrich
    Grammar School, 3
Grawitz, Ernst-Robert, 92, 132–3
Grönke, Erich, 62–3
Grüner, Regina, 206

Haas, Senior Storm Command
    Leader, 172
Hans-Jürgen, 21, 196
Harding, Thomas, 52–5, 194–5
Härtel, Mrs., 9, 12–13
Hartjenstein, Friedrich, 58, 92,
    141, 143
Hauptsanitätslager (HSL) [Principal
    Medical Store], 134
Hausner, Gideon, 162, 166–7
Heger, Leopold, 33–4
Hensel, Hedwig, 21, 52
Herff, Maximilian von, 24
Hergt, Oskar, 17–19
Heydrich, Security Service Chief,
    97, 112
Himmler, Heinrich, 21, 25, 28, 30, 32,
    38, 40–1, 43–4, 46–8, 54, 66, 86–7,
    89–91, 93–6, 98–9, 102–6, 109–10,
    112, 117, 124, 130, 133, 138, 162,
    165, 172–3, 175, 182, 189–92
Hindenburg, Paul von, 18, 20, 32, 120
Hitler, Adolf, 6, 20, 25–6, 28, 30,
    38–40, 46, 93, 106, 114, 163, 165,
    172, 190, 192
Hodys, Eleonore, 51, 53, 57–8,
    65–8, 74
Holocaust, 30, 33, 76, 157
Holtz, Friedrich Carl, 19
Höß, Franz Xaver, 1–2, 27, 44
Höß, Maria Luise, 21
Höß, Rainer, 52–4, 58
House Elbe, 171–2, 189
Huber, Helene, 13–14
Huley, SS Storm Man Horst, 33
Hüttemann, Anneliese, 124

IBV, 61
Ingebritt, 52–5, 194–6

Jacob, Rena, 82
Jansen, Hans Peter, 51, 194, 196
Jarosiewitsch, Peter, 81
Jawohl, 11
Jehovah's Witnesses, 59, 76, 78

Jerusalem, 30, 163
Jewish camp Plaszow, 32, 198
Jewry, 39–40
Judenreferat, 105, 159
Jurisch, Bernhard, 7–9
Jüttner, Hans, 162

Kadow, Walter, 2, 5–9, 14–16, 18–19
Kaiserswaldau, 15
Kaltenbrunner, Ernst, 37–8, 97, 100,
    104–5, 197
Kammler, Hans, 29, 90, 92, 102, 104,
    110, 112–16, 173
Kamphus, Johann, 81
kapo, 57, 62, 71–2, 74, 121, 137, 179
Kauffmann, Kurt, 38
Kaul, Friedrich Karl, 168
Keitel, Wilhelm, 175
Kielar, Wieslaw, 48, 96
Klaus-Bernd, 53, 61, 193–5, 200,
    202–3
Knapp, Gabriele, 82, 84
Knight's Cross, 29, 103, 109
Kompisch, Kathrin, 58
Koolish, 195
Kopycinski, Adam, 82
Kramer, Josef, 44, 83
Krause, 144–5, 178
Kremer, Johann Paul, 102
Krüger, Waffen-SS, 165
Krupp AG, 174–5
Kuczynski, Friedrich Karl, 30
Küsel, Otto, 150

Landshut prison, 37
Lang, Franz, 174, 192, 197
Langbein, Hermann, 52, 59, 74, 79,
    160–1
Langefeld, Johanna, 90
Laponese, 107
Lasker-Wallfisch, Anita, 83
Lehmann, Julius Friedrich, 17
Leipzig, 2, 6, 8–10, 13, 15–16, 19,
    21, 68
Leischow, Kurt, 78, 88

Less, Avner, 163
Liebehenschel, 33, 86, 92, 98, 111, 123–4, 126, 128, 131, 143–4, 150, 161, 171, 173
Lietz, 193
Local Heritage Society Buberow, 207
Lockhauserbaum, Man Eduard, 72
Lolling, Enno, 92, 134, 189
Loritz, 23, 146
Lübeck-Lauerhof prison, 67
Luftwaffe, 112, 115, 152, 166, 173
Lukans, Vera, 149
Lüneburg Heath, 169
Lüth, Wolfgang, 192
Luwow, Man Ewald, 81

Mahler, Gustav, 83
Majdanek extermination camp, 33, 36
Major Bramwell, Captain Alexander, 197
Malorny, Gertrud, 69
Mandl, Maria, 54–5, 83, 91
Mannheim, 1–3, 11, 14, 16, 21, 59, 206
Martini, Emil de, 149
Mathey, Private Karl, 81
Maurer, Gerhard, 40, 92, 111, 140, 144, 151, 154, 172–3, 178, 182, 191–2, 194
Mayr, Franz Xaver, 44
Meer, Fritz ter, 180
Meier, 146–7
Meseberg castle, 53
Mesopotamia, 4
Meyer, 147–8
Mildner, 162–3
Mináriková-Fuchs, Martha, 61
Moll, Otto, 34–7, 149
Morgen, Konrad, 57, 65–8
Mrugowsky, Joachim, 92, 133–4
Mulka, Robert, 90–2, 118–22
Müller, 47, 69, 72–3, 81, 91, 97–8, 105, 164–6
Murr, Gustav, 178
Mutz, 198–202

MV, 134
Mythus des 20. Jahrhunderts [The Myth of the 20th Century], 39

Naczelny Trybunal Narodowy (NTN), 198
Naujoks, Harry, 42, 76
Nazi regional leadership [Gauleitung], 25
Neuengamme, 74, 143, 157, 189
Niedner, Alexander, 8
NSDAP, 6, 18, 25–8, 31, 47, 66–7, 106, 130, 136, 138, 145

Obergruppenführer or Lieutenant General, 29
Oberscharführer or company sergeant major, 22
Ochshorn, Isaak Egon, 31
Operation Barleycorn, 193
Operation Reinhardt, 29–31, 117, 125, 128
Orchestra of Auschwitz, 81

Palitzsch, Gerhard, 93, 145–50
Patriotic Prisoners Aid, 19
People in Auschwitz, 59
Pfeiffer, Georg, 6–8
Piening, Holger, 191
Pilecki, Jan, 46
Pohl, Oswald, 30–1, 52, 90–2, 99, 171, 182, 189
Polenz, 131
Poznan Citadel, 205
Pressac, Jean-Claude, 8
Pritzokleit, Herbert, 86
Prützmann, Adolf, 191

Rakers, Bernhard, 186
Rantum, 192–3
Rascher, Sigmund, 166
Rathenau, Walther, 13
Rau, Jörg, 207
Rawic, Jerzy, 63
Regensburg, 136

Regenscheidt, 73
Reich Physician SS and Police
    (RP SS), 132–4, 156–7
Reich Security Main Office
    [Reichssicherheitshauptamt], 37
Reichenbacher, 60
Reichsgau [Reich region], 205
Reichsmark, 11–12, 19, 45, 55,
    128, 180
Reichstag, 17–20, 29, 40
Reichswehr, 5, 112, 141
Reimers, SS Storm Man, 81
Remmele, Josef, 186
Rhenish Palatinate, 106, 110
Riedle, Andrea, 26
Rönisch, Erich, 120
Roosevelt, 40
Rosé, Alma, 83–4
Rosen, Groß, 145, 168
Rosenberg, Alfred, 28
Rott, Franz, 81
Royal Horse Artillery (RHA), 197
RSHA, 47, 50–1, 91, 97–8, 100, 112,
    117, 156, 158–9, 161, 169
Rudolf Hoess komendant Auschwitz
    na szubienicy, 205
Ruhr, 6–7, 9, 14, 18

Saucke, Labour Minister, 113
scallywa', 79, 86
Scharführer, 21–2
Schebeck, 59–60
Schenck, Ernst Günther, 101
Schill Youth, 13
Schillhorn, Hans, 161
Schirach, Baldur von, 28
Schlageter, Albert Leo, 6, 161
Schleswig-Holstein, 7, 51, 189–90, 196
Schmelt, Albrecht, 30
Schmidt, Cesrin, 206
Schmincke, SS Head Storm
    Leader, 174
Schnütgen, Rudolf, 7, 12
Schöttl, Vinzenz, 185
Schultz, Ernst Philipp, 171

Schütter, SS Storm Man Alfred, 86
Schwarzhuber, 148
Seckendorff, Artaman Ilse von, 52
Seeckt, Hans Von, 25
Sehn, Jan, 37, 60, 75–6, 80, 198
Seidler, 147, 149
Setkiewicz, Piotr, 188
Shala, Stefanie, 206
Siemann, Werner, 13, 129, 191
Sierek, Robert, 63
Skrein, Friedrich, 60
Sola River, 44, 81, 177, 179–80, 206
Sönke Dwenger, 193
Sports School Ekkehard, 13
Springorum, 47
St Michaelis, 195
St Michaelisdonn, 51, 191–4, 196
Stanislaw Dubiel, 57, 59–60, 80, 99
Stasi Documents Office, 206
State Food Agency, 189
Stolten, Richard, 81
Storfer of the Vienna Central
    Office, 164
Strauß, 180
Streckenbach, Bruno, 92, 111
Strobel, Karen, 14, 206
Stürmer [Attacker], 39
Sturmmann or lance corporal, 22
swastika, 82
Szcurek, Janina, 64

Tauber, 73
Techow, Hans-Gerd, 13
Thederjahn, Richard, 158
Tiergarten police station, 19
TREBLINKA, 46–7
Treuenfels estate, 6
Trowitz, Adolf, 121

UEBERREUTER, 50
Ullstein dictionary, 11
Urząd Bezpieczeństwa (UB), 205

Veesemayer, Edmund von, 162
Viviani, Annalisa, 207

Vogel, 89
Völkischer Beobachter [National
    Observer], 27

Wagner, Bernd C., 188
Weinbergstraße, 1
Weiseborn, Mia, 54
Westküste 1945 [Western Coast
    1945], 191
WHVA, 174
Wider das Vergessen [Against the
    oblivion], 82
Wiebeck, Judge, 74
Wiegandt, Leader, 43–4
Wiemeyer, Emil, 7–8
Winkelmann, 162

Wirth, 134, 156
Wirths, Eduard, 93, 135, 154–8
Witzmann, Regina, 206
WOLZEK, 47

Zabel, 7–8
Zaremba, Reverend Tadeusz, 204
ZBL, 29
Zenz, 8
Zimmersitz, 73
ZLB, 174–5
ZNP, 198
Związek Nauczycielstwa Polskiego
    (ZNP), 198
Zyklon B, 49, 133, 136, 155, 157